Studies in Economic History

Series Editor

Aims and Scope

This series from Springer provides a platform for works in economic history that truly integrate economics and history. Books on a wide range of related topics are welcomed and encouraged, including those in macro-economic history, financial history, labor history, industrial history, agricultural history, the history of institutions and organizations, spatial economic history, law and economic history, political economic history, historical demography, and environmental history.

Economic history studies have greatly developed over the past several decades through application of economics and econometrics. Particularly in recent years, a variety of new economic theories and sophisticated econometric techniques—including game theory, spatial economics, and generalized method of moment (GMM)—have been introduced for the great benefit of economic historians and the research community.

At the same time, a good economic history study should contribute more than just an application of economics and econometrics to past data. It raises novel research questions, proposes a new view of history, and/or provides rich documentation. This series is intended to integrate data analysis, close examination of archival works, and application of theoretical frameworks to offer new insights and even provide opportunities to rethink theories.

The purview of this new Springer series is truly global, encompassing all nations and areas of the world as well as all eras from ancient times to the present. The editorial board, who are internationally renowned leaders among economic historians, carefully evaluate and judge each manuscript, referring to reports from expert reviewers. The series publishes contributions by university professors and others well established in the academic community, as well as work deemed to be of equivalent merit.

More information about this series at http://www.springer.com/series/13279

Kazuo Wada

The Evolution of the Toyota Production System

Springer

Kazuo Wada
Tajimi, Gifu, Japan

ISSN 2364-1797 ISSN 2364-1800 (electronic)
Studies in Economic History
ISBN 978-981-15-4927-4 ISBN 978-981-15-4928-1 (eBook)
https://doi.org/10.1007/978-981-15-4928-1

This Springer imprint is published by the registered company Springer Nature Singapore Pte Ltd.
The registered company address is: 152 Beach Road, #21-01/04 Gateway East, Singapore 189721, Singapore

Preface

Toyota currently represents one of the largest automobile companies in the world because the company manufactures and sells its cars globally. However, Toyota was not always a dominant company in the auto industry. In the mid-twentieth century, Toyota was a small company that manufactured and sold its cars almost exclusively in Japan. To illustrate, while General Motors (GM) manufactured about five million cars in 1955, Toyota manufactured only about 23,000 the same year. As a further indication of Toyota's humble beginnings, Ford produced, monthly, approximately 22,000 cars between April and June of 1913 (before assembly lines were installed); Toyota's annual output reached this production level only in 1955.

In the 1980s, however, the export volume of Japanese auto manufacturers increased rapidly. The drastic increase in Japanese auto exports caused Toyota (as the largest Japanese auto manufacturing company) to attract significant attention from academics and journalists. Since the 1980s, the substantial literature on Toyota has amassed. The researchers and journalists responsible for this work have repeatedly claimed that Toyota has produced high-quality automobiles at a low cost. Many believe that Toyota achieved this efficiency through the development and application of the Toyota Production System (TPS).

The attention paid to TPS to date has stimulated extensive and diverse literature on the system. Although the diversity of the work on TPS has induced companies to implement the system using a plethora of methods, most individuals typically explain TPS based on Taiichi Ohno's book, *Toyota Production System*. This book describes TPS as follows. Toyota uses "Kanban" to produce requirements "just-in-time" for each step of the production process. Some may readily grasp the meaning of unfamiliar terms such as Kanban. Others are often too occupied with Toyota's shop floor operations alone to grasp the meaning of Kanban. Consequently, the uniqueness of TPS is often emphasized without consideration of the development of general production models.

Most researchers have shown little interest in discussing Toyota's development as a company while outlining the evolution of TPS. In contrast, this present book offers an explanation of Toyota's historical development to provide a more comprehensive (and contextualized) discussion of TPS.

The path to interchangeable production in Japan was convoluted. However, after World War II, Toyota and its practices began to take root. TPS emerged from Toyota's struggle to survive in the postwar environment. Considering this context, this book contextualizes the evolution of TPS in Toyota's historical development in postwar Japan.

Ford's production methods galvanized the pursuit of Japanese production engineers. In this way, the evolution of TPS can be attributed to Japanese efforts to catch up with US production methods before World War II. Specifically, Japanese production engineers sought to mass-produce high-quality products modifying Ford's approach. Rather than referring to the "assembly line approach," however, Japanese engineers used the "flow production" method. The flow production method proliferated across the Japanese manufacturing industry (particularly assembly) during and after the War (see Chap. 2).

Although the concept of flow production had a gradual effect on the production of Japanese automobiles, the establishment of the Japanese automobile manufacturing industry posed a daunting challenge. Ford demonstrated mass production at a low cost, but replicating Ford's production method in Japan proved difficult. The production of interchangeable parts was complex, taking years in some cases. As a result of these difficulties, entrepreneurs that established the automobile manufacturing industry in Japan were forced to use inferior materials and had an insufficient number of machines for production.

Despite these hardships, Kiichiro Toyoda was one of the early entrepreneurs to launch an automobile manufacturing business. Before entering the automobile business, Toyoda worked in the textile machinery industry. The history of Toyoda's transition to the automobile industry and the construction of the production facilities is described in Chap. 3.

When first established, Toyota's production system was relatively small in scale. Even during World War II, however, its limited scale and capacity became problematic. Toyota attempted to reform the ways in which the shop floor was controlled through the company's rationalization movement. When the company resumed its automobile production after the war, Toyota further pursued its rationalization movement. Shop floor reform was an attempt to implement the flow production approach. However, this attempt was curtailed in 1950 when deteriorating economic conditions brought the company to the edge of bankruptcy. Following the settlement of the labor struggle in 1950, the company reformed its organization and changed its shop floor data collection methods (see Chap. 4).

After the labor struggle was settled, two Toyota executives traveled to the USA. What they found there had a significant effect on production control at Toyota. Notably, these executives returned to Toyota realizing that new equipment could pave the way for the establishment of flow production at the company (see Chaps. 5 and 6). To effectively execute the flow production approach, Toyota developed and implemented some unique ideas, particularly with respect to material handling (see Chap. 7).

By 1963, Toyota and its suppliers comprehensively changed the company's parts numbers. This led to the introduction of Kanban inside Toyota's plants, although the adoption of Kanban for purchasing parts did not occur until much later. Many researchers have claimed that by using Kanban, Toyota could effectively implement just-in-time production. Some researchers have even argued that Kanban would facilitate Toyota's production activities even in the absence of a definitive production scheme. In this book, I argue the importance of completing a Bill of Materials (BOM) based on a digitalized punch-card system (see Chap. 8).

Many articles in the early twentieth century highlighted the importance of BOM. However, a single passenger car comprises well over 20,000 parts and materials. The sheer number of parts necessary to produce a car renders production difficult if the system relies on a paper-based BOM. By the early twentieth century, Toyota successfully transformed its BOM completely to a fully digitalized BOM. This new BOM aided Toyota's global advancement coupled with the rapid development of its international communication network.

Tajimi, Japan Kazuo Wada

Contents

About the Author

Kazuo Wada is a professor emeritus of The University of Tokyo. He also taught at Nanzan University and Tokaigakuen University. Professor Wada obtained his Ph.D. in economic history at the University of London (London School of Economics) in 1989. He edited *Fordism Transformed: The Development of Production Methods in the Automobile Industry* (Oxford University Press, 1996) with Haruhito Shiomi. He also compiled and edited *Corpus of Kiichiro Toyoda's Documents* (Nagoya University Press, 1999). He published *Courage and Change: The Life of Kiichiro Toyoda* (Toyota Motor Corporation, 2009) with Tsunehiko Yui. His research interests include international comparisons and long-term changes. His recent achievements include *The Fable of Manufacturing: From Ford to Toyota* (Nagoya University Press, 2009), *Beyond Manufacturing: From Imitation to Building Toyota's Individuality* (Nagoya University Press, 2013) and "Automobiles," with Patrick Friedenson, in *The Routledge Companion to the Makers of Global Business* (2020).

Chapter 1
Introduction

Toyota Motor Corporation (Toyota) is currently one of the largest automobile companies in the world, manufacturing and selling its cars globally. However, Toyota was not always a dominant player in the auto industry. In the mid-twentieth century, Toyota was a small company that manufactured and sold its cars almost exclusively in Japan. While General Motors (GM) manufactured about five million cars in 1955, Toyota manufactured only about 23,000 that same year (Schifferes 2007). As a further indication of Toyota's humble beginnings, Ford Motor Company (Ford) produced approximately 22,000 cars monthly between April and June of 1913 (before assembly lines were installed) (McCalley 1994, p. 462); Toyota's annual output only reached this production level in 1955.

In the 1980s, however, the export volume of Japanese auto manufacturers increased rapidly. The drastic increase in Japanese auto exports resulted in Toyota (as the largest Japanese auto manufacturing company) attracting significant attention from academics and journalists. Since the 1980s, substantial literature on Toyota has amassed. Researchers and journalists responsible for this work have repeatedly claimed that Toyota has produced high-quality automobiles at low cost. Many believe that Toyota achieved this efficiency through the development and application of the Toyota Production System (TPS).

To date, attention paid to the TPS has inspired extensive and diverse literature on the system. Although the diversity of the work on the TPS has encouraged companies to implement the system using a plethora of methods, the TPS is usually explained based on Taiichi Ohno's book, *Toyota Production System* (Ohno 1978). This book describes the TPS as a system in which Toyota uses *Kanban* to produce requirements "just in time" for each step of the production process. An article on this topic by Sugimori and others was published in a professional journal in 1977 (Sugimori et al. 1977). Next, the Oxford English Dictionary recorded the peculiar Japanese word, *Kanban*, and defined it as follows:

> a card or sheet displaying a set of manufacturing specifications and requirements, which is circulated to suppliers and sent along a production line to regulate the supply of components (Proffitt 1997).

K. Wada, *The Evolution of the Toyota Production System*,
Studies in Economic History,
https://doi.org/10.1007/978-981-15-4928-1_1

Public interest in the Toyota production system was motivated by interest in the factors behind the company's robust performance after the oil shock in 1973. At the same time, many people wanted to know the meaning of the unfamiliar and strange terms "Kanban" and "just in time." Interest in these terms was found not only outside of Japan but also within Japan. In response to these requests, many business books on Toyota or the Toyota production system were published in Japan. In 1983, Shigeo Shingō published a book on the Toyota production system from an industrial engineering perspective (Shingō 1984). Outside of Japan, Monden published a book about the Toyota production system in English in 1983 (Monden 1983); Ohno's book was also published in English in 1988 (Ohno 1988). By the end of the 1980s, the Toyota production system was understood to some extent even in English-speaking countries.

When the book *The Machine that Changed the World* was published in 1990 and called the Toyota production system a lean production system, interest in the production system was regenerated (Womack et al.1990). This book has been published in various countries over many years. The version published by Free Press in 2014 was subtitled *The Story of Lean Production—Toyota's Secret Weapon in the Global Car Wars that is now Revolutionizing World Industry*, demonstrating the continued public interest. Books by Fujimoto (1999) and Liker and Franz (2012) have also attracted readers with the same interests while expanding the subject area.

Excellent studies on the Toyota production system have been published in English. However, many of them are focused on explaining the current status of Toyota. Most researchers have shown little interest in discussing Toyota's development as a company while outlining the evolution of the TPS. In contrast, this book offers an explanation of Toyota's historical development to provide a more comprehensive (and contextualized) discussion of the TPS.

The path to interchangeable production in Japan was convoluted. However, after World War II, Toyota and its practices began to take root. The TPS emerged from Toyota's struggle to survive in the postwar environment. Within this context, this book contextualizes the evolution of the TPS in Toyota's historical development in postwar Japan.

Ford's production methods galvanized Japanese production engineers to pursue the same methods and goals. In this way, the evolution of the TPS can be attributed to Japanese efforts to catch up with the production methods that existed in the United States before World War II. Specifically, Japanese production engineers sought to mass-produce high-quality products by modifying Ford's approach. Rather than referring to the "assembly line approach," however, Japanese engineers used the "flow production" method. The flow production method proliferated across the Japanese manufacturing industry (particularly in assembly work) during and after World War II (see Chap. 2).

Although the concept of flow production had a gradual effect on the production of Japanese automobiles, establishing the Japanese automobile manufacturing industry posed a daunting challenge. Ford demonstrated mass production at low cost, but replicating Ford's production method in Japan proved difficult. The production of interchangeable parts was complex, taking years to achieve in some cases. These difficulties meant that entrepreneurs who were working to establish the automobile manufacturing industry in Japan were forced to use inferior materials and had an insufficient number of machines for production.

Despite these hardships, Kiichiro Toyoda was one of the early entrepreneurs to launch an automobile manufacturing business. Before entering into the automobile business, Toyoda worked in the textile machinery industry. The history of Toyoda's transition to the automobile industry and the construction of his production facilities is described in Chap. 3.

When first established, Toyota's production system was relatively small in scale. As early as during World War II, however, its limited scale and capacity became problematic. Toyota attempted to reform the ways in which the shop floor was controlled through the company's rationalization movement. When the company resumed its automobile production after the war, Toyota continued to pursue its rationalization movement. Shop floor reform was an attempt to implement the flow production approach. However, this attempt was curtailed in 1950 when deteriorating economic conditions brought the company to the edge of bankruptcy. Following the settlement of the labor struggle in 1950, Toyota reformed its organization and changed its shop floor data collection methods (see Chap. 4).

After the labor struggle was settled, two Toyota executives traveled to the USA. What they found there had a significant effect on production control at Toyota. Notably, these executives returned to Toyota realizing that new equipment could pave the way for the establishment of flow production at the company (see Chaps. 5 and 6).

Toyota had to face the problem of product quality as its production increased. Because Toyota used a lot of external parts, it was necessary to improve the quality of external parts as well as in-house parts in order to improve the overall quality of the cars. In addition, Toyota also addressed the problems associated with aging automobiles (the so-called recall problem) in 1969 by creating a history file of individual vehicles using an information system (see Chap. 7).

By 1963, Toyota and its suppliers had made comprehensive changes to the company's parts numbers. This was an opportunity for Toyota to increase the use of computers in various fields. In addition, Toyota deepened its relationships with affiliated companies through information systems. This plan was accelerated by changing the basis on which the bill of materials (BOM) was processed from paper to digital (see Chap. 8).

Toyota's information system has been indispensable for formulating production plans and facilitating efficient production. However, Toyota's official histories reveal little about information systems and production planning, even though use of BOM is essential for efficient production in operations that use a large number of parts, including production at Toyota. While Toyota successfully converted from paper-based BOM to a digital system in the 1970s (see Chap. 8), Toyota's company histories rarely mention this step.

European and American researchers are likely to consider that even if Toyota's company history does not deal with particular topics, research could proceed by using the minutes of board meetings and similar documents as references. However, researchers do not have access these board minutes, even though Toyota maintains a company archive and an industrial museum. Furthermore, researchers do not have access to internal newsletters or magazines within the Toyota organization.

Some of the newsletters and magazines cited in this book were handed over personally by people who worked for Toyota for a long time; others were purchased from secondhand bookstores by the author. While interviews with many people also provided material for this book, the author has opted not to use quotes from those people directly but instead to rely on as much verifiable literature as possible.

References

Fujimoto, T. (1999). *The evolution of a manufacturing system at Toyota*. New York: Oxford University Press.

Liker, J. K., & Franz, J. K. (2012). *The Toyota way to continuous improvement: Linking strategy and operational excellence to achieve superior performance*. New York: McGraw-Hill.

McCalley, B. W. (1994). *Model T Ford: The car that changed the world*. Wisconsin: Kraus Publications.

Monden, Y. (1983). *Toyota production system: Practical approach to production management*. Norcross, Georgia: Industrial Engineering and Management Press.

Ohno, T. (1978). *Toyota seisan hōshiki: Datsu kibo no keiei o mezashite* (Toyota production system: Beyond large-scale production). Tokyo: Daiyamondo sha.

Ohno, T. (1988). *Toyota production system: Beyond large-scale production*. Portland, Oregon: Productivity Press.

Proffitt, M. (1997). *Oxford english dictionary additions series*: Vol. 3. New York: Oxford University Press, Incorporated, 1997. Internet resource.

Sugimori, Y., Kusunoki, K., Cho, F., & Uchikawa, S. (1977). Toyota production system and Kanban system Materialization of just-in-time and respect-for-human system. In *International Journal of Production Research*, vol. 15, no. 6. Oxford: Taylor & Francis.

Shingō, S. (1984). *Toyota seisan hōshiki no IE teki kōsatsu* (The industrial engineering perspective of Toyota production system). Toyota production systemTokyo: Nikkan kōgyō shinbun sha.

Schifferes, Steve (2007), "The Decline of Detroit," BBC News. http://news.bbc.co.uk/2/hi/business/6346299.stm (accessed July 5, 201.

Womack, J. P., Jones, D. T., & Roos, D. (1990). *The machine that changed the world*. New York: Free Press.

Chapter 2
Acceptance of the Ford Production System by Japanese Manufacturing Industries

2.1 Influence of Ford Production System on Japanese Manufacturing Industries

In 1925, Ford Motor Company established its branch plant in Yokohama, Japan. As Ford accepted visitors, many visited its plant and gazed at the moving assembly line or conveyor system. By then, the concept of the "Ford production system" had spread among Japanese engineers. However, the Ford system's conveyors were rarely a focus of any explanation of the concept. Moreover, it is noteworthy that Japanese engineers rarely mentioned Ford's production system or even the term "mass production," particularity after 1937 when Japan declared war with China. Instead, two terms were gradually adopted and used extensively in books and articles on production control: "flow production" and "high-volume production." This implies that Japanese engineers rejected the Ford production system. In reality, however, engineers kept a watchful eye on the achievements of Ford.

Both the terms "flow production" and "high-volume production" prevailed in Japanese literature on production control during World War II and immediately after. The Japanese used these terms to address pressing matters: increasing aircraft production during the war, and, after the war, the reconstruction of Japanese manufacturing industries. Thoughts on production control had a wide influence on Japanese manufacturing industries, and Toyota's production system also evolved under theses influences. This chapter clarifies the frame of mind of Japanese engineers by considering the two terms "flow production" and "high-volume production." In addition, we examine what the Japanese implemented, or, at least, tried to implement for aircraft production during the war, and, more generally, in Japanese manufacturing industries after the war.

For most western scholars, the term "flow production" would stir memories of the book titled *Principles of Mass and Flow Production* by Frank G. Woollard, a British engineer. Woollard characterized both mass and flow production as follows: "Mass production implies the method of making vast quantities of similar articles. … Flow

K. Wada, *The Evolution of the Toyota Production System*,
Studies in Economic History,
https://doi.org/10.1007/978-981-15-4928-1_2

production, on the other hand, envisages the passage of the part from operation to operation in a direct and uninterrupted sequence" (Woollard 1954, p. 48). Woollard also explained flow production figuratively as follows:

> The ideal arrangement for flow production should resemble a watershed; the river being the main assembly track, fed by tributaries in the shape of sub-assembly lines which, in turn, would be supplied by streams representing the machine lines fed by brooks typifying the material conveyors. Each part should flow continuously forward. There should be few bends, no eddies, no dams, no storms, no freezing should impede the inevitable flow to estuarine waters—the dealers—and ultimately to the sea—the consumers (Woollard 1954, p. 48).

Admitting that the flow production technique "originated on the automobile assembly lines" (Woollard 1954, p. 19), Woollard was clearly conscious of the Ford production system and its high productivity. He insisted that the flow production methods would be "applicable to all the repetitive engineering and mechanical trades" and even "small-scale production can frequently benefit to a surprising degree by a study of the principles of flow production" (Woollard 1954, p. 15). For Woollard, smooth connection between production processes was particularly important to achieve "benefit to a surprising degree."

Before Woollard's book was published, Japanese production engineers would begin to consider organizing production processes with a focus on production flows. Consequently, the term "flow production" was often used in Japan even before the war. It became the norm to explain the Ford system's strength using the loose term "flow production."

In 1941, a committee of the Japan Society for the Promotion of Science (JSPS) surveyed flow production. This demonstrates that flow production was established as a Japanese term at that time. However, this survey was conducted in turbulent times: in July 1937, the Sino-Japanese War broke out and aggravated the confrontation with the United Kingdom and the United States. Therefore, a genuine academic interest in the situation of Japanese companies at the time and a pressing need for increased production motivated the JSPS to conduct the survey. The survey report was released in 1943 and revealed that the flow production method had not been widely adopted, even among major companies. The reason for conducting the survey was given in the report introduction as follows:

> We face an acute shortage of materials and manpower at present, and have to take measures to increase production by utilizing both existing equipment and manpower as much as possible. Implementing flow production and applying its basic principles would be absolutely essential for the challenge of production increase (JSPS 1943, p. 1).

All committee members involved in the survey, excluding the chairman, were from aircraft companies. The committee was established to study how to rationalize the production of aircraft, and the flow production survey was part of this study. However, the survey was aimed at rationalizing the production process of aircrafts rather than simply introducing flow production to engineering trades. After the confrontation with the United Kingdom and the United States began in 1941, the Japanese government endeavored to maximize aircraft production. Engineers found a solution based on flow production.

Japanese engineers defined flow production as:

> The essence of flow production is to proceed with work following the production process sequence and to close any gaps or to reduce any backflow in the course of production. The handicraft industry, which is operated just by one person, therefore, could implement flow production… (JSPS 1944, p. 2).

Some fiercely criticized this definition considering it as a retrograde notion: flow production is largely irrelevant for the primitive handicraft industry, which has no mechanical basis at all (Aikawa 1944). The JSPS report, in at later section, discussed flow production as pertaining to conveying equipment:

> All materials would move smoothly in the workplaces by combining operating machines with carrying devices; there would be no extra materials on hand as well as no waiting time for the work. Consequently, production would be based on the production schedule. Thus, this could be considered flow production (JSPS 1944, p. 29).

As described, the JSPS did not neglect the importance of "conveying equipment" nor "carrying device." However, it did attach greater importance to the smooth and continuous flow of work-in-progress rather than to mechanical devices. This approach to flow production was not unique and was prevalent in Japan. For example, a leading management scholar before the war, Yasutaro Hirai, explained flow production as:

> People would often associate flow production with conveyors, and flow production would require conveyors. But this is not necessarily the case. Conveying materials from one station to another would often be done just by hand (Hirai 1932, pp. 135–136).

Although the JSPS mentioned flow production with "conveying equipment," they prioritized the smooth flow of materials in their report. Both the JSPS and management scholars such as Hirai were typically less concerned with mechanical devices based on flow production than the time required at each process. If flow production ran steadily, the "amount of time required at each process should be the same" (JSPS 1944, p. 4).

The suggestions in the JSPS report sounded straightforward, but they were difficult to apply in Japanese factories at the time. Sadao Hatano, the chairman of the JSPS committee, recognized that the production efficiency of Japanese machine industries remained poor mainly because they produced many different product part types in small amounts at each factory. Under these conditions, Hatano attempted to find a solution that would increase production volume. He observed that some factories received a large volume of incoming orders for the same parts, and, in other factories, several parts were produced with similar operations. Hatano concluded that those factories would be likely to increase production efficiency easily: "once they rearrange both machine and jobs based on the production sequence, the work-in progress should move smoothly in the production sequence" (Hatano 1941, p. 807). This was the reason why Hatano attached such importance to flow production.

Before the JSPS report was published, Hatano died. However, in 1943, the year the JSPS survey reported on flow production, Kazuo Noda published a short article. Noda was a pioneer and the creator of the time and motion study in Japan (Sasaki

1987). He directly addressed the problem of how to increase production volume. He incisively described the nature of wars:

> As the war would inevitably lead to the consumption of goods in large quantities, production in wartime should be high-volume production. …Transforming to high-volume production would pose the greatest challenge for our country's industrial efficiency (Noda 1943, p. 2).

The term "high-volume production," was used by Noda, and this term, together with "flow production," were often used in the Japanese literature on production control, particularly during and just after the war. Noda clarified this term:

> High-volume production means the high-volume assembly of interchangeable parts. … Establishing high volume production requires "absolute interchangeability." …The essence of high-volume production is to produce absolutely interchangeable parts in high volume. Therefore, machine shops with "fitters" in large numbers implies that production methods are quite low level (Noda 1943, p. 2).

The above quotation was profoundly influenced by Henry Ford's article "Mass Production." In particular, the reference to the famous "mass production has no fitters" is obvious. Thus, it raises questions as to why Noda did not use the term "mass production" in the above quotation. He was clearly conscious of mass production, but did not dare to use the term. He made a distinction between mass production and high-volume production: high-volume production would not be equal to mass production with increased mechanization, specifically, extensive use of special-purpose machine tools. The essence of mass production is a smooth flow of production. A smooth flow of production can be achieved without any mechanization. At the time, the conditions in Japan did not allow engineers to install a large number of machines. Consequently, most Japanese engineers tried to establish flow production without extensive mechanization aiming for high-volume production. Their true intent, however, was to realize mass production with highly mechanized equipment.

A review of the books and articles on production control published during World War II and immediately after reveals that two terms, "flow production" and "high-volume production," were often used. Engineers using both terms were aware of the Ford production system, but they were also mindful that they could not adopt mass production at their plants. Their awareness was evident in an article written by a management scholar in 1945:

> Currently, the most important national policy is to increase production, especially the production of aircraft. But under the present conditions, we cannot easily produce the number of aircraft we badly require. …The production method, which would surely fulfill the requirements for increasing production, is getting a lot of attention: that is, high-volume production or flow production. To overcome the present crisis on which the Empire's fate depends, we have to succeed in implementing this production system. It is impossible otherwise. High-volume production, or flow production is typically realized as the Ford system. This was created by our current enemy, the United States, but even so, we should let the Ford system serve as an example (Nakagawa 1945, p. 151).

Some Japanese aircraft companies attempted to apply flow production to their own plants to realize high-volume production of aircraft. In the next section, we consider the attempts of Japanese engineers to increase aircraft output.

2.2 Evolution of Flow Production in the Aircraft Industry

After the Ford Motor Company successfully mass-produced cars, the company also attempted to manufacture planes during the early 1940s.

> As late as 1939, one of the largest airframe builders in the United States was turning out only three aircraft per day when foreign purchases gave him a large backlog of orders. By contrast, a typical Detroit auto manufacturer was turning out two or three cars a minute (Holley 1987, p. 578).

Ford tried to build many B-24 (Liberator) bombers. Although its "sequence of operations was complicated," Ford's engineers "were inventing a flow of manufacturing never before attempted" (Nevins and Hill 1963, p. 189). Ford applied its mass-production method to the production of aircraft at Willow Run, Ford's greenfield plant.

> The B-24 was broken down into 20,000 separate operations, while 70 major component sections were to be prefabricated in special areas and moved on conveyors to join the final assembly line. Some 29,000 dies and 21,000 jigs and fixtures (including special fixtures for all assembly operations) were developed at a total cost of $75–$100 million in order to reduce costs, increase accuracy, and ensure interchangeability (Zeitlin 1995, p. 57).

Nevertheless, this "most extreme experiment with the application of Detroit-style mass production to military aircraft" was "at best a Pyrrhic exercise" (Zeitlin 1995, pp. 56–57). Ford itself failed to apply its mass-production method to aircraft manufacturing.

Even in Japan, engineers were attempting volume production of aircraft during World War II. Yet, around this time, Japan established several auto-manufacturers in the late 1930s, who faced an uphill battle in establishing mass production or even high-volume production of cars (Wada and Yui 2002, Chap. 8). Despite the fact that Japan was rather poor at high-volume production, Japanese government policy compelled most Japanese engineers to apply high-volume production to any manufacturing sector, including shipbuilding and aircraft manufacture (Wada and Shiba 2000).

Shortly after World War I, when Japan began to produce aircraft, Japanese aircraft companies initially called in experts from the United States and Europe to build planes under their direction and to allow the Japanese to absorb the fundamentals of aircraft technology and design. By inviting several western engineers, and, later, by copying western aircraft, Japanese manufacturers gradually acquired aircraft design capabilities. However, even after Japanese aircraft companies managed to accumulate design capabilities, they needed production capabilities.

Japanese aircraft companies were poor at producing several of the same model of aircraft. Companies and military authorities were acutely aware of their poor production capabilities. As late as January 1939, 18 months after Japan opened hostilities against China, the Military Air Service Board invited two engineers, K.E. Sutton and E.B. Parke, from the Curtiss-Wright Corporation in the United States, and held a week-long course titled "Lectures on Mass Production of Aircraft Engines." The course covered a wide range of subjects from design and production to organization, cost accounting, and the layout of machine tools. At the lectures, Japanese engineers quizzed the Americans, sometimes with simple technical or managerial questions such as how to get test pieces or how to depreciate the value of buildings and machines. The two American engineers showed their plan of a plant that would produce 300 aircraft engines. The engineers at the Nagoya Engine Works of Mitsubishi Heavy Industries documented the lectures in Japanese, and these were circulated within the company as three volume typescripts (Sutton and Parke 1939). In addition, in February and March 1942, as war broke out between Japan and the United States, visiting engineers from Junkers, a famous German firm, lectured Japanese aircraft engineers on the high-volume manufacture of fuselages and engines (Nagoya Kōkūki Seisakujo, February and March 1942).

If the Japanese aircraft companies had no problem in producing large numbers of aircraft engines and airframes, American and European engineers would not have been invited in the late 1930s and early 1940s. If Japanese companies had not faced up an uphill battle to produce a large number of aircraft, they would not have made lecture notes or abstracts in Japanese. Therefore, the fact that such documents were made by the companies shows that they were aware of their own poor production capabilities. The engineers' efforts did bear fruit; the United States Strategic Bombing Survey evaluated the Japanese plants as "reasonably good" as follows:

> The overall planning and production methods employed in the original airframe and engine plants appear to have been reasonably good. Many production engineers and plant managers had served their time with Curtiss, Pratt and Whitney, Douglas and Lockheed before the war and much of the tooling and plant layout showed that such experience had not been wasted. Generally speaking, the United States' influence seemed much more apparent than German or Italian (United States Strategic Bombing Survey 1947a, p. 22).

But the good news was short-lived. "By the spring of 1945, the Japanese aircraft industry [had] reverted to an amorphous collection of job shops" (United States Strategic Bombing Survey 1947a, p. 22).

With respect to the actual output of aircraft, the Japanese aircraft industry produced less than US companies. Moreover, the production gap between the United States and Japan widened during the war. According to one estimate, the number of aircraft produced in Japan was 5,088 in 1914; in the US, the number was 19,433. The USA produced about 3.82 times more aircraft than Japan in 1914, and this factor increased to 5.58 times in 1943 (Yamamoto 1994). These production figures imply that Japanese aircraft companies achieved little during the war, even though Japanese firms increased their production to some extent (see Fig. 2.1) and adapted several western ideas on aircraft production systems to Japanese conditions.

Despite the relatively poor performance of the Japanese aircraft production industry during the war, engineers attempted to produce aircraft using flow production methods. Two aircraft companies, Nakajima and Mitsubishi Heavy Industries, produced approximately 60% of all combat aircraft during World War II (United States Strategic Bombing Survey 1947a, p. 20). The companies spent prodigious amounts of time and effort to achieve flow production at their plants. To examine how flow

Fig. 2.1 Annual aircraft production in Japan, Germany, and the USA, 1941 to 1944. *Source* Yamamoto (1994), p. 236

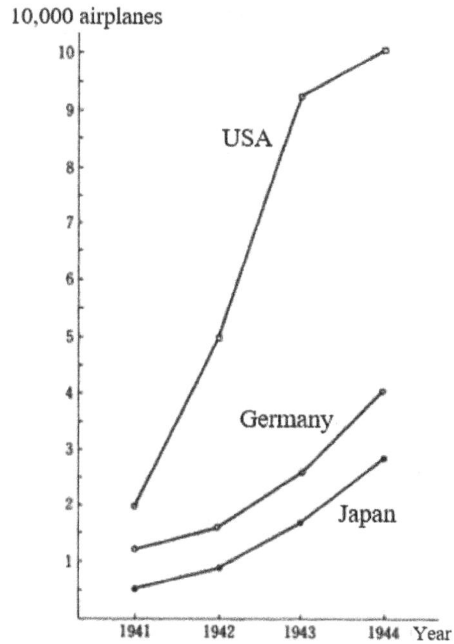

production was established in aircraft production, we divide its production process into two sections: airframe and engine.

2.2.1 *Airframe Assembly*

An engineer at the Nagoya Aircraft Works of Mitsubishi Heavy Industries asserted that there were two ways to efficiently manufacture airframes: one was sectional production and the other was the moving-forward method (Moriya 1944, p. 43). These two methods were used for airframe flow production during the war.

2.2.1.1 Sectional Production Method

In the early years, aircraft production was similar to shipbuilding: the body fuselage and wings were built first, and were then rigged up. During the war, Japanese engineers came to adopt a new way of airframe production: the fuselage and wings were divided into sections an each section was produced, fittings were installed in each section without waiting for final assembly, and then the entire sections were joined together. This was known as sectional production.

In designing the Nakajima Ki-27 fighter aircraft, the Ōta works of the Nakajima Aircraft Company took the initiative in adopting sectional production. Because its main wing was an integral structure, the whole fuselage was divided into the front and the rear part, and the airframe was assembled in separate places. Consequently, the Ōta works reduced the time required to produce an airframe: "it took within four and a half days by sectional production for the Ōta works to produce an airframe while it took about 15 days for the other companies to do the same" (Fuji Jūkōgyō Kabushiki Kaisha 1984, p. 29). The adoption of sectional production reduced the required time by creating the airframe sections simultaneously.

On the other hand, Mitsubishi's Nagoya works did not reduce airframe production time or the volume of airframe production despite expanding its airframe plant facilities greatly because the Nagoya works adhered to an old production method: a job system. Consequently "its output did not develop to the degree of its competitor, Nakajima" (United States Strategic Bombing Survey 1947b, p. 1). This comment of contrast on Nakajima and Mitsubishi was convincing because it was based on the United States Strategic Bombing Survey (USSBS). Even the USSBS wrote that "the rise in importance of Nakajima and the corresponding decline of Mitsubishi is worthy of note" (United States Strategic Bombing Survey 1947a, p. 20). The USSBS added concluding remarks: "The most important inference to be drawn from the analysis of production by the manufacturers is the growing importance of Nakajima and its final dominance of the airframe and engine industry" (United States Strategic Bombing Survey 1947a, p. 20). Most researchers accepted this view: Nakajima was a step ahead of Mitsubishi even in terms of production methods.

Opposing this view, however, the Japan Society of Mechanical Engineers (JSME) praised Mitsubishi for its sectional production method after the war: "the most advanced one [sectional production method] was Mitsubishi's Ki-67" (Nihon Kikai Gakkai 1949, p. 977). The Ki-67 was a heavy bomber, called *Hiryu* (Flying Dragon). Its production began at Mitsubishi's Nagoya works by the end of 1942. The period required for its production was reduced "generally from three months to one and a half months" (Nihon Kikai Gakkai 1949, p. 977). The production period depended largely on the type of aircraft and the weight or size of the aircraft. Mitsubishi's actual production record was not worthy of praise compared to Nakajima's Ōta works.

Why did the JSME praise Mitsubishi's Nagoya works? In reminiscing about their war experiences, engineers at Mitsubishi proudly wrote how far their attempt was advanced. They claimed that Mitsubishi's Ki-67 "was designed to adopt sectional production from its initial stage; it was also the first Japanese aircraft with a design that would emphasize better performance as well as an easy production process" (Nihon Kikai Gakkai 1949, p. 977). This statement might have served to merely glorify the past, but we can follow how the sectional production was developed for the Ki-67 bomber.

The Nagoya Aircraft works completed the first Ki-67 prototype in December 1942, and high-volume production began in April 1944. In total, 606 Ki-67 were produced (Nagoya Kōkūki Seisakujo 1988, p. 368). Before designing the Ki-67, the primary concern was the time it would take to complete a prototype aircraft. Production based on a prototype took longer because outfitting was done inside a narrow airframe. Consequently, the works could not implement high-volume aircraft production. For the Ki-67, however, policy changed with a strong emphasis on "how the prototype would incorporate the ideas of high-volume production, and, also, how quickly workers could move from experimental production to volume production" (Okuda 1943; Nagoya Kōkūki Seisakujo 1988, p. 130). This statement was written and circulated in the works soon after production of the Ki-67 shifted to high-volume production in September 1943. Thus, some engineers recognized that the production method of the Ki-67 was something new and innovative, and the statement was not made simply to glorify an older engineer.

Mitsubishi's Nagoya Aircraft works introduced a complete sectional method for the design stage of its Ki-67 bomber. Before starting the Ki-67 design, the works reorganized its design engineers on a functional basis, such as wing, fuselage, or hydraulic system. The works also created a department of production engineering, which controlled all the production techniques on site. This department also established a committee that oversaw production techniques, and included a person in charge of the specialized departments such as the wing, for example, at each plant. In designing a prototype, a design team would often consult the committee for production techniques to confirm that its original designs were suitable or amenable to high-volume production. Based on the advice of the committee, the original design was changed and adapted for easier and quicker production. In accordance with these changes, the blueprints for each section of the airframe, including the placement of all necessary fittings, were redrawn.

The adoption of "complete sectional methods" for the Ki-67 caused significant changes in blueprints. The blueprints for the Ki-67 were prepared for each production process showing the number of personnel required, the number of days needed to complete each section, and other factors. These changes in the blueprints facilitated practices whereby each section of airframe was outfitted before each section was joined to form a complete airframe. Jigs and fixtures for volume production were also prepared in advance and were tried and checked for their suitability for high-volume production.

This was the rudimentary practice of product and process design in manufacturing. In a sense, this could be considered the embryonic stages of the modern Japanese engineering practice of "concurrent engineering." After the production of the Ki-67 bomber began, one engineer wrote "we came up with a breakthrough in production methods, such as sectional production and so on, only by fundamentally changing the organization to enable close cooperation between design and production sides" (Okuda 1943; Nagoya Kōkūki Seisakujo 1988, p. 141).

The Japanese aircraft engineers at that time were familiar with sectional production having learned it from Germany, particularly from Junkers. The engineers probably considered Mitsubishi's attempts to be a modification of the German concept or even innovation. For this reason, the JSME praised the Ki-67 bomber as "the first memorable aircraft in Japan" in its fiftieth anniversary history published in 1949, although the actual number of bombers produced was less than 1,000 (Nihon Kikai Gakkai 1949, p. 977).

Japanese companies could not fully realize volume production of aircraft during World War II. However, attempts to achieve sectional production of airframes were made in which the design stage of a prototype attached importance to the level of ease in volume production.

2.2.1.2 Moving-Forward Method

While engineers began to seriously consider the adoption of sectional construction for airframes, they gradually realized the possibility of introducing flow production to airframe assembly. By 1943, Mitsubishi's Nagoya Aircraft works had successfully implemented a flow production method initially called the moving-forward method among Japanese airframe manufacturers. One observer visiting the works summarized this method as "moving-forward type flow production inspired by the German takt system," describing it:

> At each assembly station, workers worked on the sections of airframe under the direction of their squad leaders. ...Then the whole plant suddenly turned quiet. The allocated time for assembly operations was over, ...the workers pushed the section of airframe moving forward to the next assembly station. Next, the rising sun flag was hoisted, and all the workers came together in the center of plant and lined up ....Then, they returned to their original locations to continue working.... (Nihon Sangyō Keizai Shimbun 1943, pp. 7–10).

In September 1941, this moving-forward method was experimentally implemented at Mitsubishi's Nagoya Aircraft works. After two years, the works implemented the moving-forward method, but it was found that airframes did not move forward smoothly within the plant. When the works experienced a problem in moving the airframe forward from one assembly station to another, the problem was fixed step by step. Such incremental changes resulted in successful implementation of the method at the Nagoya works, which received an official commendation from the Japanese Army for implementing the moving-forward method in April 1943 (Aikawa 1944, p. 193).

After this commendation, the method was open to the other manufacturers (Aikawa 1944, p. 193). The USSB noticed the method at Nakajima: "The plane was mounted on wheels and rolled from station to station in the shop as the various parts and sub-assemblies were added to it..." (United States Strategic Bombing Survey 1947c, p. 80). This was the moving-forward process that originated at Mitsubishi's Nagoya Aircraft works. One scholar wrote that one of the Nakajima plants implemented this method to produce Zero fighters, but only one or two aircraft per day on average. Even at this low level, Nakajima's works could not stably maintain aircraft production (Yamamoto 1994, Chap. 4).

For other small-scale manufacturers, one book compiled after the war explicitly referred to the production methods of five companies that implemented the moving-forward or takt method. The Showa Aircraft Company, for example, introduced the sectional construction method for airframe production, and the moving-forward method for fittings with 14 stations. However, the result or the production volume was not reported. The Kawasaki Aircraft Company "made efforts to increase the output rapidly," but never referred to the actual output. In addition, the Japan Aircraft Company "failed to get a result from the introduction of the moving-forward method because the company had difficulty obtaining the necessary materials for production." The Kyushu Aircraft Company "intended to adopt the moving-forward method but could not implement it smoothly" (Kōkūki Kōgōshi Editorial Committee 1948, pp. 53, 94, 88, 143).

Thus, at least several aircraft companies managed to implement the moving-forward method during the war. Although the method might have contributed to increased output to some extent, companies that implemented the method still suffered from bombing raids or faced imminent shortages of materials for production. Therefore, the moving-forward method did not significantly increase aircraft production. The compiled history of the aircraft industry during World War II addressed whether the method was adopted, but does not report actual output.

However, production engineers often praised the adoption of the moving-method at Mitsubishi's Nagoya Aircraft works even after the war. One famous Japanese efficiency engineer, Kenichi Horigome, stated: "after the introduction of the takt system [the moving-forward method at the Nagoya works], Mitsubishi rapidly changed its system into the takt system at all plants relating to the Army's production. That was brilliant" (Horigome 1967, p. 563). As previously mentioned, the USSB generally downplayed the significance of Mitsubishi compared to Nakajima in terms of aircraft output. For production methods, the USSB also used a similar line: Mitsubishi's "expansion of airframe plant facilities was large, but because of job-shop origin, its output did not develop to the degree of its competitor, Nakajima, which, after the adoption of true assembly-line techniques in 1942, expanded its production by 1944 to more than eight times its former capacity" (United States Strategic Bombing Survey 1947b, p. 1). This USSB opinion is in sharp conflict with Horigome's evaluation of Mitsubishi.

In addition to the abovementioned analysis at the company level, the USSB made a detailed assessment of Mitsubishi's particular plants:

> The assembly of aircraft was on a modern production-line basis at the Ōe-machi plant in Nagoya after January 1944. The Chita plant also was equipped modernly and final assembly was on a line basis. Wing and fuselage assembly was on a job-shop basis (United States Strategic Bombing Survey 1947b, p. 156).

The USSB astonishingly gave a precise account of the Ōe-machi plant of the Mitsubishi Nagoya works. The moving-forward method was referred to by the USSB as "on a modern production-line basis" (United States Strategic Bombing Survey 1947b, p. 156). The USSB also said that after January 1944, the plant introduced a modern production-line method. The USSB gave the date of introduction with remarkable accuracy considering that the Japanese Army officially praised the moving-forward method in April 1943. This method was later moved to the Chita plant, where final assembly of the Ki-67 bomber was carried out (United States Strategic Bombing Survey 1947b, p. 156).

The USSB recognized that the moving-forward method operated on a modern production-line basis and was highly regarded by the Japanese engineers. After the aircraft companies successfully carried out the sectional production of wings and fuselage, they attempted the assembly of airframes on a production-line basis. Mitsubishi's Nagoya Aircraft was the first company to implement the moving-forward method.

Horigome also mentioned the person who promoted the implementation of the moving-forward method at the works: Doi explained why and how the method was introduced at the works:

> Mitsubishi did not intend to implement flow production at the onset. We just wanted to make our operations easier, and to increase the production. To collect every part rationally or more easily, we wanted to pull parts from the final assembly. Therefore, we acted at the assembly plant. In fact, it might be more rational to begin with parts plants based on the production plan. Actually, we made a start on the final assembly just because it was much easier for us to attack on this project (Doi 1943, p. 10).

For the current situation, Doi insisted that the necessary parts could not be delivered on schedule. Facing this situation, Doi and other members decided to collect the necessary parts for the final assembly from its previous process. According to Doi, it resulted in the implementation of flow production.

Notably, Nakajima took a different approach to factory improvements. In August 1939, the Ōta plant reformed its organization and its ad hoc steps in production control: until then the plant had focused on final assembly. Consequently, the production process had suffered. At that time, final assembly experienced delays. The production of parts plants increased, which also did the same thing to its suppliers. As the reorganization did not change Nakajima's situation, process improvement at parts plants began as late as September 1941. The department managing the whole process within Nakajima's plant, however, was not responsible for placing orders with suppliers. Therefore, parts purchasing often did not correspond to the pace of production inside Nakajima's plant. Again, Nakajima reformed its organization in November 1941. By then, Mitsubishi's Nagoya Aircraft works had already begun to implement flow production on an experimental basis. Considering this situation, Nakajima was not one step ahead of Mitsubishi's Nagoya works in terms of production control, although Nakajima increased its output compared to Mitsubishi.

However, Mitsubishi's Nagoya works did not attain a high standard of production control. This is evident from the works' processes before the introduction of the moving-forward method. At first, the works analyzed its operations process, and created its assembly order sheet showing the sequence "which parts would go from and enter into the assembly plant." Then, the works "made its assembly operation schedule and combined the assembly order sheet with operation analysis on each process;" the works clarified its assembling sequence, machining sequence, machining time, number of personnel required for each process, and also divided each process between the main task and its preliminary work (Doi 1943, p. 10).

To achieve this, the works obtained the necessary information and training through a training session for production engineers, which was sponsored by the Japan Management Association (JMA). For the training session, Doi was sent from the works, and learned about Therblig analysis and how to measure processing time for each process for three months. At that time, even large Japanese companies such as Mitsubishi had rudimentary ability only for production control. Thus, they had to learn basic production control knowledge and absorb it through a process of trial and error. This resulted in the introduction of sectional production and the moving-forward method.

2.2.2 *Parts Manufacturing*

For airframe assembly and parts manufacturing, Japanese production engineers attempted to implement flow production during World War II. Once the moving-forward method was implemented in the final assembly, engineers directed their attention to making parts and their delivery. Particularly, as mentioned earlier, the moving-forward method was adopted because it could collect every part rationally or easily. Consequently, the production engineers attempted to pull necessary parts from final assembly (Doi 1943, p. 10). For smooth operation of the flow production method, they gradually recognized that the smooth delivery of necessary parts was essential. One engineer said: "The greatest enemy of the moving-forward method was late [delivery of] parts. If parts are delivered on time, the method could work. If the method could work, facilitating the delivery would be much easier" (Moriya 1944, pp. 45–46). In fact, the Nagoya works produced and circulated a secret document in 1943, noting the difficulty in parts making:

> We, Mitsubishi's Nagoya Aircraft works, implemented the moving-forward method at the assembly plant; we completed flow production in the assembly operations [for airframe]. But the problem now remaining is how to establish the planned flow production for parts making… This is a very difficult task to accomplish… but, in order to utilize [the virtues of the method] fully, we should also prepare for flow production in parts making (Takagi 1943, pp. 1–2).

This lengthy report shows that the works recognized the necessity of smooth parts supply. However, this concept was not fully implemented at the works, probably because acquiring materials in time and controlling suppliers became increasingly difficult as the war accelerated. However, engineers developed formulas to overcome the parts delivery problem. The following sections describe two of them: the semi-flow production method and the propulsive storage method. The latter was called the *suishin-ko* method, in rather awkward Japanese.

2.2.2.1 Semi-flow Production

Necessary parts should be delivered without delay to maintain the pace of final assembly. To achieve this, engineers first applied the flow production method to parts making. However, flow production was difficult to implement in making parts, which was a low volume process. As one solution, Nakajima's Musashino works found a compromise in the form of the semi-flow production method (Sakuma 1943, p. 128). This method of parts making required low volume with effects similar to flow production where possible. Some parts differed in size and shape but were produced through identical or similar processes. Even if each of these parts was required in a small amount, they could be economically produced through joint production, according to advocates.

Semi-flow production was often illustrated with a specific example: the production of gears. At that time, an engine used almost 50 different types of gears. Three of each type of gear was used in each engine. If the production of engines was 300 per month, the gears would not reach over 3,000, which was thought to be economical through flow production. However, the monthly output of all gears would reach over 45,000. Those gears would differ in size and shape, but the necessary steps of production process would be similar. By dividing these gear groups according to similar processes, engineers sought to apply the semi-flow production method to each group of gears, which would reach well over 3,000 per month.

While reading through the semi-flow production reports, some were reminded of Woollard's comments on a group production system:

> Progressive firms are finding there are many useful lessons to be learned from flow production techniques which can be applied to small outputs and that when this is done a very near approach will be made towards achieving flow production costs. Products based on engineering practice usually fall into recognizable categories, such as casings, covers, shafts, pulleys, gears, cams, and so forth. Moreover, since most concerns deal with allied or at least similar products, these components although varied are, quite frequently, suitable for flow production under what is known as the group [production] system.

The method employed is to analyze and classify the running jobs and to group the components in such fashion as to permit a layout of the machines in operation sequence (Woollard 1954, p. 42).

Woollard's thought on the group production system were equally applicable to semi-flow production. Advocates of the semi-flow production attached substantial value to the organizing of "a layout of the machines in operation sequence" (Woollard 1954, p. 42). Machines were arranged by type and several same-type machines were grouped. Several groups of machines, such as milling machines, were grouped according to operation sequence. An area that contained the same types of machines was called a work area, although a different type of machine could be placed there if necessary. Thus, a whole plant was divided into several work areas. For example, the operation would start with work area A, and then the next operation would be done in work area B. In this way, the necessary operations would be done while moving from one work area to another (see Fig. 2.2).

Operations at each work area were followed by an inspection process, then work-in-progress was moved into a pool, which was located at the beginning of the next work area (see Fig. 2.2). These pools were the warehouse of each work area, which buffered the differences in working time between the work areas. Despite great effort, each work center was unable to achieve the same processing time unless they processed the same parts. The differences in processing times of the work centers were accounted for by installing a pool in each work area.

In addition, the fact that the production site became composed of several production areas induced an unexpected effect: the management of the production site became decentralized. As the inspector was stationed in each work area, the inspection function was delegated to the work site to a certain extent. Moreover, both a group

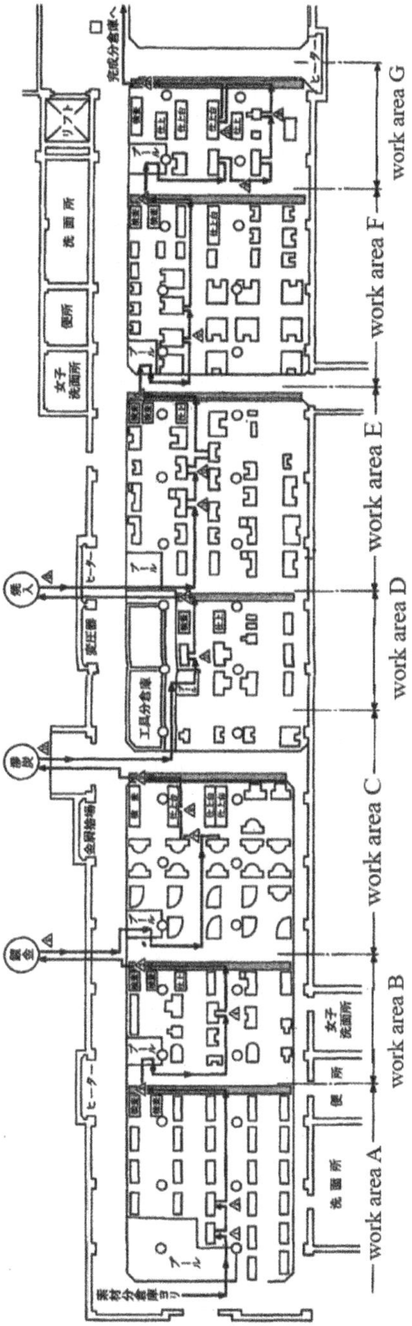

Fig. 2.2 Layout of machine-tools at a workshop adopting semi-flow production. Arrows indicate the flow of work-in-progress. Various shapes inside each area indicate the types of machine tools. *Source* JSPS (1944, Fig. 6)

leader and a progress chaser were also stationed in each work area. These personnel were responsible for production and its progress within each work area. This labor-intensive control of scheduling was, in a sense, substituted by more capital-intensive controls such as mechanical conveyors.

The production site devised a solution to facilitate the management of in-process parts:

> Tote-boxes were, in principle, to accommodate one lot per box. But if one lot of parts could not fit in one box, more than two boxes with a continuous sign were used. The information such as the time of completion, process sequence, machine number, and delivery place were clearly displayed in the tote box. For example, the tote-box was painted in white, and its symbols were written in black enamel. Separately, some parts that could work in a hurry, or special parts, were stored in tote-boxes, painted in red, and with a specified delivery order (Sakuma 1943, p. 141).

Through these actions, the worker was immediately able to confirm the information about the processing instructions without any slips. Similar ideas were also proposed to Japan's shop floors after the war.

However, the semi-flow production method applied only to parts with similar processes, and such parts were limited.

Moreover, changes in the design and processing technology of manufacturing methods were required, which changed the arrangement of machines. The semi-flow production method had a limit to its benefits. Overcoming this to a certain extent, therefore, the Musashino works quickly rearranged its machine tools in devising the required jigs and tools. In fact, the works did not fix its machine tools to the factory floor but simply installed them with wedges to minimize movement and vibration. Because the machine tools used electric power directly without belts or shafts, the locations of the machine tools could change. It was possible to rearrange "two hundred machine tools into a new array in just three days" (Nihon Keizai Renmeikai Chōsa-ka 1944, pp. 31–32). This made it possible to rearrange the layout of machine tools swiftly as design and manufacturing methods changed, although problems remained as to whether the fine machining process would be possible using this type of machine-tool fixing.

The layout of machine tools could be changed swiftly, however, only if each machine tool was equipped with its own electric motor for operations. Therefore, it was only possible for larger establishments, such as the Musashino works, to implement this swift rearrangement of machines. Most Japanese factories supplied power to their machines through belts or shafts.

2.2.2.2 Propulsive Storage Method

When inexpensive electric motors emerged in Japan, the electrification of small and medium-sized factories proceeded rapidly after World War I compared to western nations (Minami 1976). Individual operations of machine tools were also increasingly adopted. However, the literature also shows that engineers in some factories still had to manage operations that mostly used belt-driven or shaft-driven machines. Engineers tried to increase efficiency even in such factories.

Their idea was simple: the total processing route for all parts machined inside a factory should be shorter. When a factory processed several types of parts, the work-in-progress for each part type would move and their routes would cross each other inside the factory (see Fig. 2.3). Even in such a factory, the engineers would insist on moving the work-in-progress as a whole, without turning back, through the factory. Engineers tried to reduce the number of part types or tried to process parts with a similar type of machining process, but their attempts were rarely successful or succeeded only temporarily. The types of parts processed were frequently changed and the operations were unstable. Furthermore, the types of parts produced in the same factory as well as their production processes frequently changed. Toward the end of the war, reorganizing the insides of factories became difficult because of material shortages: "Unless they had enough materials, no machine shop could realize their own ideal factory operations" (Nainen Kikan Henshūbu 1944, p. 139).

Except for some large-scale factories, most factories became woefully insufficient in maintaining production. Even if any factories had enough materials for production, process managers often run from one place to another inside a factory because changes in design and working methods were frequent. Once changes were made, managers had to identify the work-in-progress that needed to be changed and replace the identification tags. The military authorities also asked munitions factories to submit accounting documents to maintain control over costs. Consequently, Japanese factories issued many slips: it was said "An aircraft-producing factory used hundreds of thousands of slips during the war" (Nihon Nōritsu Kyōkai Sagyō-bu 1946, p. 69), or "A factory was said to use a truck-load of slips on the shop floor in the war" (Ono 1952, p. 69).

Workers handled numerous slips and undertook unfamiliar tasks such as writing necessary information on slips and handing them over to other sections. Thus, these tasks were often left incomplete, and slips were lost while waiting to be handled. One observer described the situation during the war as follows:

> Slips often became detached from the work-in-progress on the shop floor of a general factory. The process managers chased after the work-in-progress inside the factory. Officers on the shop floor were busy handling and putting the work-in-progress in order. They were too busy to improve operations to increase production. For officers, the days were laborious (Niizaki 1945, p. 5).

Consequently, slips did not reflect the actual conditions on the shop floor, and the daily production schedule based on such slips became meaningless.

Despite this situation, a new attempt at production control emerged. At the end of the war, the Japan Management Association (JMA) proposed a way to control production based on goods in-kind, not reliance on the information of goods on slips (Niizaki 1945). The JMA proposed setting up units in the workplace that would take responsibility for the daily production of parts and process control. This unit was called *Suishin-ko* in Japanese, which literally meant "propulsive storage." An organization with a higher level of management could achieve coordination between

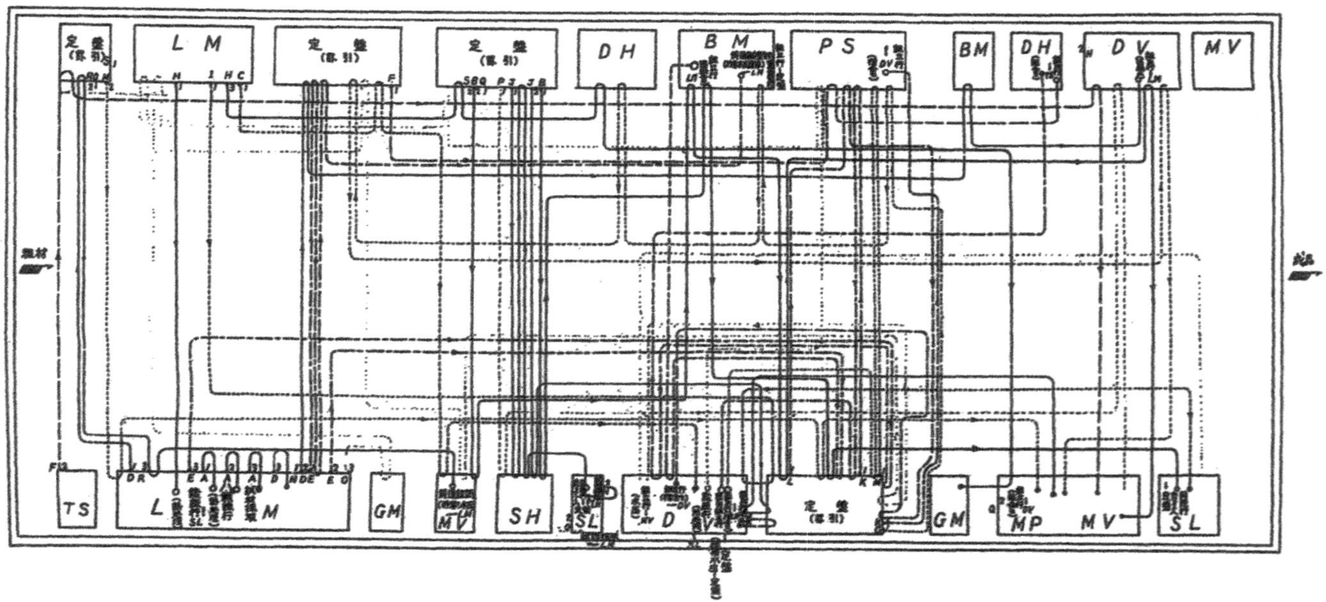

Fig. 2.3 Routing of all work-in-progress at a machine shop. Arrows indicate the flow of the work-in-progress for each part type. *Source* Nihon Keizai Renmeikai Chōsa-ka (1944, appendix table)

units. For each unit, propulsive storage meant that three men would be assigned: a group leader, one in charge of production progress, and one inspection clerk. Once they accepted work-in-progress from a previous process, they would inspect it and keep it in their own store. According to daily production, they would take it from the store and begin processing when required. As a group leader at each unit would take care of paperwork, the amount of paperwork for workers on the shop floor was significantly reduced.

Advocates of this method considered that it might have applicability not just to parts factories but also to other industries. However, this practice was experimentally introduced to just several aircraft companies. By the end of the war, use of this method was not widespread.

2.2.3 The Gap Between Vision and Reality

For airframe assembly, two methods emerged to achieve flow production during World War II: sectional production and moving-forward. But both methods were not unique to Japan. In fact, the moving-forward method was an iteration of the German "takt system" (Araki 1985, pp. 89–90). Even Japanese literature often called the moving-forward method the takt system. In addition, the sectional method was also an imitation of American and German concepts.

Once Japanese companies managed to emulate concepts from foreign countries and implemented flow production to the airframe assembly, parts production for aircraft required a major overhaul of production methods. However, as the volume of parts production was limited, most factories attempted to supply enough parts by modifying their own existing facilities, not by installing assembly lines. Consequently, the semi-flow production method was common during the war, although it was applicable to only limited types of parts. In contrast, the propulsive storage method was considered to be universally applicable. Both methods had several characteristics in common. First, they created a buffering area, as storage, between production processes. Both methods divided the shop floor into small groups. Each of the small groups was in control of their own storage. These small groups would establish a foundation for production control for the whole factory.

However, the original aims of these attempts or methods would not be easy to attain because even large-scale factories had to rely on the supply of many parts from many small-scale factories. In the case of Nakajima Aircraft Company, for example, its engines department dealt with 84 affiliated firms, which amounted to approximately 70% of the total works in the department. In addition, Nakajima ordered small parts for 320 subcontracting firms (Kōkūki Kōgōshi Editorial Committee 1948, p. 223). Therefore, one of the most critical challenges for production control at the aircraft manufacturing companies was the control of affiliated or subcontracting factories. Nakajima had regular meetings with most of its affiliated suppliers to rigorously demand maintenance of the required quality and quantity, as well as the delivery dates (Egi 1955, p. 12). However, even most large-scale manufacturers could not afford to raise the level of technology of their suppliers.

As the Japanese economy faced the shortage of materials during the war, parent companies tended to provide subcontracting factories with as little material as possible. In turn, under such economic situations, factories would often have an incentive to eke out a profit by saving materials provided by parent companies and sell them in the market. Even if a parent company provided its subcontracting factories with superior quality materials, those factories often used inferior materials instead of those that the parent company provided. Quality materials easily fetched a good price in the economic environment.

The government attempted to decrease the number of subcontracting firms with the expectation that they would grow in size and sophistication, but this goal remained unrealized as late as the early 1940s. Then the government suggested that each subcontracting firm should work for one specific parent company, but this was also in vain. Some large-scale companies, such as the Mitsubishi Heavy Industries, took a stake in their own affiliated or subcontracting firms to put them under their full control (Shiba 1986).

To increase aircraft production, the major aircraft companies attempted to establish aircraft production flow by implementing several production methods. The companies achieved flow production to some extent but only within a few large plants. However, the complete process of aircraft production, that is, from part manufacture to final assembly, was unbalanced. Unused materials or partly finished products often piled up within factories, or production delays for a few types of parts led to slowdowns in aircraft production. Although engineers tried to establish aircraft flow production, their efforts were not rewarded until Japan was defeated.

2.3 Postwar Diffusion of the "Work-Center Method"

2.3.1 An Advocated Method After World War II

After World War II, the Japanese aircraft industry was obliterated. Thus, terms such as the sectional production method and the moving-forward method are not found in any journals from the war. The term semi-flow production is also not found. Furthermore, the propulsive storage method, which was promoted as applicable to processes other than parts manufacture for aircraft, is not discussed. Were these ideas or methods just in vain? Did they have any significant effect on the Japanese manufacturing industry after the war?

For a short period after the war, one production control method, the work center method, was widely adopted in many manufacturing companies. In Japanese, this was called *Suishin-ku*, which literally means "propulsive unit." As the Japanese term would suggest, it originated from the propulsive storage method, which was refined and sophisticated after the war and added a new twist to daily production scheduling.

In June 1949, Tsuneo Ono and other JMA members began a two-year trial survey of this method at Kōsoku Kikan Kōgyō, one of the early automobile manufactures in Japan aimed at perfecting the method (Nakaoka 1981, p. 164). After these experimental years, the JMA actively encouraged this work-center method. By the end of the 1950s, many Japanese companies had implemented the propulsive unit method: Canon, Victor Company of Japan (JVC), Nippon Air Brake, Diesel Kiki, Nagoya Machinery Works of Mitsubishi Heavy Industries, Aichi Tokei Denki Company, Kayaba Industry Company, Toyota Auto Body Company, Okuma Machinery, and others (Kyanonshi Henshū Iinkai 1987; Manejimento 1955; Takada 1952; Jīzeru Kiki Kabushiki Kaisha 1981; Mitsubishi Jūkōgyō Kabushiki Gaisha 1991; Yoshida 1954; Kayaba Kōgyō Kabushiki Kaisha 1986; Toyota Shatai Kabushiki Gaisha 1975; Mizuno 1954).

This method essentially divided up the entire plant into many self-contained units, each of which was controlled as a work center. Each work center would serve as the smallest unit of process control: the whole process of production flow would be supervised by a sequence of work centers. Through these work centers, the headquarters would control the whole production plan, and coordinate among all work centers. Consequently, the plant's organization chart would be often explicitly drawn on work centers supervised by headquarters.

Each work center would have 20 to 30 workers, who were closely supervised by a foreman, a progress manager, and an inspection clerk. Inspection of work-in-progress was conducted within each work center; completed work was immediately inspected in each work center and then sent on the next work center. The progress manager of each work center would closely monitor the progress of production in accordance with the production schedule.

If the planned volume of monthly production were simply assigned to work centers, the actual production would tend to surge during the last several days of the month to achieve the target production volume for the month. Figure 2.4 shows the typical fluctuations in daily production in a factory producing aircraft parts by the end of the war. When this "end-of-month problem" occurred, the plant should have extra facilities for production. Moreover, it would hamper leveling production. With no resolution to the problem, production would not smoothly flow: flow production would not be realized at all.

As the work-center method aimed at solving the end-of-month problem, it tried to subdivide the whole plant into many work centers, by which work centers would closely supervise small areas. However, advocates of this method also recognized the importance of providing production schedule information to the workers. If such information were provided to workers by tags or slips on the work-in-progress, workers would tend to put off handling or writing necessary information on slips or tags as had occurred during the war. Therefore, the method attempted to provide workers with the information of the scheduled completion dates: a combination of lead time and serial number.

Through operation process analysis, each work center would identify the length of product lead time within its work center. For this method, the serial number would not indicate the batch or lot number but a numerical number specifying a final product.

Fig. 2.4 Daily aircraft production results for the Navy in July 1944. *Source* Nihon Kikai Gakkai (1949, p. 973)

Typically, the serial number would represent the cumulative production number of the final product but, for this method, the serial number would show the date of completion and its completion sequence on the day. If a product would be assembled as the twelfth final product completed on December 3 in 2018, for example, its serial number would be assigned as 2018120312 or 18120312 and further shortened to 120312. The same numerical number would be assigned to the final product and all parts used for its completion.

This use of serial numbers reflected the production control experience of aircraft companies during the war.

> During the war, a model of aircraft was newly designed and passed through its experimental stage of production. Then, when preparation for volume production began, changes in the engineering design of the model often occurred based on its experimental flights. In those days, most factories used slips or tags to determine the particular parts or work-in-progress on the shop floor. Thus, once changes in engineering design were made, every slip or tag associated with the changes had to be recovered, rewritten, and a new tag issued. Because the number of tags or slips was numerous, the tasks of recovering and reissuing them was not fully implemented. This created a persistent and considerable stir among aircraft factories. Military engineers were responsible for the majority of this confusion because they desperately kept pushing for a new model aircraft for aircraft production. However, the factory still could not escape responsibility because it improperly prepared for aircraft production by assembling a large number of parts (Morikawa 1950, pp. 179–180).

The advocates of the work-center method claimed that even if the engineering changes had to be made, the readjustment would be easy because every part of a final product was allocated with the same serial number as the final product. Thus, it would be easy to find out what parts had overs and shorts because of the serial numbering. In addition, as the lead time of each process was previously projected, it would be easy to identify whether production delays occurred. This would also reflect the chaotic experience in factories during the war: as missing parts were often found when assembling parts as a final product; the slips or tags with "express" were dispatched to rush the production of parts. Then, the number of those slips or tags with "express" steadily grew and the factories would be mired in confusion (Murai 1951, p. 94). These experiences during the war led to a new method proposed by the JMA.

2.3.2 Introducing the Work-Center Method

Looking at several examples, we discuss how the work-center method became a strong influence on Japanese companies after World War II.

First, we discuss the case of Canon. In 1957, the company won the Third Ōkochi Memorial Production Prize from the Ōkochi Memorial Foundation. This prize was awarded to individual researchers and business organizations that made major contributions to the field of production engineering including the development of production technology and the implementation of advanced production methods. Canon received the award because the company established a method of volume production for a high-performing camera. One reason for this recommendation was "the implementation of the work-center method" (Kyanonshi Henshū Iinkai 1987, p. 70). Canon's company history was the reason for the introduction of the method: "The company arranged to dispatch a fixed volume of parts for each production lot by a voucher system… As the scale of production was increasing, however, it was increasingly difficult to know how many parts there were and where a particular type of part was" (Kyanonshi Henshū Iinkai 1987, p. 44). When the company decided to consolidate its production facilities into one site, it adopted the work-center method under the guidance of the JMA from January 1952. According to its company history, Canon improved its production management through "visual management" (Kyanonshi Henshū Iinkai 1987, p. 44; Wada and Shiba 2000, p. 330).

Toyota Auto Body adopted the work-center method in July 1949 (Toyota Shatai Kabushiki Gaisha 1975, p. 197). As "the company faced management complexity by increasing the types of motor vehicles," it invited engineers from the JMA to implement the work-center method (Toyota Shatai Kabushiki Gaisha 1975, p. 72). In July 1953, Diesel Kiki Co. implemented the work-center method introduced by the JMA (Jīzeru Kiki Kabushiki Kaisha 1981, p. 108). The company tried to overcome the limitations to centralized control by delivering orders through office ladders. The company introduced the work-center method based on the autonomous control of work centers (Jīzeru Kiki Kabushiki Kaisha 1981, pp. 108–109).

The work-center method had significant effects on the block-construction method, which contributed to the development of the Japanese shipbuilding industry after the war. In designing a ship, the block-construction method would divide entire sections of a ship into many blocks. After building all blocks on land, the blocks were transported to the ship for final assembly (Wada and Shiba 2000, p. 322). In Japan, this block-construction method was successfully employed at the Kure Shipyard run by National Bulk Carriers Ltd. (NBC), a US shipping firm (Chida and Davies 1990).

Many Japanese shipyards tried to implement the block-construction method to realize higher output with shorter production times, and it became an industry-wide standard. As the scale of production increased, however, the block construction method could not work effectively: without precise production control of blocks, the shipyards adopting this method often faced a chaotic situation in which some necessary materials were not delivered to designated locations and some were delivered in more than the required quantity. For example, as output at Mitsubishi Nagasaki Shipyard began to increase around 1956, the shipyard began a program primarily intended to ensure that blocks were "produced at the right time, in the right order, in the right quantity" and it also initiated a rework of the entire production process (Kita 1957, p. 34). The shipyard commissioned the JMA to perform its management diagnosis. For the diagnosis, the shipyard divided its whole process, from the full-size drawing of each part to the final assembly of blocks as a ship, into 16 stages (Miyashita 1960, p. 183). In addition, "by making detailed schedules of every block for each ship, the shipyard monitored the production progress of each block from the receipt of steel materials to assembly and followed-up the progress of its production according to lead time" (Kita 1957, p. 34). On the advice of JMA engineers, the shipyard reorganized its production around flow production, which consisted of a sequence of stages. Consequently, "Mitsubishi's Nagasaki Shipyard, following the model of NBC Kure Shipyard's block assembly method, achieved this method faster than any other Japanese shipyard beginning with basic research such as the detailed production flow" (Miyashita 1960, p. 188).

As stated, the work-center method had widespread influence for a time following the war on industries such as shipbuilding. In particular, people involved with the JMA aggressively disseminated information about the work-center method.

2.3.3 Decline in Influence of the Work-Center Method

Although the work-center method was eagerly introduced in Japanese manufacturing sector for a time after World War II, it began to fade in importance in the late 1950s. Many companies started to lose interest in this method. As Nakaoka stated accurately, "the work-center method achieved great success in the early 1950s, and that just for the period" (Nakaoka 1981, p. 49). Some companies that had adopted this method soon abandoned it. This stemmed from the defects inherent in the work-center method.

As this method placed many work centers in the whole production process, the number of people employed in the production site was larger than traditional production methods. Companies that had to suppress the rise in personnel found it difficult to adopt this method. As stated earlier, Toyota Auto Body adopted this method, and the company was appreciative of its advantages: "it achieved a growing awareness of inventory management and restrained losses caused by delays in the delivery of parts," and "it standardized the control process." However, the company "regarded its drawback as a necessity to increase administration personnel." In 1956, when the company had to downsize, it abandoned the work-center method of production (Toyota Shatai Kabushiki Gaisha 1975, pp. 72, 197).

Before its full-scale implementation, the work-center method required a survey of current process and various materials on operation process. If a company implemented this method without such a survey or detailed information on operation processes, it would have to spend a lot of time on preparation up front. This applied to the case of Diesel Kiki. In July 1953, accepting a recommendation from the JMA, Diesel Kiki adopted the work-center method. However, because the company did not allow a sufficient preparation period for its adoption, the company experienced substantial hardship before the method was firmly entrenched: "The company made many changes in collected materials for formulating the plans. Lead times went through changes. The company had to correct orders on regular stocks. In addition to these, the layout of machines had to be rearranged to simplify the progress control. Moreover, it became clear that the production capacity of subcontracting factories should increase" (Jīzeru Kiki Kabushiki Kaisha 1981, pp. 110–111). Canon implemented the method successfully, but the person in charge explained: "Four years have passed since Canon adopted the work-center method. We consistently opposed the method from its introduction" (Kōjō kanri 1955, p. 32). The difficulties, which both companies encountered in trying to implement the method, would be largely attributed to most Japanese companies' inexperience in detailed analysis of production processes. This intractable situation, which both companies faced, also showed how difficult it was to analyze the production processes to obtain useful information on production control because of unstable processing or machining operation.

The cooperation of subcontracting firms was essential to implement the work-center method because the method intended to control the link with those firms as part of production control. This was because production leveling was essential to implementing "the work-center method, which had a slogan of *reducing work-in-process*" (Jīzeru Kiki Kabushiki Kaisha 1981, p. 111). Despite adopting the work-center method, Diesel Kiki made some modifications to the method because its purchaser's plant often ordered schedules. By 1958, the company had to announce its policy officially: it would make sales forecasts two months in advance and would hold inventories for two months (Jīzeru Kiki Kabushiki Kaisha 1981, p. 148). Finally, the company abandoned the method.

The disappearance of the work-center method after the late 1950s could be due to the defects inherent in the method. However, we consider the cause to be changes in the nature of production control, which changed production processes because of increased mechanization. Canon's case showed this: the company shifted away from the method although it implemented it successfully. Around the end of the 1950s, Canon began "to mechanize and automate its parts processing," and "to install conveying equipment" for its assembly process. It also "abolished the finishing department... and prohibited the use of files and hammers for fixing parts" in 1960. This shows how the company achieved a higher level of machining accuracy. In addition, the company "accelerated the introduction of single-purpose or automated machinery into the production process as far as possible." As a result, the company allocated workers with less experience instead of skilled workers with traditional practices to form production lines (Kyanonshi Henshū Iinkai 1987, pp. 68–69).

The advancement of the situation at Canon showed that the role of the work-center method had ended. The method was essentially formulated to suit the specific situation in Japan during the postwar years. The situation in those years was described as:

> The production time at each process is not standardized nor stable at all in this country. Even if we tried to enhance and expand an efficient division of labor within workplaces, we could not ensure stable and sufficient supplies of high-grade special-purpose machinery. Most subcontracting parts manufacturers still use similar production facilities such as those in small factories. Furthermore, industrial standards in Japan as a whole are yet to become widespread. Therefore, we have much work to do to improve industry efficiency in many ways (Morikawa 1950, p. 172).

The work-center method aimed to fit into this context: the method was considered a transitory measure before increasing mechanization and enhancing the stability of production time. In fact, Morikawa said: "the work-center method was to prepare, train, or practice how to control the production effectively in the forthcoming enhancing mechanization years" (Morikawa 1950, p. 173).

The work-center method had no meaning for the companies such as Canon, which were able to analyze their own production process in detail by themselves, introduce automated machinery, and even establish conveyor systems. Canon abolished the work-center method (Kyanonshi Henshū Iinkai 1987, pp. 68–69).

In the late 1950s, just like Canon, many companies increasingly endeavored to construct plants for volume production by installing special-purpose machines. In addition, companies installed many high-performance machine tools and moved in the direction of mechanized conveyor lines. Consequently, Japanese production engineers began to become aware of "the statistical approach of analyzing data on mass production" (Okuda 1985, p. 518). The case of Canon indicates how Japanese companies paid attention to these trends. As stated earlier, the company received the Okochi Memorial Production award in April 1957 partly because of the implementation of the work-center method. In the same month, Canon implemented training on statistical quality control by inviting a lecturer from the Union of Japanese Scientists and Engineers.

The work-center method disappeared as Japanese companies became interested in installing many machine tools in their plants. After the 1950s, American ideas on production control were introduced and rapidly spread among Japanese companies.

2.4 Acceptance of the Ford Production System by Japanese Manufacturing Industries by the Early 1950s

Ford's production system had a significant impact on production engineers in Japan and other countries. Engineers typically focused on high-performing moving assembly lines. Japanese production engineers were astonished by the efficient production, but they placed less emphasis on its mechanical devices. They conceptualized Ford's production system as a flow production system: it would be almost impossible for many plants to install many special-purpose machine tools to achieve high-precision machining of parts in Japan. Japanese production engineers aimed to ensure smooth flow of work-in-progress through the entire process. Consequently, they focused their energy on ensuring the same processing time for each process.

During World War II, Japan attempted to increase the production of aircraft. Japanese production engineers strived to ensure the smooth flow of airframe assembly by introducing sectional production and the moving-forward method. Once they established smooth airframe assembly technically, the challenges they faced were how to obtain high-volume, precision-processed parts. In this case, the term high-volume just meant large volume, which could not justify the installation of many special-purpose machine tools for precision work following Ford's production system. Simply copying Ford's production system with volume production could not achieve low-cost production. Therefore, production engineers increased the volume production of parts by organizing production plants in which work-in-progress might pass smoothly through the whole manufacturing process. Because they could not rely on many machine tools or mechanical conveyors, they divided the manufacturing process into small sections to better trace the location of work-in-progress. However, the lack of materials and the impact of bombing raids prevented them from achieving their intention during the war.

After the war, production methods were systematized through much trial and error by the work-center method. This method was adopted by many Japanese manufacturing companies, particularly during the early 1950s, and was the outcome of attempts to smooth the flow of work-in-progress throughout the entire process under poorly mechanized conditions. After emphasizing this as a unique and original method, Nakaoka claimed:

> It was awful, particularly compared to control systems in later years. Nevertheless, it was really adapted to the level of the machinery industry in Japan at that time. Japan experienced how to control their own production process using this system before overall technology transfer from the United States began. This was of great significance. We should not overlook this (Nakaoka 1981, p. 48).

This chapter has discussed how the Ford production system was received in Japan. The work-center method could be regarded as a milestone in Japanese manufacturing. However, this chapter has not addressed how Japanese automobile companies received these developments and applied them to their own production processes. For Toyota, this topic has been widely discussed as the Toyota Production System or "Toyota's Kanban method." It should be noted that the work-center method "quite resembles Toyota's Kanban method because the work-center method would minimize the volume of work-in-progress if it were well implemented" (Nakaoka 1981, p. 47). Many Japanese manufacturing companies tried to achieve smooth production flow, realize level production, and minimize the volume of work-in-production. The efforts at Toyota are an example of these practices, and, not surprisingly, the company learned from previous production control concepts and many other company experiences. If the Toyota Production System was as innovative as some claim, we should analyze and understand this level of innovation. In the following chapters, we investigate how and why Toyota created its own production system.

References

Aikawa, H. (1944). *Gijutsu- oyobi ginou kanri* (Technology and Craft Administration), Tokyo: Tōyō Shokan.

Araki, T. (1985). Nōritsu ichidaiki: keiei komon 30 nen (A Biography in Pursuit of Efficiency: 30 Years as A Management Consultant), Tokyo: Nihon Keiei Nōritsu Kenkyūjo.

Chida, T., & Davies, P. N. (1990). *The Japanese shipping and shipbuilding industries: A history of their modern growth.* London: Athlon Press.

Doi, M. (1943). "Kumitate sagyō ni okeru zenshin sagyō jisshi ni tsuite" (On the implementation of the moving-forward method on the assembly operations), *Nihon Nōritsu* (Japan Efficiency), vol. 2, no. 9.

Egi, J. (1955). Gaichū kanri to shitauke kōjō (Outsourcing Management and Suppliers' Factories). Tokyo: Nikkan Kōgyō Shinbunsha.

Fuji Jūkōgyō Kabushiki Kaisha. (1984), *Fuji Jūkōgyō 30 nenshi* (The Thirtieth Anniversary of Fuji Heavy Industries). Tokyo: Fuji Jūkōgyō.

Hatano, S. (1941). "Genka no kikai kogyo no seisan zouka no shudan to shiteno seisan gijutsusha no kyouiku yousei to nagare sagyou no jisshi" (The Education and Training of Engineers, and the Implementation of the Flow Production as the Main Means of Increasing Production in the Machine Industry under the Current Situation), *Sngyō Nōritsu* (Industry Efficiency), vol. 14 no. 9.

Hirai, Y. ed. (1932). *Sangyō gōrika zuroku* (Graphical Catalogue on Industrial Rationalization) Tokyo: Shunyōdo.

Holley, I. B., Jr. (1987). A Detroit Dream of Mass-Produced Fighter Aircraft: The XP-75 Fiasco. *Technology and Culture, 28*(3).

Horigome, K. (1967). "Nihon kōgyō kyōkai no koro wo kataru" (Talking about the Years at the Japan Industry Association), in *Indasutorial Enginiaringu* (Industrial Engineering), *9*(6).

Jīzeru Kiki Kabushiki Kaisha. (1981). *Jīzeru Kiki 40-nenshi* (Forty Years' History of Diesel Kiki Co., Ltd.). Tōkyō: Jīzeru Kiki.

JSPS (1943). *Waga kuni ni shiyo seraruru nagare sagyo oyobi kore ga gensoku no ohyo ni kansuru chosa houkoku* (The Report of Survey on the Flow Production and the Application of its Principles used in Our Country). Tokyo: Shibun Shoin.

JSPS. (1944). *Seisan ryoku to nagare sagyo* (Production Power and the Flow Production). Tokyo: Dainihon kogyou gakkai.

Kayaba Kōgyō Kabushiki Kaisha. (1986). *Kayaba Kōgyō 50-nenshi: 1935–1985* (Fifty History of Kayaba Industry Co., Ltd.). Tokyo: Kayaba Kōgyō Ka-bushiki Kaisha.

Kita, K. (1957). "Kōtei kanri no kaizen de kenzō kikan wo ōhaba ni tanshuku: Mitsubishi zosenjo·-Nagasaki zosenjo ni okeru ōgata yusōsen kenzō no jitsurei" (Significant Reduction of Construction Period by Improvement of Process Control: The Case of the Construction of a Large-Scale

Tanker at Mitsubishi's Nagasaki Shipyard). *Manejiment* (Management), vol. 16, no. 4. Tokyo: Nihon nōritsu kyōkai.

Kōjō kanri. (1955). "Seisan no baratsuki wo nakushita suishin ku sei kōtei kanri" (Production Control Eliminated Variations in Production, the Work-Center Method). *Kōjō kanri* (Factory Mangement). Tōkyō: Nikkan kōgyō shinbunsha.

Kōkūki Kōgōshi Editorial Committee, ed. (1948). *Minkan kōkūki kōgōshi* (The History of the Civil Aircraft Manufacturers) [mimeograph] n. p.

Kyanonshi Henshū Iinkai. (1987). *Kyanon shi: Gijutsu to seihin no 50-nen* (The History of Canon: Fifty Years' History of Technology and Production). Tōkyō: Kyanon.

Manejimento. (1955). "Kōjō tanbō: Menmoku wo isshin shita Nihon bikutā" (Touring Factory: JVC Underwent a Complete Change). *Manejiment* (Management), vol. 14, no. 10. Tokyo: Nihon nōritsu kyōkai.

Minami, R. (1976). *Dōryoku kakumei to gijutsu shinpo: Senzenki seizōgyō no bunseki* (Power Revolution and Technical Progress: Analysis of Prewar Manufacturing Industry). Tōkyō: Tōyō Keizai Shinpōsha.

Mitsubishi Jūkōgyō Kabushiki-kaisha. (1991). *Mitsubishi jūkō nagoya kiki seisakujo sanjūnenshi* (Thirty Years' History of Mitsubishi Heavy Industries' Nagoya Machinery Works). Nagoya: Mitsubishi jūkōgyō Nagoya kiki seisakujo.

Miyashita, T. (1960). "Zosen gyō no hatten to kōzō" (Development and Structure of the Shipbuilding Industry), in Hiromi Arisawa ed., *Gendai nihon sangyō kōza: kikai kōgō 1* (Modern Japanese Industry Course: Machine Indusry 1), vol. 5. Tokyo: Iwanami Shoten.

Mizuno, M. (1954). 'Danzoku kobetsu seisan ni okeru kōtei kanri no kaizen' (Improvement in Process Control of Intermittent Job Shop Type Pro-duction). *Manejimento* (Managemnet), *13*(2).

Morikawa, K. (1950). *Keiei gōrika no jōshiki* (The Common Knowledge of Management Rationalization). Tōkyō: Daiyamondosha.

Moriya, G. (1944). 'Kōkūki no taryō seisan'(The High-Volume Produc-tion of Aircrafts), in Kichijirō Kobayashi ed., *Taryō seisan kennkyū* (Study on the High-Volume Production), vol. 2. Tokyo: Gunji kōgyō shinbun kyoku shuppan kyoku.

Murai, I. (1951). *Kigyō gōrika no tameno seisan gijutsu* (Production Technique for the Enterprise Rationalization). Koronasha.

Nagoya Kōkūki Seisakujo (Nagoya Aircraft Works at the Mitsubishi Heavy Industries, Ltd.) (Feburary 1942). 'Hikōki no taryō seisan soshiki ni tsuite' (On the Organization of Producing a High-Volume of Aircraft) in *Sankō shiryō* (Reference Material), no. 36.

Nagoya Kōkūki Seisakujo (Nagoya Aircraft Works at the Mitsubishi Heavy Industries, Ltd.) (March 1942). 'Kōkūki kōgyō keizaiteki shidō mondai' (Findings on the Economic Problems of Aircraft Industry) in *Sankō shiryō* (Reference Material), no.38.

Nagoya Kōkūki Seisakujo (Nagoya Aircraft Works at the Mitsubishi Heavy Industries, Ltd.). (1988). *Meikō kōsakubu no senzen sengo shi: watashi to kōkūki seisan Moriya sōdanyaku* (The Pre- and Postwar History of the Nagoya Aircraft Works Machining Division: Aircraft Production and Me – Advisor Moriya). Nagoya: Nagoya Aircraft Works at the Mitsubishi Heavy Industries, Ltd.

Nakagawa, A. (1945). 'Fōdo shisutemu'(Ford System), in Yojiro Mauji ed. (1945), *Seisn kanri no riron* (The Theory of Production Control). Tokyo: Nihon hyouron sha.

Nakaoka, T. (1981). 'Senchū-sengo no kagaku teki kannri undō: Ni-hon nōritsu kyōkai to Nikka giren no katsudō ni sotte (2)' (Scientific Management Movement during and after the War: On the basis of activities by JMA and the Union of Japanese Scientists and Engineers) (2). *Keizaigaku Zasshi [Osaka shiritu daigaku]* (Economics Magazine of Osaka City University), *2*(3).

Nainen Kikan Henshūbu. (1944). *Kōkūki no taryō seisan hōshiki* (The High-Volume Production Method of Aircraft). Tokyo: Sankaidō.

Nevins, A., & Hill, F. E. (1963). *Ford: Decline and rebirth, 1933–1962*. New York: Scribner.

Nihon Keizai Renmeikai Chōsa-ka ed., (1944). *Sangyō nōritsu to seisan gijutsu oyobi soshiki mondai* (Industry Efficiency and Indusrial Technology as well as Organizational Problems). Tokyo: Sankaidō.

Nihon Kikai Gakkai (Japan Society of Mechanical Engineers), ed. (1949). *Nihon kikai kogyo 50 nen* (The Mechanical Engineering in Japan: 50 Years). Tokyo: Ni-hon Kikai Gakkai, 1949.

Nihon Nōritsu Kyōkai Sagyō-bu. (1946). 'Suishin-ku sei kōtei kanri hōshiki' (The Work Center Process-Control Method), *Nihon Noritsu* (Efficiency in Japan), *5*(4).

Nihon Sangyō Keizai Shinbun ed. (1943) *Zenkoku mohan kōjō shisatsu ki* (The Observation Record of Model Factories across the Nation). Tokyo: Kasumigaseki Shobō.

Niizaki, K. (1945). 'Kōtei kanri no ichi hōshiki' (One Method for Process Control), *Nihon Noritsu* (Efficiency in Japan), vol. 3, no. 5(1945).

Noda, N. (1943). 'Zosan kessen to taryo seisan' (The Decisive Battle for Increasing Output and High-volume Production), *Nihon Noritsu* (Efficiency in Japan), vol. 2, no. 5.

Okuda, K. (1985). *Hito to keiei: Nihon keiei kanrishi kenkyū* (People and Management: Study on Business Administration in Japan). Tokyo: Manejimentosha.

Okuda, K. (1943) 'Ki-67 Hiryu no seisan gijutsu kakumei' (The Production and Technological Revolution of Ki-67 Flying Dragon), in Nagoya Kōkūki Seisakujo (1988).

Ono, T. (1952). 'Mada mada unyō no myō ni kurai kōtei kanri: kongo wa jimu gijutsu men no kairyō ni matsu' (Yet Falling A Long Way Short of Good Process Control: From Now On, Office Management Should be Improved), in *Manejiment* (Management), *11*(5).

Sakuma, I. (1943) 'Seisan-ryoku to nagare sagyō' (Productive Power and Flow Production Methods). In N. K. Renmei Chōsaka (Ed.).

Sasaki, S. (1987). 'Mitsubishi Denki ni miru kagaku teki kanri dounyu katei: jikan kenkyu hou dounyu wo chushin ni shite' (The Introduction Process of Scientic Management Method: Focusing on the Introduction of Time and Motion Studies), *Keiei shi gaku* (Japan Business History Review), vol. 21, no. 4 (1987).

Sutton, K. E., & Parke, E. B. (1939). *Satton Pāku ryōshi kōkūki hatsudōki tairyō seisan ni kansuru kōshūroku* (Notes of Lectures on the Mass Production of Aircraft Engines by both Messrs. Sutton and Parke), vols. 3 (Typescript). vol.1 *Kōshūroku* (Notes of Lectures); vol. *Shitsugi outō* (Question and Answer); vol.3 *Kōkūki hatsudōki gessan 300 dai no kōjō keikaku* (The Plant Plan of Producing 300 Aircraft Engines per Month). Mitsubihi jūkō Nagoya hatsudōki seisakujo (The Naogya Engine Worksn at the Mitsubishi Heavy Industries, Ltd).

Shiba, T. (1986). 'Senji taiseiki ni no zaibatsu kei jūkōgyō no kabushiki shoyū no kōzō: Mitsubishi Jūkōgyō no baai' (The Stock Ownership Structure of Heavy Industries Companies in Zaibatsu Business Combines: The Case of Mitsubishi Heavy Industries). *Osaka Daigaku Keizaigaku* (The Economics of Osaka University), *35*(4).

Takada, Y. (1952). 'Kanri hōshiki ni shin kijiku: damu hōshiki wo kami shita kōtei kanri no jissai' (A New Departure in its Management Procedure: Process Control Procedure Adding a Creating Dams Method). *Manejiment* (Management), vol. 11, no. 12. Tokyo: Nihon nōritsu kyōkai.

Takagi, S. (1943), *Keikaku sekinin nagare seisan ni okeru sagyo kanri ni tsuite* (On the Shop Floor Control, Being Responsible for the Planned Flow Production) [mimeograph]. Naogya: Mitsubish Nagoya Aircraft Works.

Toyota Shatai Kabushiki Gaisha. (1975). *Toyota shatai sanjūnenshi* (Thirty Years' History of Toyota Auto Body Co. Ltd). Kariya: Toyota Shatai.

United States. (1947a). *U.S. Strategic Bombing Survey: Japanese Aircraft Industry.*

United States. (1947b). U.S. *Strategic Bombing Survey: Mitsubishi Heavy Industries (Mitsubishi Jukogyo K K).*

United States. (1947c). *U.S. Strategic Bombing Survey: Nakajima Aircraft Company, Ltd (Nakajima Hikoki K K).*

Wada, K., & Yui, T., translated by Scrzypczak, E. R. (2002). *Courage and Change: The Life of Kiichiro Toyoda.* Toyota: Toyota Motor Corporation.

Wada, K., & Shiba, T. (2000). 'The Evolution of the "Japanese Production System": Indigenous Influences and American Impact,' in *Americanaization and Its Limits: Reworking US Technology and Management in Post-War Europe and Japan*, edited by Jonathan Zeitlin and Gary Herrigel. Oxford: Oxford University Press.

Yamamoto, K. (1994). *Nihon ni okeru shokuba no gijutsu-rōdōshi: 1854-1990 nen* (Technology and Labor History of Shop floor in Japan: 1854–1900). Tokyo: University of Tokyo Press.
Yoshida, K. (1954). 'Sushin-ku sei kōtei kanri jisshi no taiken' (The Ex-pericne in the Implementation of Work-Center Process Control Method). *Ma nejimento* (Managemnet), vol.13, no. 2. Tokyo: Nihon nōritsu kyōkai.
Woollard, F. G. (1954). *Principles of mass and flow production*. London: Published for Mechanical Handling [by] Iliffe.
Zeitlin, J. (1995). 'Flexibility and Mass Production at War: Aircraft Manufacture in Britain, the United States, and Germany, 1939–1945,' T*echnology and Culture, 36*(1).

Chapter 3
The Foundation of the Japanese Automobile Manufacturing Industry: Attempts to Adopt Ford's Production System

3.1 The Nascent Years of the Japanese Automobile Manufacturing Industry

In 1907, the year before Ford began to sell its Model T in the USA, Japan domestically produced its first gasoline-powered passenger car, called *Takuri-gō*, which was assembled with imported parts. From that time, Japan's manufacturers, such as Masujirō Hashimoto and Miyata Works, tried to produce automobiles: "However, neither attempt was a business success at all" (Tōyōkeizai Shinpō 1942, p. 75). This early stage was simply an experimental time for automobile manufacturing in Japan and far from volume production.

Some Japanese entrepreneurs set out to produce a large number of automobiles during the 1920s, when US companies, such as Ford and GM, built assembly plants in Japan; Ford began to assemble cars in Japan in 1925, and GM did so in 1927. These two US companies soon supplied most automotive demand in Japan, and vividly showed that there was strong demand for automobiles in Japan. Faced with the fact that popular cars sold well in the Japanese market, some entrepreneurs devised a countermeasure: either enter the market for popular cars in Japan, preparing for tough competition against US companies; or enter the market by avoiding tough competition with the US companies. In fact, entrepreneurs chose the latter option and avoided severe competition with US firms.

Automobiles that foreign companies imported and assembled as kits dominated automobile production in Japan from 1929 to 1935, increasing its share during these years (see Table 3.1). Furthermore, the number of small automobiles increased rapidly after 1932 when this category first appeared (see Table 3.1). The volume of small automobile production increased 28 times in the five years to 1935, and its share in the Japanese automobile market reached 70%. In fact, the small automobile category triggered increases in car production in Japan. Nevertheless, neither foreign popular cars nor Japanese small vehicles continued to dominate the Japanese market.

K. Wada, *The Evolution of the Toyota Production System*,
Studies in Economic History,
https://doi.org/10.1007/978-981-15-4928-1_3

Table 3.1 Production volume of vehicles and assembled units of imported kits in Japan (1929–1935)

Year	Production volume	Number of small-sized vehicles	Assembled units of imported kits
1929	437		29,338
1930	458		19,678
1931	434		20,109
1932	840	144	14,087
1933	1,612	557	15,082
1934	2,701	1,366	33,458
1935	~5,350	4,170	30,787

Source Shōkoshō Kōmukyoku (1936)

The Japanese government pursued volume production of popular cars by Japanese companies, because these cars were often "regarded as utility cars, possibly for conversion into army trucks" (Ōshima and Yamada 1987, p. 64). In 1936, therefore, the government enforced the Automobile Manufacturing Industries Act, sup-porting the volume production of popular cars by Japanese vehicle companies. After 1938, the government restricted the supply of raw materials for companies producing small vehicles. These companies had to reduce the size of their businesses or abandon them altogether. Based on the 1936 legislation, the government authorized three companies to produce vehicles in Japan: Nissan Motor Co. Ltd., Toyoda Automatic Loom Works Ltd. (now Toyota Industries Corporation), and Tokyo Automobile Industries Ltd. (now Isuzu Motors Limited). As a result, these three companies dominated automobile production in Japan.

The 1936 Act required companies producing more than 3,000 vehicles per year to obtain licenses from the government (Cusumano 1985, p. 17). This set a high target, reminiscent of an episode in which Tokyo Ishikawajima Shipbuilding and Engineering Co. (later, Tokyo Automobile Industries Ltd., one of the three companies authorized to produce cars under the 1936 Act) domestically produced automobiles under license from the Wolseley Motor Company. Ishikawajima sent an engineer to Wolseley to acquire skills. The engineer looked back on his journey:

> I set sail from Yokohama at the end of 1918… [and] entered Britain via America. On my way, I made a visit to Detroit and looked around Ford and other factories. Ford already began to operate so-called mass production, producing a complete car per minute. This production method really impressed me. At the same time, I lacked confidence in establishing a new business of manufacturing automobiles in Japan, by investing just 1 million yen. After I arrived in England, I visited Wolseley's factory and found that they did finishing jobs by using files, just like the operations in Japanese factories. Seeing this, I was encouraged and worked hard to master skills. (Isuzu Jidoshiyashi Hensan Iinkai 1957, p. 337).

The engineer thought it would be tremendously difficult to manufacture automobiles following the production method of the Ford Model T. In the early years of the industry, most Japanese businesspeople were happy to share such opinions.

Achieving volume production of vehicles in Japan was very difficult at this time. One company managed to produce many vehicles by hand with meticulous fitting or filing, but such a production method could by no means realize volume production at low cost. Many people assume that the strength of Ford's production method was the conveyor or assembly line, but Japanese engineers placed particular importance on the smooth flow of work-in-progress through the entire production process rather than the existence of mechanical conveyors. Furthermore, without achieving interchangeability of parts assembled, it would be difficult to attain smooth production flow. On this matter, Fred H. Colvin, who was versed in Ford's production system, wrote as follows:

> It was not very long, however, before most of Ford's competitors had adopted the conveyer-line assembly system when they found that it not only sped up production but also resulted in better machining of sub-assemblies, thus eliminating the need for hand fitting when the parts reached the assembly line (Colvin 1947, pp. 131–132).

Still, the automobile industry drastically changed during the 1920s, while some Japanese companies struggled to acquire the skills for making cars. The passenger car itself was transformed significantly; for example, even the Ford Model T became outdated. Ford produced 2 million Model T cars and trucks in 1923, the peak of Model T production (Hounshell 1984, p. 268). However, the company experienced a "rapid fall from the heights of production and market share in 1923 to the end of Model T production in mid-1927" (Hounshell 1984, p. 274). During the 1920s, all-metal enclosed bodies came to dominate the market, at least for passenger cars. However, "Ford had manufactured cars with a wooden-framed body covered with sheet steel" (Hounshell 1984, p. 274). As a result, Ford introduced an all-steel enclosed model, Type A. In addition, the main production site of Ford moved from the Highland Park plant to the River Rouge plant, which changed the structure of factory buildings. After "building hundreds of acres of floor space in multiple story buildings" at Highland Park, Ford "concluded that raising materials to upper floors by elevators was an economic waste because of the time consumed by men and the cost of transporting materials." Ford had "the courage to practically abandon the enormous Highland Park plant for the River Rouge development" where there was "adequate room for one-story structures, and opportunity for more economical production" (Bucci 1993, pp. 57–58).

Impressed with Ford's production system, Japanese engineers tried to establish an automobile manufacturing industry that could achieve volume production of vehicles at low cost. With almost the same intention, the government selected the abovementioned three companies. Therefore, to analyze the development of volume production of vehicles based on a case study of one company, each of these three companies could be examined.

In this book, we selected Toyoda Automatic Loom Works as a case study of how a Japanese company evolved its automobile business. However, it is also worthwhile explaining why the other two companies, Nissan and Tokyo Automobile Industries, were not selected for this study. Tokyo Automobile Industries concentrated on trucks as its manufacturing base, a focus that had originated in part from Tokyo Ishikawajima

Shipbuilding and Engineering Co. As the reminiscences of one engineer at this shipbuilding company suggest, the firm began to enter automobile manufacturing but avoided making interchangeable parts. Meanwhile, Nissan Motor Co. notably entered this business by importing a set of manufacturing machines and equipment from the USA. It would have been rational for latecomers to adopt advanced technology to some extent. However, as we intend to explore how Japanese companies embraced and absorbed Ford's production method, the case of Nissan is inappropriate for our research aim. Furthermore, briefly considering Nissan's history, it would be obvious that the very plant location and size of Nissan constrained its development in later years. On this rather simple selection criterion, only Toyoda Automatic Loom Works remained as a candidate for this research.

The question is whether this company is worthy of investigation. To answer this, we should set some judgment criteria. First, was the company aware of the importance of interchangeable parts while entering the production of automobiles? Second, did the company clearly understand the transformation of the plant itself, such as Ford's move from a multistory building at Highland Park to a group of one-story buildings at River Rouge? Third, did the company intend to produce passenger cars enclosed all in steel rather than cars with wooden-framed bodies?

Toyoda Automatic Loom Works meets the first two of these three criteria. We discuss the first criterion in detail in the next section and assert that the founder of this company's automobile business understood the importance of making interchangeable parts (Wada and Yui 2002). In addition, the Koromo Plant for volume production consisted of many single-story buildings, thereby clearly fulfilling the second criterion (see Sect. 3.3). With regard to the third criterion, the answer is not clear-cut. After the company launched its automobile business, the main product was not passenger cars. During the war years, the government was forced to produce mainly trucks. In fact, the majority of car production at Toyota Motor Co., which took over the automotive business of Toyoda Automatic Loom Works, concentrated on trucks until 1966. Kiichiro Toyoda, the founder of this automobile business, clearly perceived the need for all-metal enclosed bodies for passenger cars, and, in fact, produced such passenger cars (see Sect. 3.3).

In the next section, we explore why Toyoda Automatic Loom Works entered the automobile business.

3.2 The Importance of Allowance: From Textile Machinery to Automobiles

3.2.1 From Textile Machinery to Automobiles

Just as the name suggests, Toyoda Automatic Loom Works engaged in the manufacture of textile machinery. First, we explore why this company decided to enter the automobile manufacturing business. In making its decision, the company understood the importance of making interchangeable parts. In producing any products assembled with interchangeable parts, "one of the most important aspects is to understand the concept of allowance, which without fail would be noted in production drawings together with dimensions. Once every part was shaped within an allowance limit, assembly operations could be done without fitters, and save man-hours greatly" (Nakaoka 2006, p. 458).

Even if a company were prepared to launch a business of manufacturing vehicles without using interchangeable parts, it would be next to impossible to reduce costs and prices even if producing many products. Then, we should ask how Toyoda Automatic Loom Works, or, more precisely, Kiichiro Toyoda, the founder of the automobile business, was able to learn about the concept of allowance, or whether both he and the company began to produce vehicles recklessly.

Initially, Toyoda Automatic Loom Works had no connection at all with the automobile business. Moreover, Kiichiro Toyoda did not learn anything about the manufacture of automobiles at university. If he had any chance to learn about automobiles, it would have been while he toured several factories during a two-month work experience at Kobe Steel Works in 1919. On that occasion, he had an opportunity to look at automobiles at the Osaka Armory. He wrote the following in his diary of his work experience:

> Here they [Osaka Armory] make automobiles for military use…. I wanted to see things in detail, but our guide rushed through in a hurry, so I had only a quick passing view of everything (Wada and Yui 2002, p. 57).

As Toyoda wrote, he knew about automobiles through "a quick passing view." Even if he were interested in automobiles, he was not familiar with the manufacturing process at all. "As he himself said in later years, he may have been a specialist in textile machinery but he was only an amateur when it came to automobiles" (Wada and Yui 2002, p. 78). In fact, he received a commendation from the Imperial Institute of Invention and Innovation in the form of an Imperial Commemorative Award in recognition of his shuttle-change automatic loom (Patent No. 651569, the basic patent of the Type G automatic loom) (Wada and Yui 2002, p. 280).

Naturally, most readers would question whether any technological connections existed between automobiles and textile machinery. It is often said that the casting in making textile machinery provides a technological bridge to engines for automobiles. Indeed, there is a connection between textile machinery and automobiles regarding the raw material of cast iron. However, the quality of cast iron used in the frame of an automatic loom is very different from that used in cylinder blocks and other important functioning parts of an automobile.

Indeed, Junya Toyokawa, the owner of Hakuyo Company, which had already attempted to enter the automobile business and failed, lamented that his "greatest problem was casting." Other predecessors of Kiichiro Toyoda also had considerable trouble with the production of cylinder blocks—in other words, casting (Jidōsha Kōgyō Shinkōkai 1973, pp. 11, 14). However, Toyoda felt that his own company had an advantage, at least over other companies in Japan. In fact, when the members of the Machinery Society visited Toyoda Automatic Loom Works in 1930, "everyone particularly admired its equipment in the foundry, where they were using an electric arc furnace to melt pig iron and were using dozens of molding machines in an orderly series" (Kikai Gakkai-Shi 1930, p. 100). In other words, the company had the most modern casting equipment at the time in Japan.

Becoming confident in the quality of casting at the company, Kiichiro Toyoda spoke about casting:

> In the area of casting, now, this was something we had studied for years and in which we [Toyoda Automatic Loom Works] had plenty of confidence, so, confident that we could solve any problems in castings for something like an automobile, we set to work [manufacturing automobiles] (Toyoda 1936a, p. 103; Wada and Yui 2002, p. 249).

Despite his belief, the company could not produce cylinder blocks easily. The casting of cylinder blocks and cylinder heads caused enormous headaches. The company made considerable mistakes, before it achieved a success rate of 90% or more making cylinder blocks. Finally, the company succeeded "in a little over a year," but only after it "melted down some five or six hundred faulty cylinders" (Toyoda 1936a, p. 104).

After succeeding in production of cylinder blocks, Toyoda wrote:

> The experience in using molding machines at Toyoda Automatic Loom Works and in making difficult castings, like the thin castings for spinning machines, with an electric arc furnace paid off in the end (Toyoda 1936a, p. 103).

As is clear from the praise reaped on it by the members of the Machinery Society, Toyoda Automatic Loom Works had modern equipment in these years, which "paid off in the end" for its entry into the automobile business. We should draw attention to the reason for the company installing such modern equipment. Notably, the company admitted that molding machines were "considered difficult to use" by others in the casting business at the time, and that electric furnaces were "not required for manufacturing spindles and looms" but were installed for research on high-grade castings (Toyoda Jidōsha Seizō Kabushiki Kaisha 1937, p. 213; Toyoda 1937a, p. 194). Why did the company install unnecessary electric furnaces for its main business? In addition, why did the company undertake research on high-grade castings? On the first anniversary of Toyota Motor Co., Kiichiro Toyoda wrote:

> Since I wanted… to try my hand at automobile manufacturing, and I considered the production of spindles and looms more or less as really only a part of the lead-up to that, I had begun designing and doing research on engines from early on (Toyoda 1936b, p. 105).

In summary, Kiichiro Toyoda had already moved from decision to action for entering the automotive manufacturing business while he was engaged in the textile machinery business. Therefore, we should investigate what Kiichiro Toyoda used from the manufacture of textile machinery and how he did so.

3.2.2 Recognizing the Importance of Allowance in Making Automatic Looms

Sakichi Toyoda, Kiichiro's father, was undoubtedly one of the greatest inventors in Japan. In fact, Sakichi received the Second Imperial Commemorative Award in September 1926. In particular, his invention contributed to providing inexpensive looms for common people, "not for the producers of Nishijin-brocade and other figured cloths" (Tōjō 1940, p. 159). He invented his looms while good-quality materials, such as good-quality iron, were difficult to obtain. He applied for his first patent for the Toyoda wooden hand loom in 1890. Thereafter, Sakichi Toyoda's inventions continually moved toward compositions based on iron and wood, but were mainly iron-made machines. Considering his invention from another perspective, the power source for his invention changed from human power to steam power. Then, Sakichi Toyoda moved toward the development of automatic power looms. Under the restrictions of Japanese technological development, he struggled to offer solutions in quick succession. Although Sakichi Toyoda made many inventions and produced a number of patents, one of the most striking setbacks was that "casting technology for producing each machine's part could not catch up with improving looms" (Tōjō 1940, p. 159).

Here, we draw attention to Kiichiro Toyoda's review of the development of Toyoda's textile machinery, rather than giving a detailed description of Sakichi Toyoda's inventions. The Engineering Society of Japan hosted the World Engineering Congress from October 29 to November 7, 1929, in Tokyo. For Japan, a late industrialized country, this congress played a role in introducing new developments in Japanese industries. There were about 4,500 participants in total, of which about 1,500 were from 42 countries other than Japan. There were 813 papers presented in total, of which 371 were presented by Japanese delegates. The congress was divided into 12 sections (Doboku Gakkai 2004, pp. 62–63; Bankoku Kōgyō Kaigi 1931, pp. 410–411). Kiichiro Toyoda prepared a paper titled"The Toyoda Textile Machinery" (Section VIII), dealing with the refrigeration industry, textile industry, and automotive engineering (Toyoda 1931; World Engineering Congress 1931), but he unable to present the paper himself, because he had left the country. Toyoda had set sail for the United States on September 12, 1929, and then for England, to sign an agreement with Platt Brothers in December 1929; he returned to Japan on April 2, 1931 (Wada and Yui 2002, Chap. 6).

Kiichiro Toyoda's English-written paper has rarely been referred to, even by scholars who studied Toyoda's textile machinery. In his paper, Kiichiro Toyoda summarized his father's career as an inventor simply:

> The automatic loom is his [Sakichi Toyoda's] principal achievement. Throughout his career as an inventor, this loom has been the constant goal toward which all his efforts have been directed. The first model was completed as early as 1903. From that time onward, modifications and improvements followed in quick succession until the inventor at last pronounced himself satisfied with the fruits of his labor (Toyoda 1931, p. 152).

In fact, the first "patent for an automatic loom registered under a Japanese name" (patent number: 6787) was secured by Sakichi Toyoda on August 6, 1903; until then, several patents for automatic looms had been secured by foreigners. In addition, among earlier automatic looms, only two patents by Japanese (Nos. 6787 and 7433) were "actually perfected and placed in the market": both patents were secured by Sakichi Toyoda. In 1904–05, the looms based on these patents were produced on a commercial basis but "the total number of looms sold amounted to some 500" (Toyoda 1931, p. 154). However, these looms were "soon abandoned" because their operation was not financially efficient and there were "defects in manufacture, imperfect designs, and unskilled operatives." Although Japan imported some automatic looms, such as Northrop Looms, Japanese "operatives had not yet mastered the art of manipulating automatic looms. Thus, the import of these looms ceased" (Toyoda 1931, p. 154). Subsequently, research was undertaken on the automatic loom adapted to Japanese conditions, and Kiichiro Toyoda concluded:

> The Toyoda machine recently perfected has the weft-replenishing motion embodied in Patent No. 65156, the outcome of the builder's concentrated effort towards the solution of most of the problems here discussed, and actual experiments prove that the loom stands up to 300 rpm (Toyoda 1931, p. 168).

According to the above statement, Patent No. 65156 led to the perfection of Toyoda's automatic looms. This patent was secured not by Sakichi Toyoda but by his son Kiichiro on August 10, 1925. To weave continuously, the weft-replenishing motion is necessary: a weft is wound around a bobbin, which is placed in a cop; a shuttle is the piece carrying the cop. Generally speaking, the automatic looms at the time carried out the weft-replenishing motion in one of two ways: either by replacing a cop with another new cop, or by changing the shuttle. Toyota's automatic loom adopted the structure of a shuttle change in order to secure "the maximum allowance" (Toyoda 1931, p. 168).

The reason for the abovementioned patent being required is noteworthy:

> A basic solution, at least as regarding the structure of a shuttle change, was made by Sakichi Toyoda's invention (the automatic shuttle changer) Patent No. 17028, but from the viewpoint of a more practical automatic loom, a few problems remained. These were the problems of the temporal margin of error, at the time of the shuttle change, between the insertion of the replacement shuttle and the ejection of the old shuttle. In those days, looms were already running at 200 picks per minute.
>
> Therefore, the shuttle would be parked inside the box for only an extremely short period of time, during which time the shuttle change had to be executed. If the change were delayed by even a fraction of a second, it would immediately lead to snapping of some warp yarn. With Patent No. 17028, even though there had been not the slightest problem in the experimental stage, when it was produced in large quantities, the tiniest margin of error in motion timing turned into a huge problem. The root of the problem was that the insertion of the replacement shuttle and the upward ejection of the old shuttle took place separately (Ishii 1979, p. 23).

The structure of a shuttle change was essentially solved by Sakichi Toyoda's invention, for which he took out Patent No. 17028 on the "automatic shuttle changer" in 1907. However, even with this shuttle changer, his looms could not operate smoothly owing to "the tiniest margin of error in motion timing." Consequently, Toyoda struggled to produce a large number of looms with automatic shut-tle changers.

Toyoda Loom Co. (now, Hōwa Machinery Ltd.) was established to market Sakichi Toyada's inventions commercially. Right from the beginning, the company encountered problems, as its president, Fusazō Taniguchi, pointed out in a general meeting of shareholders held in April 1907.

> Mr. [Sakichi] Toyoda has added essential improvements to many different previous inventions, so that today the Toyoda loom is so advanced that I would not hesitate to claim that it is nearly as perfect as it can be in structure. Still, while it definitely has advanced, the equipment needed to produce this loom in its entirety is still lacking, a fact that is very regrettable (Hōwa Kōgyō Kabushiki Kaisha 1987, pp. 11–12).

However, the production of this loom did not proceed smoothly. The company had invited "Mr. Charles A. Francis, an American instructor at Tokyo Higher Technical School (present-day Tokyo Institute of Technology)," whose job was to inculcate the importance of uniform standards by means of complete furnishing of the tools involved in the design and to aim for technical improvement and efficiency, but he was unable "to easily correct the inexperience, oversights, and mistakes of the workers" (Toyota-shiki Shokki Kabushiki Kaisha 1936, p. 30).

As "the techniques for producing castings and steel were not yet developed before the 1910s in Japan" (Tōjō 1940, p. 160), Toyoda Loom Co. had to use nonuniform materials, which made it difficult to produce uniform precision parts. Under such conditions, Sakichi Toyoda made every effort to achieve workable automatic looms. For example, one engineer made the following observation about one of Toyoda's inventions, which evidently showed how he responded to these conditions:

> Both Northrop's automatic loom of 1894 and Toyoda's automatic loom of 1903 were equipped with a warp halting device [which automatically shut down the machine when the warp thread broke]. Northrop's device functioned with a thin metal plate-like form's dropper. But, as it would be difficult to produce plates with uniform thickness in Japan, Toyoda's device was made simply from wires (Kikai Shinkō Kyōkai Keizai Kenkyūjo 1990, p. 41).

Sakichi Toyoda invented automatic looms in an environment in which thin metal plates could not be obtained. In fact, Sakichi and Kiichiro Toyoda managed to invent automatic looms within the constraints of poor materials and processing technology.

Sakichi Toyoda devoted every effort to working on the automatic shuttle change. However, Toyoda Loom Co. did not have sufficient spare funds to funnel money into leading-edge inventions, and the very survival of the company was in jeopardy. Finally, Sakichi Toyoda resigned from the company in 1910. He resolved to entrust research and development on the automatic looms to his subordinates and his son Kiichiro, while supplying the money required for their experiments (Toyoda Jidō Shokki Seisakusho 1967, p. 80).

Tracing Kiichiro Toyoda's research and development through the patents he acquired, we find that he acquired his first patent for an "automatic cop changer," Patent No. 66012 (applied for in June 1924 and registered in September 1925). This was the cop change invention, and not the shuttle change invention of his father

Sakichi. Kiichiro and Sakichi's subordinates on the research team "were of the opinion in the beginning" that their research on the automatic loom showed that the cop change method "was better in form" (Toyoda 1927, p. 54). Nevertheless, they soon changed their minds and favored the shuttle change method. Sakichi Toyoda also took out a patent for the cop change method but afterwards he was "firmly convinced that the shuttle change method was better" (Toyoda 1927, p. 54).

Once Kiichiro Toyoda decided to develop the shuttle change method, the best and shortest way to do so was to improve his father's invention. Kiichiro wrote about this:

> We hauled out the automatic loom Father [Sakichi] had made years ago, and we made three exactly like it. Next, we spent two years making sure we could get thirty looms operating. During that time, the original looms underwent quite a lot of modification. Then we had the thirty looms to the point where they were all working perfectly. When Father [Sakichi] came back from Shanghai and saw them, he was very happy (Toyoda 1952, p. 41).

At this time, their goal was to perfect Sakichi Toyoda's invention of the automatic shuttle changer, Patent No. 17028. In particular, the automatic shuttle changer was not the whole but a part of the automatic loom. Therefore, after the inventors perfected the automatic shuttle changer, Kiichiro Toyoda wrote about the further challenges he and his team faced:

> We attached the automatic loom part [the automatic shuttle changer as an attachment] to 200 new ordinary looms and tried them out in the Kariya plant [of the Toyoda Boshoku]. It was a disaster. In hindsight, it sounds like a stupid thing to do. At the time, though, we went to a lot of trouble to adjust the automatic looms, and when unexpected breakdowns occurred and things somehow just wouldn't work well, we felt as if the automatic looms were possessed by the Devil. Before we had installed the 200 looms, we had tested 30 of them fully and were sure we had ironed out all problems, but then, when we went ahead and installed 200, and the above problems kept occurring, we sometimes were ready to give up altogether. From this bitter experience, we became convinced that it was absolutely impossible to attach this automatic part to earlier ordinary looms, especially the older ones (Toyoda 1927, p. 62).

Consequently, Kiichiro Toyoda abandoned his idea to attach the automatic shuttle changer to normal looms. He instead decided to produce the whole automatic loom with the shuttle change method, and completed the Type G automatic loom. By the end of March 1926, Toyoda Boshoku had produced 520 automatic looms and had begun to operate them on an experimental basis. The result was successful. Later, when Platt Brothers made this Type G automatic loom under the Toyoda–Platt Agreement, it tested the looms at the Lancashire Cotton Corporation Ltd. in 1931 (for details on the Toyoda–Platt Agreement, see Wada 2006). The official report accurately pointed out its external characteristics:

> One of the main features of the loom is an excellent warp let-off motion. There are rather too many set screws and bolts, which may slip, and the loom gives the impression of having had an attachment built into it instead of being a fully automatic weaving machine (Lancashire Cotton Corporation Ltd. 1932, p. 26).

With expert eyes, it would be obvious that the Type G automatic loom had "rather too many set screws and bolts." Without any other explanation, the official report accurately concluded that the automatic shuttle changer would be attached to normal looms.

From the beginning, Sakichi and Kiichiro Toyoda pursued their research into automatic shuttle changers as attachments to normal looms, not fully automatic looms. After Sakichi left the company, Toyoda Loom Co. kept trying to successfully manufacture the automatic looms based on Sakichi's patent. One article in an industrial journal noted as follows: "Toyoda Loom Co. finally almost completed its Toyoda type shuttle changer *attachment* under research" [emphasis in the original] (Bōshoku-kai 1929, p. 11). As this article plainly explained, Sakichi Toyoda's invention was the attachment: the apparatus of the automatic shuttle changer fitted on a normal loom.

Nonetheless, a question remained as to why Kiichiro Toyoda decided to produce fully automatic looms, not just automatic shuttle changers. As mentioned earlier, he "went to a lot of trouble to adjust the automatic looms" (Toyoda 1927, p. 62). He also stated: "In hindsight, it sounds a stupid thing to do" (Toyoda 1927, p. 62). This meant that he found out why he faced such trouble: "…the old ordinary looms take too great an allowance, and it is inviting disaster to attach an automatic part with a comparatively small allowance to an old ordinary loom" (Toyoda 1927, p. 62). To make matters worse, if some parts of old normal looms had warped or been worn out, the automatic shuttle changer showed only a small allowance before it could not function at all with such looms.

When Kiichiro Toyoda changed his research and development policy from an automatic cop changer to an automatic shuttle changer, he considered that it would secure "the maximum allowance in respect to the relative positions of S_0 and S_1" (S_0 refers to the shuttle or cop in the lathe of a loom that is to be replaced; S_1 refers to the shuttle or cop in the magazine to be replaced, S_0). Furthermore, he took into account the constraints of poor materials and processing technology. Consequently, he chose the automatic shuttle change method, rather than the automatic cop change method, to "secure the maximum allowance" (Toyoda 1931, p. 168).

As just described, Kiichiro Toyoda certainly took into account the allowance between switching shuttles or cops, in choosing which type of automatic change apparatus: shuttle or cop change. Nevertheless, such an automatic change apparatus had to be used in combination with a normal loom. Even in operating such an automatic changer, allowance would be quite important. However, Kiichiro Toyoda might have overlooked the question of allowance in combining the use of the automatic changer and normal looms. In particular, the condition of old normal looms would vary widely. Therefore, he encountered "a disaster" in adjusting automatic changers to normal looms. Then, he discovered why things had not been working well. After he solved the problem, he wrote: "In hindsight, it sounds a stupid thing to do," because he surely knew the importance of securing the allowance. Therefore, he wrote: "It is inviting disaster to attach an automatic part with a comparatively small allowance to an old ordinary loom [with too great an allowance]" (Toyoda 1927, p. 62).

3.2.3 *Why Toyoda Automatic Loom Works Moved Quickly into the Automobile Business*

Following Toyoda Automatic Loom Works, Kyugorō Sakamoto of Enshū Loom Manufacturing Co. (now Enshu Ltd.) made automatic looms with the cop change method. Sakamoto was listed in the *Selection of 50 Distinctive Japanese Inventors*, as was Kiichiro Toyoda (Matsubara 1952, pp. 70–76). Furthermore, the Ministry of Commerce and Industry provided a financial incentive to Enshu Loom Manufacturing Co. in 1926, and approved the completion of the automatic loom in 1929 (Enshū Seisaku Kabushiki Kaisha 1971, pp. 204–206). During that year, the volume of shipments was 2,398 automatic looms for Toyoda Automatic Loom Works, and 2,603 for Enshu Loom Manufacturing Co. Sakamoto also made a start in inventing automatic looms with shuttle change.

In 1908, Sakamoto graduated from the Department of Machinery of Osaka Technical High School (now the Department of Engineering of Osaka University), and got a job at Kimoto Iron Factory, producing wool looms and silk-spinning machines using British machine tools. In 1921, he was hired as a manager and chief engineer at Suzumasa Loom Manufacturing Co., which changed its corporate name to Enshū Loom Manufacturing Co. in 1923. Sakamoto published a book on power looms at his own expense in 1925, emphasizing the importance of the gauge system for producing interchangeable parts (Sakamoto 1925, p. 125). By 1923, Enshū Loom Manufacturing Co. prepared gauges for increasing production efficiency and total unification of products (Enshū Seisaku Kabushiki Kaisha 1971, p. 435).

The limit gauge system is essential for the manufacture of parts within prescribed limits of allowance. The extent to which the use of the limit gauge system was dispersed in the manufacturing setting would clearly show how the concept of allowance prevailed among Japanese manufacturers. A book titled *Compendium of Japanese Industry* published in 1930 reported a brief survey of implementing the limit gauge system. This survey listed the names of 23 private companies, including Toyoda Automatic Loom Works and Enshū Loom Manufacturing Co., in addition to the Armories of Army and Navy as well as the factories of the Ministry of the Railway. Furthermore, the survey noted that in 1924, an association for the use of the limit gauge was founded in the Kansai region (Kōgakkai 1930, p. 347), which shows that the use of the limit gauge began to increase among Japanese manufacturers after the mid-1920s. Japanese manufacturers came to recognize the vital importance of allowances in manufacturing interchangeable parts.

More than 20 companies moved toward production of inter-changeable parts. Indeed, Toyoda Automatic Loom Works did not stand out among other Japanese manufacturers in this respect. This finding triggers a new question: why did Toyoda Automatic Loom Works enter the automobile business earlier than other competitors? To answer this question, we should draw attention to the attempt to manufacture automobiles by Suzuki Loom Manufacturing Co. (now Suzuki Motor Corporation).

This company was founded as Suzuki Loom Manufacturing Works in 1909, and was incorporated as Suzuki Loom Manufacturing Co. in 1920. The company was located in central Japan, as were Toyoda Automatic Loom Works and Enshū Loom Manufacturing Co. In 1936, Suzuki Loom Manufacturing Co. tried to manufacture small automobiles. In autumn 1937, the company succeeded in manufacturing engine prototypes for motorcycles. In the same year, the company began to research the manufacture of automobiles by purchasing an Austin sedan car. Nevertheless, the company abandoned manufacturing automobiles, because the Army ordered it to increase production of munitions. Although the company manufactured crankshafts and pistons for six-cylinder engines as a subcontractor, it did not produce any four-wheeled vehicles (Suzuki Jidōsha Kōgyō Kabushiki Kaisha 1970, p. 20).

As the case of Suzuki Loom Manufacturing Co. illustrates, textile machine manufacturers had their sights set on entering automobile manufacturing during the 1930s. However, Suzuki Loom Manufacturing Co. moved to the manufacture of munitions. Enshū Loom Manufacturing Co. also moved in the same direction. Although these textile machine makers acquired sophisticated processing technologies, they did not make serious attempts to enter automobile manufacturing in the 1930s. Consequently, they started manufacturing munitions during the war. After the war, these companies entered new business fields in search of new opportunities. Suzuki moved into motorcycles and automobile manufacturing, while both Enshū and Toyoda Loom Co. entered the production of machine tools.

However, Toyoda Loom Co. had earlier joined the so-called Chukyo Detroit Project, which aimed to turn the Chukyo region around Nagoya City into another Detroit by developing an automobile industry in the early 1930s. In the summer of 1932, Toyoda Loom Co. produced a prototype vehicle called the "Atsuta" based on an American Nash vehicle. However, while lessons were learned from this project, it did not aim to produce popular cars in Japan or to produce cars by assembling interchangeable parts. As a result, the project came to its conclusion and Toyoda Loom Co. was forced to enter production of machine tools.

In contrast to these companies, Toyoda Automatic Loom Works deliberately attempted to enter the automobile manufacturing business as early as the spring of 1930. Several years later, Suzuki Loom Manufacturing Co. also tried to move into the same business, but the intervening years made a substantial difference in this regard: Toyoda succeeded whereas Suzuki did not. It became increasingly difficult for companies that did not obtain licenses from the government under the Automobile Manufacturing Industries Act in 1936 to acquire materials for manufacturing automobiles, and, ultimately, they had to abandon the manufacture of automobiles. Even with sophisticated processing technology, the companies developing their own business fields, like those in the textile machinery, were very unlikely to have the ability to produce more than 3,000 vehicles per year to obtain a license under the 1936 Act.

3.3 Constructing Automobile Manufacturing System on a Small Scale

3.3.1 Conceptual Planning

Toyoda Automatic Loom Works faced many challenges before it brought its product to the market. Kiichiro Toyoda, who promoted this venture, was surely aware of the difficulties—not only of manufacturing automobiles, but also of facing competition from overseas vehicles.

> First of all, to build up an automobile industry, one needs a huge amount of capital, one has to master the very difficult techniques of manufacturing all the different parts, and one has to acquire the skilled techniques of assembly. Even if one looks only at the raw materials, there are steel, cast iron, rubber, glass, paint, and other materials that cover a wider range of industrial products, with the result that, unless these products have been developed up to at least a certain level, turning one's hand to the automobile industry is quite risky. Moreover, the finished automobile, from the very time it comes out into the market, has to be ready to engage in a one-on-one fight with a foreign vehicle that has a history of almost half a century behind it and that has acquired an international market. In the company of all these various difficulties comes a whole host of economic sacrifices. One may well ask whether an automobile for the masses can really be made in Japan (Toyoda 1937b).

Kiichiro Toyoda's decision to enter the automobile business was not just based on rosy analysis. Rather, he had carefully done the spadework for entering the business.

From the late 1920s to the early 1930s, most parts or even some materials for manufacturing automobiles were not easily obtainable in Japan. Under such conditions, what was Kiichiro Toyoda's business plan for entering the automobile business? He wrote: "It would be much easier and more economical to bring materials, machines, and even some parts from outside Japan" through a partnership with a foreign company (Toyoda 1940, p. 355). However, Kiichiro denied this course of action, because he strongly adhered to a policy of producing automobiles inside Japan.

However, Kiichiro Toyoda had to admit that it would be impossible to produce the same volume of production in Japan as Ford or GM did in producing more than 1 million cars per year in the USA. He also noticed that some automobile companies producing tens of thousands of vehicles per year still existed in the USA. He did not wish to imitate such companies, because they produced "high quality or specialized cars" without pursuing the production of popular passenger cars. Based on Kiichiro's observations, it would only be possible to establish an assembly plant by purchasing many parts from the market in the USA. However, if someone were to try to found a company just by assembling passenger cars in Japan, the company had to depend exclusively on imports of almost every material and parts from the USA. Kiichiro Toyoda asserted that cars assembled in this way were not "truly domestically produced cars" (Toyoda 1940, p. 356).

Kiichiro Toyoda envisaged the foundation of an automobile industry in Japan in which the assembly of cars should be based on the "basic industry" of producing materials and parts for cars in Japan (Toyoda 1940, p. 355). Once he understood the importance of allowance and aimed to establish interchangeable production in Japan, he had no time for the idea of importing precision-worked parts from outside Japan and assembling them in Japan.

Then, how did Kiichiro Toyoda consider creating an automobile manufacturing business in Japan? It would take a long time to establish the parts and material industries for automobiles. Therefore, while steadily developing such new industries, it would be essential to acquire assembly technology. Once starting large volume production, of about several hundred thousand cars per year, it would be difficult to master assembling technology as well as the process of how to make parts or materials. Therefore, Kiichiro conceived his idea for a new business: starting with small-scale production volume to judge whether it would be possible to enter the automobile manufacturing business over time.

> At first, we began to produce 200 passenger cars a month. The most difficult thing for producing popular cars existed in producing passenger cars, especially producing their bodies at inexpensive cost. Therefore, we decided to start producing passenger cars (Toyoda 1937a, p. 194).

Kiichiro Toyoda certainly knew that all metal-enclosed bodies would become dominant, at least, in the market for passenger cars, during the 1920s. To enter the manufacture for passenger cars during the 1930s, it would have been necessary to equip a vehicle with an all-metal enclosed body. In particular, as Toyoda Automatic Loom Works had never made bodies by pressing sheet steel, Kiichiro worried whether the venture would succeed in manufacturing bodies with a high degree of accuracy. Furthermore, the adoption of an all-metal enclosed body would require large investment in costly dies and pressing machines. If passenger cars were not selling well because of the automobile exterior and if bodies had to be reshaped, the company would have to rebuild costly dies from the ground up. Even though body making raised such a management headache, Kiichiro decided to start the automobile business with small-scale production in order to acquire the technology for automobile manufacturing.

Using this business concept, Toyoda Automatic Loom Works attempted to enter the automobile business. In 1937, a separate company, Toyota Motor Co., was established and became fully engaged in the automobile manufacturing business. In the next subsection, we examine how this project developed.

3.3.2 *Plant Location and Expansion*

Around May 1930, Kiichiro Toyoda set up a laboratory for automobiles at Toyoda Automatic Loom Works and began to research the automobile business. In September 1933, the company established the Automotive Production Division. In January 1934, the company formally approved the establishment of the automobile business at the general meeting of shareholders. Finally, in March 1934, the company began operating its newly built experimental plant. Until this plant was built, the company had been exploring ways to manufacture automobiles within the premises of the Toyoda Automatic Loom Works.

The prototype plant comprised an area of approximately 9,100 m^2, within which four buildings were located: a sheet-metal and assembly shop (floor space of 3,600 square meters); a machining and finishing shop (3,600 m^2); a warehouse (1,700 m^2); and an office for materials testing and research (700 m^2). The outstanding feature of this prototype plant would be the materials testing and research office, which comprised a mechanical property testing room, a physical property measurement room, a microscope test room, a chemical analysis room, a paint testing room, a combustible material testing room, and an electro-metallurgy testing room. "This was comparable to material testing laboratories at universities and laboratories in those days" (Toyota Jidōsha Kōgyō Kabushiki Kaisha 1967, p. 55). Companies like Toyoda Automatic Loom Works that were located in a country with little accumulation of automobile experience had to start with research and consideration of materials.

In addition, a steel mill was completed in July 1943, 4 months after the start of operation of the prototype factory. The company had two objectives in building the steel mill. One was the manufacture of steel materials that were not made in specialized steel mills owing to specialized requirements; the steel mills would not make even ordinary steel with special dimensions. The company's primary objective was to manufacture such steel materials on its own. The second objective was research on automotive steel materials. Together with the material testing and research office of the prototype plant, this steel mill also served as a research facility to examine the material. Located on the south side of the factory of Toyoda Automatic Loom Works, the steel mill was adjacent to the prototype plant (Toyoda Jidō Shokki Seisakusho 1967, p. 235; Toyota Jidōsha Kabushiki Kaisha 1999, p. 40). In other words, its location was convenient for studying steel materials.

Furthermore, in June 1936, the Kariya Assembly Plant, with a total floor space of about 24,800 m^2, was built about 1 km from the prototype plant. The Kariya Assembly Plant was "a pilot plant before launching construction of a large-scale mass production plant" (Toyota Jidōsha Kōgyō Kabushiki Kaisha 1967, p. 53). Equipment relating to assembly was transferred from the prototype plant to the Kariya Assembly Plant. Within the prototype plant, a press shop was newly set up and the existing foundry shop, engine shop, and axle shop were improved and upgraded.

By constructing the Kariya Assembly Plant, the Automotive Production Division of Toyoda Automatic Loom Works was made up of two divisions: manufacturing shops from raw material production to machining and an assembly plant from car body processing to final assembly. At the same time, the research and design departments, such as the tool design department, engine and body design department, and automobile research laboratory, were established (Toyota Jidōsha Kōgyō Kabushiki Kaisha 1967, p. 83). In addition, in June 1937, a machine plant for producing machine tools and jigs for automobile production was set up in Toyoda Automatic Loom Works. Finally, the production system for small-scale automobile manufacturing was completed.

Despite these developments, preparation for the construction of a large-scale factory was also advanced. Toyoda Automatic Loom Works resolved to acquire more than 400 acres in Koromo-cho of Aichi Prefecture at a board of directors meeting on July 30, 1934, and the land acquisition was completed in December 1935. This be-came the site of the Koromo Plant built for large-scale automobile business (completed in February 1938).

Toyoda Automatic Loom Works successively expanded its investment in the automobile business, because the company had its eye on the rapid movement of the Japanese government's automobile industry policy. In August 1935, the Cabinet approved an outline of the Automobile Industry Bill. Its preamble referred to the automobile business promoted by Nissan Motor Co. and Toyoda Automatic Loom Works; even though the automobile manufacturing projects of the two companies had not yet reached completion, the government committed to giving them guidance and subsidies if their plans were appropriate and reasonable. Toyota's plan to purchase a vast factory construction site seemed to have greatly contributed to this reference to Toyota's automobile project in the legislation of the government. Furthermore, Toyoda Automatic Loom Works held an exhibition commemorating the completion of the domestic Toyoda popular car in September 1936 at which it displayed its passenger cars, trucks, and buses. Thanks to these efforts, Toyoda Automatic Loom Works became a licensed company under the act in September 1936, together with Nissan Motor Co. In the same year, Toyoda Automatic Loom Works began production of trucks, and for the first time, the production record of the company was recorded in October.

Then, the Toyota Motor Co. was established in August 1937. Although the completion of Koromo Plant had been planned for Au-gust 1938, it was not completed until November 3 of the same year. The factory began full operation in the spring of the following year. The company did not utilize its entire site of 400 acres: at first, the factory used only about 50 acres for its operations, spreading to about one-quarter of the entire site.

3.3.3 Changes in Production Volume

How did the production of automobiles increase with the development of facilities? Figure 3.1 shows the monthly production up to April 1939.

First, it took about 5.5 years for the company to produce its first vehicle in October 1935 after the company began researching its automobile manufacturing business in the spring of 1930. Even after the company started the operation of its prototype plant in March 1934, it did not produce any vehicles for at least 1 year.

Second, the company rather steadily produced its vehicles after producing its first. At the prototype plant, the company produced fewer than 100 vehicles per month, but after the Kariya Plant started operating in March 1937, its monthly production reached 400 units in just a few months. The monthly production volume remained steady for 1 year until August 1938. Thereafter, production declined as the company was busy dealing with preparatory work for the completion of the Koromo Plant.

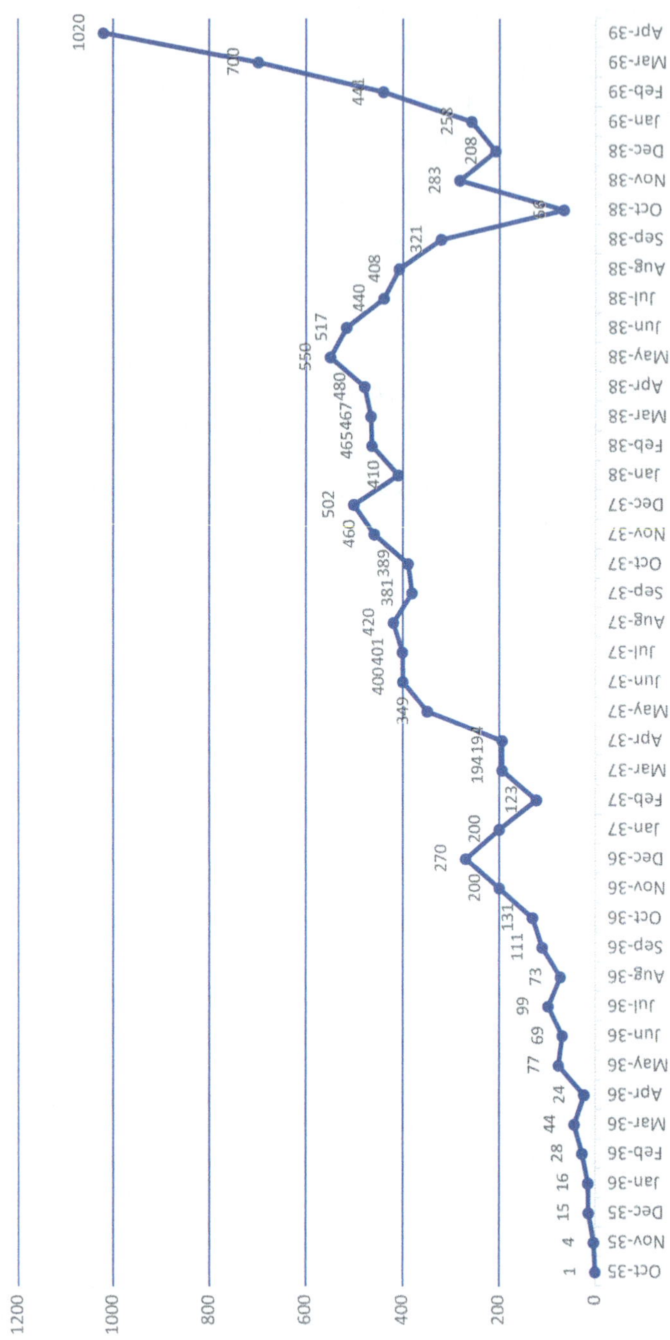

Fig. 3.1 Monthly production volume of vehicles at Toyota (October 1935 to April 1939). *Source* Toyota Jidōsha Kōgyō Kabushiki Kaisha (1958), p. 702

When the plant began to operate at full capacity, monthly production soon reached 1,000 units in April 1939.

Third, after the Koromo Plant began operating at full capacity, the company's monthly production swung wildly from one month to the next (see Fig. 3.2). Without paying attention to such large fluctuations in monthly production, we note that the average monthly production was more than 1,000 vehicles (precisely, 1,052.4) for the 77 months from April 1939 to August 1945. By the end of World War II, it became difficult for the company to procure materials and execute production.

Even a brief examination of the production volume raises some questions. After 5.5 years of preparation, the company man-aged to produce its first vehicle. What kind of problems did it face during this period? Considering only the monthly production figures, it seems that the transition from the prototype plant and Kariya Plant to the Koromo Plant proceeded smoothly. However, considering Kiichiro Toyoda's goal was to produce cars in competition with foreign-made cars, the number of cars produced was not the most important factor. What was important was whether the cars could compete with foreign cars in terms of quality and cost. Furthermore, it has often been assumed that the Koromo Plant assembled and produced cars on a moving assembly line. However, the volume production at the plant varied greatly from month to month (see Fig. 3.2). Was it possible or rational to make cars on a moving assembly line in such a situation?

The following subsections consider the three issues mentioned above: the long preparation period, the quality and cost of cars, and the question of the adoption of an assembly line.

3.3.4 The Long Preparation Period

After conducting research on entering the production of automobiles in the spring of 1930, Toyota took another 5.5 years to produce its first vehicle in October 1935. What did the company do during this period?

Until recently, it had been emphasized that the company struggled to manufacture engines. The company would have met manifold problems in manufacturing many different parts, but in fact, there was little discussion of problems other than those relating to engines. When it produced its first vehicle, the company did not produce every kind of part. It produced "just the cylinder head, the cylinder block, the housing, and the transmission case, and some other parts by itself, but it mostly used Chevrolet's genuine parts" (Toyota Jidosha Kōgyō Kabushiki Kaisha 1958, p. 37). In fact, to advance into automobile manufacturing, it was essential for Kiichiro Toyoda to judge whether the company could manufacture engines. For that reason, the manufacture of other parts was postponed.

The company had finished the experimental production of a small engine modeled on the Smith Motor by the middle of October 1930. The Smith Motor was a popular engine in Japan at the time. It was normally attached to a bicycle or tricycle by means of what was known as the Smith Motor Wheel to produce a convenient self-powered

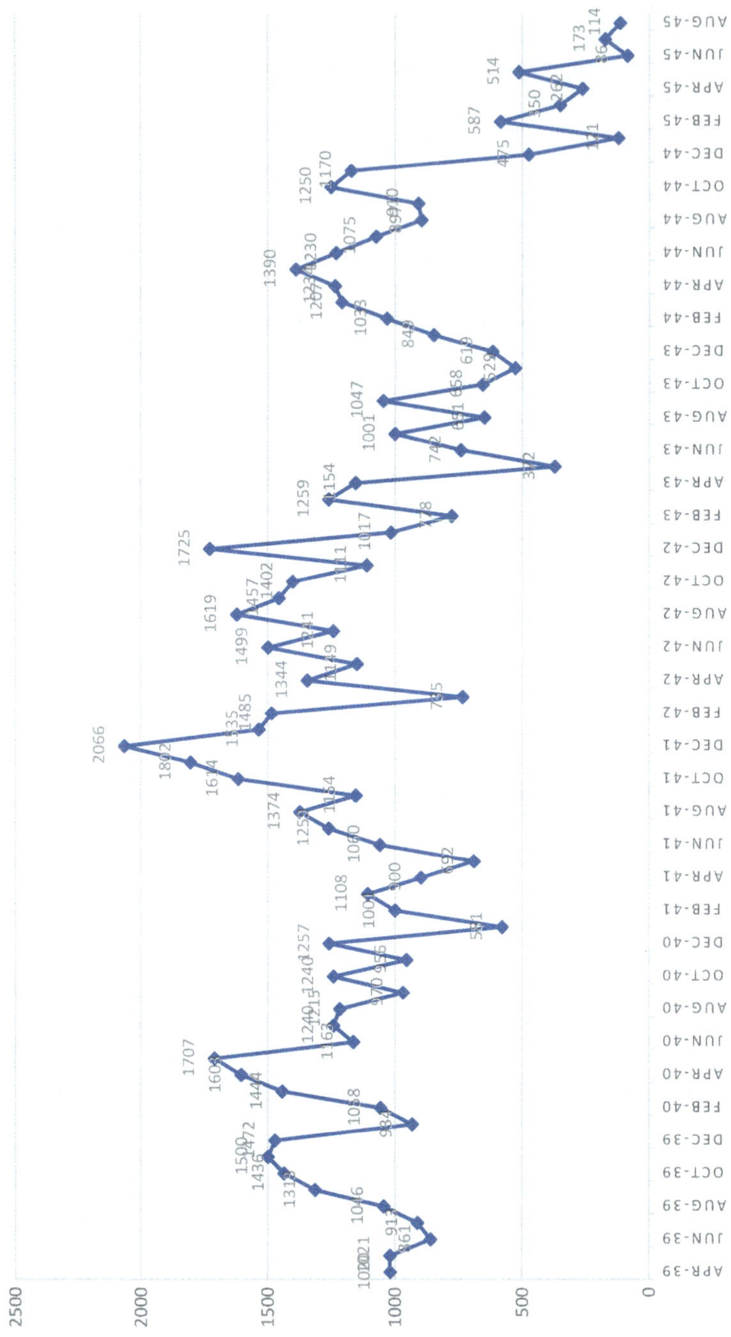

Fig. 3.2 Monthly production volume of vehicles at Toyota (April 1939 to August 1945). *Source* Toyota Jidōsha Kōgyō Kabushiki Kaisha (1958), p. 702

vehicle used to transport goods. Because it was a simple means of propulsion, the Smith Motor was imported in large numbers to Japan in the 1920s. Following the entry into Japan of this small engine, Toyota continued to manufacture several types of prototype engines. The prospect of engine manufacturing led the company to establish the Automotive Production Division in September 1933. In January 1934, the company formally approved the automobile business at an extraordinary general meeting of shareholders. Nevertheless, the company completed the first prototype engine only in September 1934.

The company was unable to produce engines based on its experience of casting production with automatic looms. One of the biggest bottlenecks was the problem of the core. The core is indispensable for making the interior of a hollow casting, such as a cylinder block. The company had to produce castings without any mold cavity. It took a little more than 1 year, but the problems with casting were eventually all resolved. The experience in using molding machines at Toyoda Automatic Loom Works and in making difficult castings, like the thin castings for spinning machines, with an electric arc furnace paid off in the end.

The company began to design a new engine in May 1937, and completed the design in October. Prototype production of this new engine, the B engine, started in March 1938 (Toyota Jidōsha Kōgyō Kabushiki Kaisha 1967, p. 153). With the completion of the Koromo Plant in November 1938, the company began full-scale production of this engine. Furthermore, the company initiated design of another engine (the C-type engine) in May 1937 and began its prototype production of a new car with this C-type engine in July 1938 (Toyota Jidōsha Kōgyō Kabushiki Kaisha 1967, p. 161). By the time of the completion of the Koromo Plant, Toyota had acquired the ability to produce engines.

In addition to the production of engines, the company faced another important problem: the adoption of an all-steel body. Kiichiro Toyoda intended to advance into the automobile business with the manufacture of passenger cars. By the early 1930s, it had become impossible not to adopt an all-metal enclosed body for the manufacture of passenger cars. However, the adoption of an all-metal body would cause the company two major problems. First, Toyoda Automatic Loom Works had never pressed thin steel sheet until then. The company had to work on the critical issue of whether it could make a whole body using high precision without technical accumulation. Second, the adoption of an all-metal body meant that large investment would be required for dies and press machines. Moreover, since the body would be closely related to the styling of the car, if the car was to sell slowly and the appearance of the car should have to change, it would be necessary to recreate the dies. Therefore, the company would require not only the initial investment but also a large amount of investment intermittently. Kiichiro Toyoda was aware of such problems and wrote in a booklet published in 1937:

> One of the factors behind the lack of progress by the automobile industry in our country is the fact that we cannot produce bodies in the large quantities in which this is done in the United States, and as long as we're beating them out by hand, establishment of the automobile industry is difficult. How to solve this problem was always one of the things that caused people in the industry a lot of headaches. Some people suggested that we should hire

> foreigners, but this would mean importing the US-style large-quantity production system lock, stock, and barrel, a thing that does not fit in with conditions in our country. And yet, in the present state of our country, manufacturing in this area is practically nonexistent, and people are making bodies just by beating them out by hand. True, because the Japanese are relatively good with their hands, what they beat out by hand is quite good, but for producing in large quantities, you just have to have presses. And yet, since we cannot make them in their tens of thousands the way they do in the United States, we cannot spend a lot of money on making dies. We have to come up, somehow, with a method that is unique to Japan. Unless we can make the main parts by press and do the rest by hand, there's no way we can adopt the United States method just as it is (Kato 1937; Wada 1999, p. 133).

Kiichiro Toyoda aimed to produce at least 200 passenger cars per month (Toyoda 1937a, p. 194). However, this goal was not achieved even by 1955, when he died; in the same year, the company produced only 1,857 passenger cars. In fact, only 19 trucks were produced in 1935, when the company began to record its production figures, and not a single passenger car was produced. An employee at the time said in a retrospective article in the company's in-house magazine:

> As we wanted to produce passenger cars as a start of this project, we were beating out the bodies of seven cars out of ten cars by hand. … [But it took too long to complete and we had to indicate the actual production figures.] So, we temporarily stopped the production of passenger cars (Gijutsu no Tomo, 1956, p. 108).

The company began to produce passenger cars in 1936, but the numbers remained quite low: 100 units in 1936 and 577 in 1937. During World War II, the company produced only 1,912 passenger cars in total. This level meant that the production of passenger cars accounted for just 2% of the company's total production volume.

This low level was due to the lack of materials, as well as to the substantial prohibition of passenger car production by the government during the war. In fact, there was little demand for passenger cars during the war years. In addition, it was difficult to mass produce steel bodies with high precision by machine equipment at the Koromo Plant. As long as the production volume of passenger cars remained small, there was no substantial increase in machine equipment, and low-precision body manufacture by hand tapping continued. This did not change until the early 1950s.

In the 1930s and 1940s in Japan, passenger cars were sold as bodies with chassis. However, trucks were normally supplied as a chassis and bodies for the chassis were produced by rural body makers. Therefore, truck companies did not need to manufacture bodies themselves. Moreover, wooden cabinets and platforms were still mainstream for trucks. The Toyota Body Co. Ltd., which was responsible for Toyota's car body manufacturing, began to produce steel cabs at full scale after World War II (Toyota Shatai Kabushiki Gaisha 1975, pp. 21, 42, 44–45).

3.3.5 Poor Quality of Vehicles Produced at Koromo Plant

The engine and body were only parts of the car. What was the quality of the cars themselves? Kiichiro Toyoda frankly said, "As we had to say sorry to everyone who used our cars, I was in a cold sweat" (Toyoda 1939a; Wada 1999, p. 280). The quality of cars produced at the Kariya Plant was poor.

The manufacture of automobiles requires many parts. The Toyoda Automatic Loom Works could not afford to manufacture all parts internally, and had to outsource or purchase many parts. As the market size of automobile manufacturing itself was small, the company had to rely on smaller and medium-sized enterprises to obtain such parts. One book published in 1938 pointed out the state of Japanese small and medium-sized enterprises as follows:

> Whatever they make, they would make without using any drawings. They did not have any ideas of dimensions. Little do they know how to use any gauge. They were using inexpensive materials without any respect to strength or durability. In the manufacturing process for any item, they did not consider any complicating matters, such as allowances. If items were regular in shape, and if the place to go around could be rotary, the process would be entirely satisfactory. In this situation, they could not manufacture any good-quality item at all (Waratani 1938, p. 9).

Therefore, Kiichiro Toyoda's assertion that the outsourced parts played a considerable role in the poor quality of cars might not just be a wild allegation (Toyoda 1938a; Wada 1999, p. 272).

Kiichiro Toyoda had thought that the quality of cars should still be improved after a certain period. As no automobile business had been developed in Japan, "there were no adequate facilities in Japan that could produce good quality parts at all" (Toyoda 1938a; Wada 1999, p. 272). Nevertheless, "we have ordered parts without stopping because we should wait for some years until a parts factory would learn how to produce parts or make arrangements for its own equipment" (Toyoda 1938a; Wada 1999, pp. 272–273). In a booklet distributed only to his company stakeholders, Kiichiro Toyoda frankly stated, "we have accepted the stigma that the quality of cars was terrible" during the period of production at the Kariya Plant (Toyoda 1938a; Wada 1999, p. 273).

The Koromo Plant, therefore, was significant not only for its large scale. The operations at the plant held the key for the success of the automobile business, which until then, had been based on trial and error at the Kariya Plant. Indeed, Kiichiro Toyoda had great expectations for the operations of the Koromo Plant (Toyoda 1938a; Wada 1999, pp. 268–269). Most of his writings penned after the Koromo Plant was built are heavily tinged with an optimism burning with hope. Not too long after operations began, his writings started giving off a slight air of impatience. "The earliest vehicles after the completion of the Koromo Plant were, contrary to expectations, not very good products," he admitted to employees (Toyoda 1939b; Wada 1999, p. 295).

Meanwhile, the government requested the company to in-crease the production of vehicles as a licensed company under the Automobile Manufacturing Industries Act.

Therefore, the company had no choice but to begin preparations to achieve monthly production of 3,000 vehicles by 1941. It started doing so in the middle of May 1939, but by the end of that month, the government decided to switch its policy. Although the government aimed to produce vehicles domestically and had been constantly requesting increased production, the instruction was withdrawn, because the quality of vehicles did not improve at all. In addition, the government became reluctant to supply the materials for vehicle production (Wada and Yui 2002, pp. 282–286).

3.3.6 Quality of Vehicles as a Management Problem

Kiichiro Toyoda gradually recognized that the poor quality of vehicles would cause a serious management problem. In June 1939, he told employees:

> The volume of production at our company has been quite low so far. Fortunately, therefore, we did not have any heavy stocks of vehicles. Once we increase the volume of production, however, it will be possible for us to have stock for a couple of months. It would be permissible, if it were only temporary. But it would be a fatal blow to our company if we had to hold a large number of vehicles as inventories, since the quality of vehicles is poor and we cannot sell our vehicles well (Toyoda 1939b; Wada 1999, pp. 294–295).

In April 1939, the company recorded a monthly production rate of more than 1,000 vehicles for the first time, and since the number of vehicles the following month also exceeded 1,000, an outsider would have surmised that the business must be running at full sail before a favorable wind. Kiichiro Toyoda, however, sensed that danger was ahead after this increase in vehicle production numbers, even though it looked good on paper. In fact, by September 1939, the company had the inventories of parts and materials for 6,500 vehicles. In other words, the company had inventories for 6 or 7 months (Toyoda 1939c; Wada 1999, p. 301). Nevertheless, complaints about quality were ongoing. Consequently, the inventory problem was recognized as a serious management problem and measures were taken to resolve it.

In 1939, war broke out in Europe and the hostilities were seen as an opportunity to set the automobile business on track. Kiichiro Toyoda immediately formulated a policy in the form of a documented titled "Management Policy Hereafter." He felt that the company had overinvested to the tune of 20 million yen because it could not ignore government demands that it should increase production rapidly. He even described this overinvestment as "the large cancer that Toyota Motor Co. was born with" (Toyoda 1939c; Wada 1999, p. 300).

To get rid of this "large cancer," in February 1940, Kiichiro Toyoda decided on a wholesale revision of the company's purchasing policies and ordered a thorough review of the parts made in-house and those ordered from suppliers. Specifically, the company decided to reduce the number of parts on order to reduce costs by "giving consideration to the geographical distribution of suppliers" (Toyota Jidōsha Kōgyō Kabushiki Kaisha 1967, p. 180). It greatly reduced the number of items ordered from the Tokyo and Osaka areas, while only slightly reducing orders from the Nagoya area near the company's location.

Before the Koromo Plant began to operate in 1938, Toyota held meetings with suppliers in Tokyo, Osaka, and Nagoya to explain the process of establishing its automobile manufacturing business. This led to a meeting with Toyota's subcontractors in November 1939. From this meeting, an organization of parts suppliers was established. However, as Toyota was trying to make many parts in-house, parts suppliers with a stance of fully engaging in automotive parts became frustrated with Toyota's purchasing policy. Therefore, Toyota established a "purchasing provision" in November 1939; once Toyota recognized a supplier as its subcontracting partner, the company would treat the supplier as its branch plant and would place orders in a stable manner with the supplier. As a result, the organization of parts suppliers developed into Kyōhōkai in December 1943, which continues to exist until now as Toyota's first-tier suppliers' organization (Kyōhōkai 1967, p. 13). In the same year, Toyota reorganized its internal organization to establish two departments: one to give technical guidance to subcontracting companies and the other to oversee the business from purchasing materials to delivery.

What were the characteristics of the manufacturers participating in the Kyōhōkai? They were manufacturers of small parts, such as screws, pins, and springs (Toyota Jidosha Kōgyō Kabushi-ki Kaisha 1958, p. 109). Most of them engaged in supplying parts for textile machinery, specifically, Toyoda Automatic Loom Works Ltd. It would be natural for them to enter manufacturing of small parts of automobiles, because the production of automatic loom parts also required precision machining, even if not as much as the production of automobile parts.

Among the members of Kyōhōkai, Kojima & Co. (now Kojima Industries Corporation) presents an interesting case study. This firm had no experience in precision machining. It was engaged in the manufacture of hand warmers and mosquito coils, employing only 15 workers (Nagoya Shōkō Kaigisho 1936, p. 137). As the founder felt uneasy about the future of the business, he repeatedly visited Toyota to win orders for automobile parts. However, the firm had no processing technology with the precision to manufacture automobile parts. Toyota first gave the product drawing of its "sand bucket" (for fire protection against incendiary bullets) to Kojima, which then looked over its workmanship requirements. Then, Toyota ordered other parts, like washers and additional parts for a truck radiator grill. Toyota guided and trained manufacturers, such as Kojima, which did not have high technical capabilities. Toyota trained some manufacturers and raised their technical capabilities, organizing them as suppliers. Without these suppliers, Toyota would not have obtained the appropriate small parts for its automobiles.

3.3.7 Production Flow Designed at Koromo Plant

Was "flow production" realized at the Koromo Plant from the beginning of operations? The Guidebook of the Toyota Commemorative Museum of Industry and Technology stated:

> The assembly line system—the forerunner of the Toyota Production System—was first utilized at the Koromo Plant from the time it opened in 1938. Assembly for completing the automobile production process was performed on two chain-conveyor lines, each 100 m long—one for passenger cars and the other for trucks. When the Koromo Plant began operations, these lines had a production capacity of 2,000 vehicles per month, making it the most productive assembly system in Japan.
>
> The line for the mass production of passenger cars actually consisted of two assembly lines. On the second floor was the body equipment line, where interior components, such as seats, instrument panels, etc., were installed; on the first floor was a chassis assembly line, where the engine and suspension components were installed. Production of Model GA trucks and Model AA passenger cars began on these lines (Toyota Commemorative Museum of Industry and Technology 2007, p. 272).

From this extract, it is easy to imagine that production capacity of 2,000 vehicles per month was realized smoothly at the Koromo Plant. However, the guidebook continued:

> Because of the low precision of body work at the time, line workers had to make on-the-spot adjustments to align each body with each chassis. They also had to manually tighten the bolts and screws with spanners, which required a great deal of time and man hours. Every vehicle that was shipped from the plant had to undergo final repair in a special shop at the end of the line and paint work in the touch-up shop. These finishing tasks required an extra number of workers (Toyota Commemorative Museum of Industry and Technology 2007, p. 272).

In other words, due to "the low precision of body work," the production flow in the final assembly process was not smooth. However, the extracts above do not explain the whole Koromo Plant. The final assembly plant, described as a "general assembly plant" in Fig. 3.3, was only a small part of the Koromo Plant, which was a collective name for various plants and workshops.

Was there an intention or ingenuity behind the realization of smooth production flow at the Koromo Plant? Looking closely at the plant, it is noticeable that there were many warehouses in the plant. From the north side of the plant, there was a warehouse near the forging plant, an iron warehouse and a warehouse near the tool and machine plant, a waste material warehouse and casting materials warehouse near the side of No. 2 special casting plant, and three more warehouses at the eastern end (see Fig. 3.3). In addition, there were three material preparation rooms next to machining plants named No. 1 to 3 material preparation rooms, which corresponded to No. 1 to 3 machining plants.

What were these material preparation rooms? Takatoshi Kan, who was in charge of the construction plan of the Koromo Plant, explained:

> I built three material [preparation] warehouses for each of these three [machining] plants. The first warehouse stores casting products, the second warehouse keeps forged products and large-sized iron bars, and the third warehouse supplies malleable casting products and steel bars. These stocked items correspond to the items made in the three plants, respectively, and are consumed in plants that follow each. As a result, I named these "preparation warehouses." In these warehouses, the materials for two weeks are always placed in piles of one day each. That is why I named it as such (Toyota Jidosha Kōgyō Kabushiki Kaisha 1958, p. 616).

Although the preparation warehouse could prepare material for the machine plants on a daily basis, it was called a "preparation warehouse" because it could stockpile

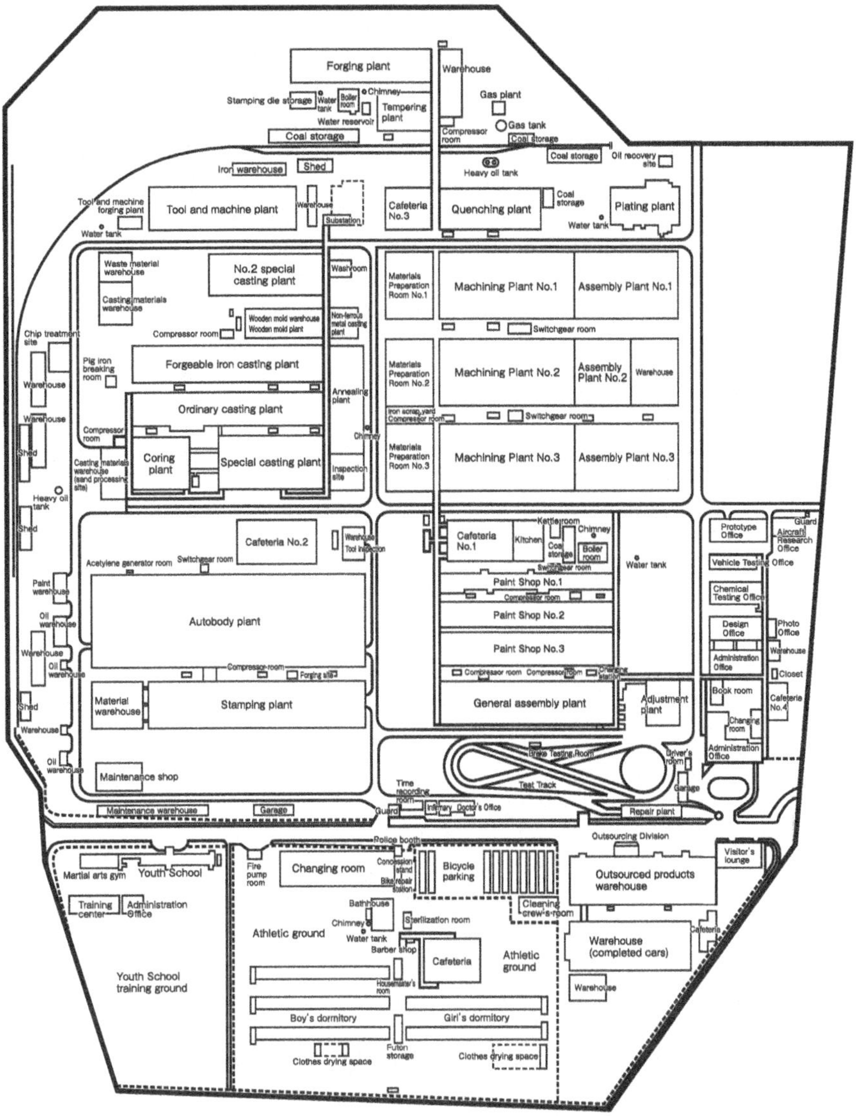

Fig. 3.3 Layout of Koromo Plant at its time of completion (around April 1939). *Source* http://www.toyota-global.com/company/history_of_toyota/75years/text/taking_on_the_automotive_business/chapter2/section4/item4.html

material for two weeks. Many warehouses, including material preparation rooms, were located at the Koromo Plant. After parts were processed or assembled, they travelled along routes from a warehouse to a plant or shop, or from a plant or shop to a warehouse, finally being collected and assembled at the general assembly plant.

The Koromo Plant used warehouses to absorb differences in production time among the various plants or workshops. This was the same idea as the semi-flow production method. High output of defective products occurred because of low-quality materials or crude-machining processes, so these defective parts were removed in the warehouses and only appropriate parts were selected and sent to plants or shops for follow-up processing. To remove the defective parts, the Koromo Plant hired many inspection workers (Kan 1940, pp. 39–40), which contributed to smooth flow of production within each plant or shop. However, the plant as a whole did not realize smooth flow of production.

Therefore, Kan did not install full conveyor coverage in the Koromo Plant. Kan had inspected Ford's River Rouge and other American plants before planning the Koromo Plant, and recognized the importance of conveyors and transportation facilities:

> This [transportation] facility is generally neglected in Japan, but how to transport the materials to each workplace is the most important thing. Nevertheless, I only installed a conveyor system partially in this factory (Kan 1940, p. 40).

Owing to lack of funds, conveyors were only installed in important places, such as the casting plants, painting shops, and general assembling plant.

Relishing the idea of establishing "the best transportation facilities in every necessary place in this plant someday," Kan stated:

> To replace the conveyor [someday], I did not put electric wires, cords, power belts in the space above the factory. All the machines were able to move separately by motors, having their respective lamps... So each machine could easily be repositioned with the lamp (Toyota Jidōsha Kōgyō Kabushiki Kaisha 1958, p. 608).

Ford equipped its factory with many special-purpose machines following process sequences. However, Toyota did not use special-purpose machine tools but rather adjustable special-purpose machine tools, making some alterations to general-purpose machines. If the company had installed many special-purpose machine tools, like Ford did, then Toyota would have had to replace those machines each time the designs or types of its automobiles changed. Production in Japan was expected to be small initially. Because of a lack of funds, Toyota could not consider reinstalling machines at short intervals. Therefore, the use of adjustable special-purpose machine tools from alterations to general-purpose machines was dictated by cost considerations. However, this strategy also caused production problems at the Koromo Plant, especially in regard to low precision in the metal body-making process.

Furthermore, the machines at the Koromo Plant were fixed to wooden floorboards, which meant that settings on the machine tools could be easily changed. This arrangement was also used at the Musashino Works of the Nakajima Aircraft Company during the war. The question then remains: did the Koromo Plant realize flow production by combination of adjustable special-purpose machine tools and an easily changeable installation? An employee at the time looked back: "Accepting visitors, machine tools were arranged in a good way [as if to perform flow production]."

3.4 Managing the Production Process at Koromo Plant

Before the Koromo Plant began operation in 1938, Kiichiro Toyoda spoke of his idea for managing production:

> In the case of automobile manufacturing, materials play an extremely important role in terms of both quality and quantity. In the types of parts alone, there are some two to three thousand different parts, and if you don't think carefully about the materials used in them or their preparation or the stocking of them, you will waste money and the number of completed vehicles will decrease. The first thing I think of is "making sure you don't have too many or too few"—in other words, making sure one doesn't use too much effort and time to produce a specific item: no waste and no surplus. When a part moves down the assembly line, you have to make sure you don't keep it waiting. I think it's important that every part be ready just in time.
>
> I believe this is the first principle in improving efficiency. If parts X are made too quickly and are piled up in excessive numbers, then parts Y will lag behind and be ready in too few numbers. Even down to a single nut and bolt, everything has to "be there just at the right time"—this has to be the greatest concern as far as making connections goes (Toyoda 1938b; Wada 1999, pp. 253–254).

When he explained this ideal, Kiichiro Toyoda knew the layout of the Koromo Plant. How could his just-in-time concept be realized in the physical restrictions of the plant? In June 1939, Kiichiro Toyoda issued a circular on the plant's operations. This circular clearly showed how he conceptualized his idea in the plant. First, he sought to coordinate the tempo of work in all plants and shops. Furthermore, workers were allowed to return home when they produced a target production volume. However, workers on a job site who had finished their job more than 1 h earlier were required to assist workers in places where work had been delayed. Those in charge of each plant and shop should strive to increase production volumes in job sites that were unable to reach target figures within normal working times (Wada and Yui 2002, pp. 288–289).

Kiichiro Toyoda aimed to synchronize the progress of production within the Koromo Plant. As the plant consisted of several plants and workshops, work in progress would be transferred from one area to another whose working time was consistently maintained. Even if the working time would differ slightly among plants or workshops, the material preparation warehouse or warehouses located between the plants and workshops could absorb the gap in working time. Toyota's official history gives strong acknowledgment to Kiichiro Toyoda's vision:

> When operations started at the Koromo Plant, a material preparation warehouse was established between the raw material divisions and machining divisions. The preparation warehouse delivered only the raw materials necessary for that day's planned production to the machining plant, which delivered completed parts corresponding to the raw materials to the assembly plant. The assembly plant produced only the number of completed vehicles based on the received parts from the machining plant. When the planning quantity was manufactured and delivered to the next process, that department shut down its line. This was an innovative management method without using any transfer slips (Toyota Jidōsha Kōgyō Kabushiki Kai-sha 1967, p. 422).

Nevertheless, the company history went on to state that this method did not match the actual situation of production sites, and was modified shortly thereafter, when the plant was managed using the Gōguchi production control system (Toyota Jidōsha Kōgyō Kabushiki Kaisha 1967, p. 422).

> In the Gōguchi production control system, a group of finished vehicles is scheduled for completion on a given day; if ten vehicles, ten of them are collectively called No. 1 Gōguchi. The next group is called No. 2 Gōguchi, then No. 3 Gōguchi, and so on. At the same time, each part necessary for assembly for No. 1 Gōguchi, No. 2 Gōguchi, and so on is referred to as No. 1 Gōguchi, No.2 Gōguchi, and so on. By knowing which process the respective Gōguchi's parts are currently in, the production progress is apparent at a glance (Toyota Jidōsha Kōgyō Kabushiki Kaisha 1967, p. 422).

Thus, the Koromo Plant attempted to control the production progress of every process by using a serial number for the final products. This idea was similar to the method adopted for Japanese aircraft production during World War II: every part in a particular final product was allocated the same serial number as the final product. After the war, this process evolved as the work center method, without the use of many tags or slips to control the progress of production.

However, the Gōguchi production control system did not achieve smooth flow of production at Toyota in the war years. Pro-duction at the plant contracted, and many "butty gangs" were com-missioned, each consisting of several workers. Due to a lack of materials or parts, automobile production itself fluctuated during the war years. Managing this situation well, butty gangs themselves attempted to secure the necessary materials or parts required for their own work to cover their living expenses. The commission of butty gangs was determined by the volume of their production. Their highest priority became securing higher piece-rate work, without considering final assembly production (Gijutsu no Tomo 1954, pp. 221–222). Even the company history acknowledged this situation in the war years:

> As each lot production was done in each Gōguchi in each production process, semi-finished products and finished products pile up at the start and end of the line in each plant. Even in the line, many works in progress are found everywhere in various places (Toyota Jidōsha Kōgyō Kabushiki Kaisha 1967, p. 422).

Toyota managed to achieve automobile production on a small scale; it produced 92,225 vehicles in total by the end of the war. At the government's request, however, most vehicles produced were trucks, of which the cabs were made from wood. Therefore, the company avoided the necessity of building all-metal enclosed bodies. The Koromo Plant was unable to achieve Kiichiro Toyoda's just-in-time idea by keeping the working time for each plant or shop constant. Furthermore, the plant's Gōguchi production control system did not realize smooth flow of production at the plant. Ohno Taiichi recalled the situation of the plant:

> In the war years, as many as 10,000 people were engaged in enhancement of production all day and night. That was a labor-intensive method indeed. …Each [butty gang] group manufactured as they desired without any permission from the company. In other words, we were obsessed with the notion of putting together even only one vehicle before being bombed (Gijutsu no Tomo 1954, p. 17).

Many works-in-progress and materials on production sites, and even finished parts, were stored. It is likely that preparation warehouses and warehouses failed to adjust the differences in processing times between plants or shops, and came to function simply as material storage places.

In the next chapter, we discuss how Toyota achieved smooth flow of production.

References

Bankoku Kōgyō Kaigi (World Engineering Congress). (1931). *Bankoku Kōgyō Kaigi hōkoku* (Report on World Engineering Congress). Tokyo: Bankoku Kōgyō Kaigi.

Bōshoku-kai. (1929). "Toyoda-shiki Shokki Kaisha no Hikae Jidōshokki no Kansei Chikashi" (Toyoda Loom Co.'s automatic Looms Nearing Completion). Bōshoku-kai (The World of Spinning and Weaving), *20*(9).

Bucci, Federico. (1993). *Albert Kahn: Architect of ford*. New York: Princeton Architectural Press.

Colvin, Fred H. (1947). *60 Years with men and machines: An autobiography*. New York: Whittlesey House.

Cusumano, Michael A. (1985). *The Japanese automobile industry: Technology and management at Nissan and Toyota*. Cambridge, Mass: Harvard University.

Doboku Gakkai (Japan Society of Civil Engineers). (2004). *Furuichi Koui to sono Jidai* (Koui Furuichi and the Modern National Land Development in Japan). Tokyo: Japan Society of Civil Engineers.

Enshū Seisaku Kabushiki Kaisha. (1971). *50nenshi Enshū Seisaku* (The 50th Anniversary History of Enshū Seisa-ku). Kamimura, Shizuokaken: Enshū Seisaku.

Gijutsu no Tomo (Friends of Technology). (1954). "Kikai Kōjō no Konjaku wo Kataru" (Talking about Machining Plants' History) in *Gijutsu no Tomo* (Friends of Technolo-gy), no. 14. Toyota: Toyota Jidōsha Kogyō Kabushiki Kaisha (Toyota Motor Co., Ltd).

Gijutsu no Tomo (Friends of Technology). (1956). "Toyota Jidōsha Oitachi no ki: zadan-kai" (A Note on Toyota Mo-tors in the Early Years: A Roundtable Discussion). *Gi-jutsu no Tomo* (Friends of Technology), no. 16. Toyota: Toyota Jidōsha Kogyō Kabushiki Kaisha (Toyota Motor Co., Ltd).

Hounshell, D. A. (1984). *From the american system to mass production, 1800–1932: The development of manufacturing technology in the United States*. Balti-more: Johns Hopkins University Press.

Hōwa Kōgyō Kabushiki Kaisha. (1987). *Hōwa Kōgyō hachi-jūnenshi* (The 80th Anniversary History of Hōwa Kōgyō). Aichi-ken: Hōwa Kōgyō Kabushiki Kaisha.

Ishii, T. (1979). "Tokkyo kara mita sangyō gijutsu shi: Toyoda Sakichi to shokki gijutsu no hatten (5)" (The history of industrial technology seen from patents: Sakichi Toyoda and the development of loom technology no. 5), in *Hatsumei* (Inventions), vol. 76, no. 5. Tokyo: Hatsumei Kyōkai.

Isuzu Jidoshiyashi Hensan Iinkai. (1957). *Isuzu Jidōshashi* (History of Isuzu Motors). Tokyo: Isuzu Motors Ltd.

Jidōsha Kōgyō Shinkōkai (Association for the Promotion of the Automobile Industry). (1973). *Nihon Jidōsha Kōgyōshi Zadankai Kirokushū* (Records of Roundtable Discussions on the History of the Automobile Industry in Japan). Tōkyō: Jidōsha Kōgyō Shnkōkai.

Kan, T. (1940). "Watashi wa nani wo kairyō shitaka—jūkōgyō ni okeru taryō seisan kōjō shisetsu" (What have I improved? High-volume production plant in heavy in-dustry), in *Kagaku Shugi Kōgyō* (Scientific Industry), vol. 4, no. 3. Tokyo: Kagaku Shugi Kōgyōsha.

Kato, S. ed. (1937). *Toyota Jidōsha Yakushinfu* (The Toyota Automobile: A Story of Rapid Progress). Aichi-ken: Toyoda Automatic Loom Works; Reprinted in Wada (1999).

Kikai, G.-S.. (1930). "Nagoya Rinji Taikai Kiji" (Notes on the Extraordinary Convention in Nagoya), in *Kikai Gakkai-shi* (Journal of the Society of Mechanical Engineers), vol. 33, no. 165. Tokyo: Nihon Kikai Gakkai.

Kikai Shinkō Kyōkai Keizai Kenkyūjo (The Economic Research Institute, the Japan Society for the Promotion of the Machine Industry). (1990). *Wagakuni sen'i kikai no gi-jutsu hatten chōsa kenkyū hōkokusho*. 2. (Report of re-search on the technological development of textile machinery in our county 2). Tokyo: Kikai Shinkō Kyōkai Keizai Kenkyūjo.

Kōgakkai (The Japan Federation of Engineering Societies). (1930). *Nihon Kōgyō Taikan* (Compendium of Japanese Industry). Tokyo: Kōseikai Shuppanbu.

Kyōhōkai. (1967). *Kyōhōkai 25nen no Ayumi* (The 25th Anniversary History of Kyōhōkai. Toyota: Tōkai Kyōhōkai.

Lancashire Cotton Corporation Ltd. (1932). "Official report con-cerning a test of automatic looms, etc., made in 1931," in *Journal of Textile Institute*, vol. 23, no. 3. Manchester: Textile Institute.

Matsubara, Kentarō. (1952). *Nihon Hatsmeika 50 Ketsu Sen* (Selection of 50 Distinctive Japanese Inventors). Tokyo: Hatsumei Tosho Kankōkai.

Nagoya Shōkō Kaigisho (The Nagoya Chamber of Commerce and Industry). (1936). *Nagoya Kōjō Yōran* (Nagoya Factory Directory). Nagoya: Nagoya Shōkō Kaigisho.

Nakaoka, T. (2006). *Nihon Kindai Gijutsu no Keisei: "Dentō" to "Kindai" no Dainamikusu* (Formation of Mod-ern Technology in Japan: Dynamics of "Tradition" and "Modern"). Tokyo: Asahi Shinbunsha.

Ōshima, T., & Yamada, S. (1987). *Jidōsha: Sangyō no Shōwa Shakaishi* 11 (Automobiles: Social History of Industry during the Shōwa Era, vol. 11). Tokyo: Nihon Keizai Hyōronsha.

Sakamoto, K. (1925). *Rikishokki no kenkyu* (Study on Power Looms). Hamamatsu: Kyugorō Sakamoto.

Shōkōshō Kōmukyoku (Ministry of Commerce and Industry Engineering Bureau). (1936). *Jidōsha Seizō Jigyō Sankō Shiryō* (Automobile Manufacturing Business Reference Material). Tokyo: Shōkōshō Kōmukyoku.

Suzuki Jidōsha Kōgyō Kabushiki Kaisha. (1970). *50 nenshi* (The 50th Anniversary History). Hamamatsu: Suzuki Jidōsha Kōgyō Kabushiki Kaisha.

Tōjō, T. (1940). "Gijutsusha Shōden: Toyoda Sakichi den" (Short Stories of Engineers: Sakichi Tyoda's Biography) (2), in *Kagaku Shugi Kōgyō* (Industries with Scientific Spirit), vol. 5, no.3. Tokyo: Kagaku Shugi Kōgyōsha.

Toyoda, K. (1927). "Toyoda shiki shokki ni hikae shi wo sayō shitaru riyū' (Reasons for Toyoda Automatic Loom Works adopting the shuttle change method), originally published in *Bōshoku-kai* (The World of Spinning and Weaving), vol. 18, no. 9 (September); Reprinted in Wada (1999).

Toyoda, K. (1931). "The Toyoda Textile Machinery" in World Engineering Congress.

Toyoda, K. (1936a). "Jumbi wa dekita, Toyota wa maishin shimasu" (Preparations are over, Toyota pushes on), originally published in *Toyota Nyusu* (Toyota News), no. 9 (November 1); Reprinted in Wada (1999).

Toyoda, K. (1936b). "Toyota Jidosha isshunen wo mukae-te" (Greeting the first anniversary of Toyota Motor Co. Ltd.), originally published in *Toyota Nyusu* [Toyota News], no. 10 no. 9 (November 1); Reprinted in Wada (1999).

Toyoda, K. (1937a). "Jidōsha seizō-bu kakuchō shuisho" (A prospectus for expanding the automobile manufac-turing division' (handwritten private memo), Reprinted in Wada (1999).

Toyoda, K. (1937b). "Toyota jidōsha no shutsugen kara gen-zai no yakushin made" (From the advent of Toyota Automo-bile to its present rapid progress). *Nagoya Shinbun* (Nagoya Newspaper), May 26.

Toyoda, K. (1938a). Koromo Kōjō e iten to shin-seihin ni-tsuite minasama e onegai (Moving into the Koromo Plant and A Re-quest to Our Customers Regarding Our New Product). Aichi-ken: Toyota Jidōsha Kōgyō Kabushiki Kaisha (Toyota Motor Co., Ltd), Reprinted in Wada (1999).

Toyoda, K. (1938b). 'Toyota-shi risō wo kataru:kisha to ichimon ittō' (Mr. Toyoda Recounts His Ideals: A Series of Questions and Answers with the Writer). *Mōtā* (Motor) July 1938 Re-printed in Wada (1999).

Toyoda, K. (1939a). Jidōsha Kōgyō no Kakuritsu ni Tsuite (On the Establishment of the Automobile Indus-try). Aichi-ken: Toyota Jidōsha Kōgyō Kabushiki Kaisha (Toyota Motor Co., Ltd), Reprinted in Wada (1999).

Toyoda, K. (1939b). "Dai 5 ki ni Okeru Warera no Kaku-go" (Our Resolve during the Fifth Period). *Toyota Bun'en* (Toyota Literally Works) [in-house magazine] Aichiken: Toyota Jidōsha Kōgyō Kabushiki Kaisha (Toyota Motor Co., Ltd), June, Reprinted in Wada (1999).
Toyoda, K. (1939c). "Kongo no Keiei Housshin" (Manage-ment Policy Hereafter) [a typescripted circular in the company], September, Reprinted in Wada (1999).
Toyoda, K. (1940). Kokusan jidōsha wa kanzen na mono ga dekiruka (Is It Possible to Make Domestic Automobiles Perfect?). Nagoya: Toyota Motor Co., Ltd; Reprinted in Wada (1999).
Toyoda, K. (1952). 'Jidōshokki oitachi no ki: Jidōshokki no omoide banashi' (A Record of the Way in which Toyo-da Automatic Loom Works Grew Up: Reminiscences on the Automatic Looms), originally published in Matsubara (1952); Reprinted in Wada (1999).
Toyoda Jidōsha Seizō Kabushiki Kaisha (Toyoda Motor Manu-factuirng Co. Ltd). (1937). "A Prospectus for Establish-ment of the Toyoda Motor Manufacturing Co. Ltd." (typescript written). Reprinted in Wada (1999).
Toyoda Jidō Shokki Seisakusho (Toyoda Automatic Loom Works). (1967). *40 nenshi* (The 40th Anniversary Histo-ry). Aichi-ken Kariya-shi: Toyoda Jidō Shokki Seisa-kusho.
Tōyōkeizai Shinpō. (1942). "Kakuritu ki ni Haitta Jidōsha Kōgyō" (Entering the Establishment Phase of the Au-tomobile Industry). *Tōyōkeizai Shinpō* (New Report on the Eastern Economy) April 25. Tokyo: Tōyōkeizai shin-pō sha.
Toyota Commemorative Museum of Industry and Technology (2007). *Toyota Commemorative Museum of Industry and Technology Guide Book*, New Edition. Nagoya: Toyota Commemorative Museum of Industry and Tech-nology.
Toyota Jidōsha Kabushiki Kaisha (Toyota Motor Corporation). (1999). *Ōinaru Yume Jōnetsu no Hibi: Toyota Sōgyōki Shashinshū* (Great Dreams, Days of Passion: Photo Collec-tion in Toyota's Foundation). Toyota: Toyota Jidōsha (Toyota Motor Corporation).
Toyota Jidōsha Kōgyō Kabushiki Kaisha (Toyota Motor Co., Ltd). (1958). *Toyota Jidōsha 20-nenshi* (The 20th Anniversary History of Toyota Motor Co). Koromo-shi: Toyo-ta Jidōsha Kogyō Kabushiki Kaisha (Toyota Motor Co., Ltd).
Toyota Jidōsha Kōgyō Kabushiki Kaisha (Toyota Motor Co., Ltd). (1967). *Toyota Jidōsha 30-nenshi* (The 30th Anniversary History of Toyota Motor Co). Toyota-shi: Toyota Jidōsha Kogyō Kabushiki Kaisha (Toyota Motor Co., Ltd).
Toyota Shatai Kabushiki Gaisha (Toyota Body Co. Ltd). (1975). *Toyota Shatai 30-nenshi* (The 30th Anniversary History of Toyota Body Co. Ltd). Kairya-shi: Toyota Shatai Ka-bushiki Gaisha.
Toyota-shiki Shokki Kabushiki Kaisha (Toyoda Loom Co.). (1936). *Sōritsu Sanjūnen Kinenshi* (In Commemoration of Thirty Years since the Company's Foundation). Nago-ya: Toyotashiki Shokki Kabushiki Kaisha.
Wada, Kazuo comp. 1999. *Toyoda Kiichiro Monjo Shūsei* (Cor-pus of Kiichiro Toyoda's Documents). Nagoya: Nagoya Daigaku Shuppankai (Nagoya University Press).
Wada, Kazuo. (2006). "The fable of the birth of the Japanese automobile industry: A reconsideration of the Toyoda–Platt Agreement of 1929," in *Business History* vol. 48 no. 1. London: Taylor & Francis.
Wada, K., & Yui, T. (2002). *Courage and Change: The Life of Kiichiro Toyoda*. Toyota City: Toyota Motor Corp.
Waratani, H. (1938). *Chūshō Tekkōgyō Josei-saku* (Subsidi-zation Policy for Medium and Small Iron Industry). Tokyo: Nihon Kōgyō Kyōkai (Japan Industry Association).
World Engineering Congress. (1931). *Proceedings of the World Engineering Congress of Tokyo in 1929*. vol. 28 (Refrigerating industry; Textile industry; Automotive engineer-ing). Tokyo: Kogakkai.

Chapter 4
Establishing Flow Production at Toyota: Collecting the Data on Shop Floors and Its Use

4.1 Organizational Reform During World War II

4.1.1 Wage System and Its Effects on Shop Floors

By the end of World War II, Toyota did not implement the just-in-time production system that Kiichiro Toyoda desired, nor the Gōguchi production control system that aimed at flow production. The preparation warehouses failed to adjust to the differences in processing times between plants or shops. Consequently, they came to function simply as material storage warehouses. However, Toyota began to collect data on each of the production processes, and its shop floors began to change in the 1950s. How and why did Toyota collect data on each production process? To understand this, we have to first examine Toyota's situation during World War II, particularly the fact that "each [butty gang] group manufactured as they desired without any permission from the company" (Gijutsu no Tomo 1954, p. 17).

The fact that each workers' group manufactured without any permission from the company demonstrates the loose control over the shop floors during the war. However, it is not clear why, or what criteria each workers' group used to select particular parts for manufacturing. If they behaved differently from the efficiency wage system, Toyota's Engineering Department that controlled its shop floors could have charged penalties or reduced payments to them. According to various existing records, the company was, however, unlikely to charge any penalties or reduce payments. If so, we might speculate that their behavior would be at least consistent with the efficiency rate plan.

Toyota paid wages to its shop-floor workers based on the efficiency rate plan from its foundation until just after the war. The efficiency wages were applied only to shop-floor workers, while the office staff received monthly salary. The shop-floor workers belonged to either the contracting department or the regular employment department. The wages of workers in the contracting department were calculated as follows:

K. Wada, *The Evolution of the Toyota Production System*,
Studies in Economic History,
https://doi.org/10.1007/978-981-15-4928-1_4

$$\text{Contract wage} = \text{Daily wage} \times \text{Man} - \text{hours} \times (1 + \text{Commission}) \tag{4.1}$$

$$\text{Commission (paid by group)} = \frac{\text{Piece rate of part} + \text{Finished Volume}}{\Sigma(\text{Daily wage} \times \text{Man} - \text{hours})} \tag{4.2}$$

The contract wages were calculated by using formulas 4.1 and 4.2. The company paid wages not directly to individual contract workers but to each group of contract workers. As such, group leaders of the butty gangs would receive their own group's wages, and then distribute wages to the group members. The wages of workers in regular employment were calculated as follows:

$$\begin{aligned}\text{Additionalwage} = {} & \text{Dailywage} \times \text{Man} - \text{hours} \times \\ & (1 + \text{Additionalwage rate for regular employment workers})\end{aligned} \tag{4.3}$$

$$\begin{aligned}&\text{Additionalwage rate for regular employment workers} \\ &= \text{Average commission of contracting department} \\ &\times \text{Factor for regular employment workers for regular employment workers}\end{aligned} \tag{4.4}$$

(Makino 1966, pp. 155–156).

According to formulas 4.3 and 4.4, the workers' commission in the contracting department had significant effects even on the wages of regular employment workers. The calculation of this commission largely depended on the "piece rate of parts" and "man-hours." This commission largely depended on the "piece rate of part" and "man-hours." These items were calculated in a very simple way. The piece rates of parts were "determined by estimating the difficulty of making parts, the quantity of parts made, and so on, comparing against other parts on the shop floors" (Makino 1966, p. 156). This was not based on the exact time that shop-floor workers actually spent on processing any particular parts. The man-hours were also calculated by a very simple method: the company perceived the working time by checking the time-clock cards of shop-floor workers (Makino 1966, p. 156). Based on the information gathered in this way, the "commission" was determined.

Such information would not reflect the actual situation of work on the shop floors. The opinion of contract workers, particularly the group leaders of butty gangs, had strong influence on the determination of piece rates of parts, because the company did not control any specific work process. Indeed, the company knew what amount of materials was input to the shop floors as well as the volume of finished products. Even if the person in charge of the production process pushed production, the speed or intensity of work was left to the discretion of the butty gangs.

Furthermore, the finished volume of parts had a significant effect over the determination of commission. As each butty gang was usually contracted with making several kinds of parts, "each butty gang preferentially chose parts with a higher piece rate among contracted parts. For the butty gangs, it was crucial that they received the necessary wages for their own lives....Without considering the production of final assembled cars, or even without considering the other butty gangs' works, each butty gang pursued its own goal of securing the necessary amount of wages" (Gijutsu no Tomo 1954, p. 41). To avoid this situation, the company gave additional wages to the office staff as reward, according to the increase in the number of completed assembled cars. This induced the office staff to propel the shop-floor workers to engage in their work ardently. However, without concrete knowledge of shop-floor operations, their encouragement did not change the attitude of the shop-floor workers. This reward was soon abolished (Makino 1966, p. 156).

Under this wage system, butty gangs produced unnecessary parts for the final assembly because of their own self-interest. These unnecessary parts were left all over the shop floors. If specific components or parts were required in the process of final assembly, they had to be produced in a hurry. This often created significant disruption in the plant.

4.1.2 Organizational Reform of 1944 and Its Consequences

How did Toyota deal with this situation? Even if the company had changed the wage system, butty gangs would continue to pursue their own interests under new constraints unless the company understood the actual working time for making each part. For a while, the company did not change its wage system. In fact, the company decided to change its organization to acquire sufficient information about the operations on shop floors. In the spring of 1944, Toyota reformed its organization, setting up the Manufacturing Department as follows:

> Traditionally, the organizations on shop floors consisted of the rough shape material department, the machining department, and the assembly department. To unify and control these departments, the Manufacturing Planning Department was separately established in spring 1944. Within the Manufacturing Department, the company simultaneously established the Engineering Works Department, which would be responsible for clerical jobs. This department would aim at maintaining basic source records on wage calculation (for continuing the employment of the butty gangs), and on cost accounting, by acquiring the number of finished products and precisely processing defective products and collecting accurate data on them. Until then, such data collection was insufficient. The data collected by this department was sent to both the wage calculation section and the cost-accounting section.
>
> President Kiichiro Toyoda strongly instructed all plants to improve this method. Because of war, it was difficult to obtain paper and other raw materials. However, to enforce this new method, the company changed administrative record files and made efforts to improve the flow of administrative work (Toyota Jidōsha Kōgyō Kabushiki Kaisha 1958, p. 193).

Thus, Toyota began to acquire data for cost and wage calculations in spring 1944. However, until this time, Toyota was not able to sufficiently collect such data on shop-floor operations. Despite this organizational reform, Toyota did not make much progress on assessing the actual situation on shop floors. Thus, the company's official history subtly describes as follows:

> Until the end of the war, for keeping records, workers were placed in the Engineering Works Department. They were taking records on man-hours [of each operation]. This worked well in theory, but this did not work well in practice. The relationship between the workers for keeping records and the workers being monitored for their own work was a delicate one on the shop floors. Despite many workers keeping records, this organizational reform had a poor record in terms of acquiring the actual data on shop floors (Toyota Jidosha Kōgyō Kabushiki Kaisha 1958, p. 291).

Within the context of a close relationship on the shop floors, the record-keeping workers did not try to acquire data on actual work processes rigorously but rather placed the top priority on creating harmonious personal relations on the shop floors.

Indeed, there were other reasons for the company's failure to acquire the actual data on shop floors. The company's official history points out:

> The Engineering Works Department issued shop-orders. However, regarding scheduling and follow-up control of work, supervisors had the real power at each plant. This was because the department had not enough information to judge the production capacity and actual condition of the shop floors. Moreover, there was no time to recruit and train people by calling from armed forces. However, it was also an important job for the department to communicate and coordinate among plants (Toyota Jidosha Kōgyō Kabushiki Kaisha 1958, p. 193).

The Engineering Works Department did not achieve the original purpose of accumulating basic data for wage calculation and cost accounting. The department's people simply served as liaisons between plants and flitted from one plant to another. Therefore, they did not have enough time to observe the shop floors. This organizational reform failed to obtain a result. Nevertheless, placing the workers for keeping records on the shop floors during the war was significant for the company given its later development (see Sect. 4.3.2).

The company did not have full control over the shop floors by acquiring the information of work processes. If so, why did the company not coerce the workers into submission? In fact, during the war, the company tried to do so regarding the central regrinding system of cutting tools. For skilled workers, it would be natural to regrind the cutting tools by themselves. In particular, in cases where wages were determined by volume (and therefore also in contracted workers), regrinding of tools had a profound effect on the efficiency of machining and directly affected their economic interests. Therefore, their resistance was strong to leave regrinding to people other than themselves. In fact, Toyota attempted to introduce the central regrinding system of cutting tools during the war. However, it failed because of workers' opposition. Consequently, each worker kept sharpening his own cutting tools afterwards (Okano 1954, pp. 73–74).

Even if Toyota had tried to acquire the information on the shop floors—at least the man-hours of each work process—it was quite difficult to obtain precise information. In addition, the company had tried to change the behavior of workers on the shop floors, but it failed. Despite the company's intentions, it did not have full control over the shop floors. Such circumstances, at least, led Toyota to not realize smooth flow of production at the Koromo Plant.

4.2 Postwar Restoration and Renovation of Production Facilities

4.2.1 Postwar Restoration of Production Facilities

Immediately after World War II, no one could see a bright outlook for the future of the automobile business in Japan. Even Kiichiro Toyoda once said, "On the automobile business for which I sacrificed life, I felt uneasy about whether there would be any way to survive. I was in a daze for a while" (Toyoda 1946a, p. 485). He also said, "In fact, I made a plan for transforming to bicycle manufacturing immediately after the war" (Toyoda 1946b, p. 513). Toyota's employees also left the company because they became concerned about the future. After students were mobilized during the war, girl volunteers as well as soldiers left the plant. On September 15, 1945, one month after the defeat, Toyota announced "We would employ 4,500 people required for the future resumption of production, but we would comb out the other jobs." However, many employees "voluntarily left the company to return home." The number of employees that left the company greatly exceeded the company's expectations. "By the end of October, the company's employees reduced to as few as 3,701" (Toyota Jidōsha Kōgyō Kabushiki Kaisha 1967, p. 240).

After the war, it was not clear whether Japanese companies would be able to engage in automobile manufacturing. For the company's survival, Kiichiro Toyoda considered transforming the company to bicycle manufacturing. Two months after the defeat, however, he finally decided to focus entirely on the automobile business. Yet the production facilities at Toyota were poorly equipped. At the end of the war, Toyota had transferred some of its machines, such as Gleason gear cutting machines, from the Koromo Plant to another location. In addition, the casting plant was bombed on August 14, 1945, just before the defeat. Therefore, even after attempting to resume automobile production, it was necessary to restore the bombed plants and reinstall the missing equipment, and to further shakedown all of the production facilities.

The Koromo Plant was restored in April of 1948 (Toyota Jidosha Kōgyō Kabushiki Kaisha 1958, p. 844). However, Toyota did not simply aim to restore the plant to its pre-bombed condition. Toyota reinforced its plant's facilities to cope with the increase in production volume. In fact, Toyota announced new cars one after another after the war. In February 1947, Toyota began to produce BM type trucks; in April, the company announced SB type small trucks; in October SA type small passenger cars. In both SB type trucks and SA type cars, the S type engine was installed. Therefore, in the manufacturing facilities of the S type engine, a monthly production capacity of 500 units was achieved by February 1948 (Toyota Jidosha Kōgyō Kabushiki Kaisha 1958, p. 844).

Given this operation, it would be assumed that Toyota added new machinery and facilities in the plants for engines, body making, and final assembly. However, the company's official history writes:

> In preparing for the production of BM, SB, and SA type cars, the company did not add new machinery equipment in the plants of machining, body making, and final assembly. However, the company tried to rationalize the production by changing the arrangement of facilities (Toyota Jidosha Kōgyō Kabushiki Kaisha 1958, p. 252).

Immediately after the war, Toyota aggressively restored and expanded production facilities. The company tried to cope with the production of newly manufactured automobiles by just "changing the arrangement of facilities" without adding new facilities in the plants for machining, body making, and final assembly.

4.2.2 Renovation of Production Facilities and Its Consequences

In 1951, Toyota launched the Facility Modernization Five-Year Plan, covering the period from April 1951 to March 1956. This plan rigorously replaced obsolete equipment with updated equipment. In addition, the company emphasized the rearrangement of equipment as follows:

> At that time [in around 1951], our company's production volume was about 1,500 units per month, even by adding the special demand of the Korean War. It was half the 3,000 units that this Plan set as its goal.
>
> Therefore, we examined which mechanical equipment would be necessary as well as adequate for achieving the monthly production of 3,000 units. Soon after reaching a conclusion on the reasonable placement of equipment, we sequentially installed it one after another. In considering the rational production factory with a monthly capacity of 3,000 units, we had to rebuild several new equipment under the new arrangement plan of equipment. (Toyota Jidōsha Kōgyō Kabushiki Kaisha 1958, p. 361)

While implementing the Facility Modernization Five-Year Plan, Toyota did not simply add more equipment by replacing older equipment with new equipment, it also considered the proper arrangement of equipment, just as it did immediately after the war. What effect did the relocation of such equipment show at specific work processes or on the shop floor? Did such rearrangement of equipment cause a significant effect on the efficiency of shop floors or increase the production volume? On the machining line for 1,000 cc engine cylinder blocks, detailed research was conducted from 1949 to 1953. The new equipment and the special-purpose machine tools were installed gradually, rather than at the one time. Although 20 machines were not replaced from August 1944 to January 1954, Toyota reduced the man-hours required on this line for making a cylinder block by 80% between January 1949 and May 1952 (Shōwa Dōjinkai 1958, p. 32). In fact, as they did not notice any drastic changes in equipment or even in its production system in this machining line, bewildered researchers concluded as follows:

> Efforts on rationalization or modernization would be made in each workplace or machine individually. If we looked at each one, it would be difficult to find any definitive one which

> would change the production system of the whole plant. However, after such efforts cumulatively reached a certain extent, we might eventually notice a heterogeneity, which was not seen in the production system in the past. (Shōwa Dōjinkai 1958, p. 34)

This field study was limited to the machining line for cylinder blocks, but other research also reported that between August 1950 and August 1957, overall, Toyota reduced of the man-hours required for standard car[1] production by 76%. During the same period, car production increased sevenfold. Toyota converted this number of actual cars produced into an equivalent production volume for standard cars. On this measure, Toyota increased its production by six times. During the same period, the personnel in the manufacturing departments increased by only 124% (see Table 4.1; Kishimoto 1959, p. 86).

The two abovementioned studies indicated that Toyota increased its production efficiency; specifically, man-hours required for making cylinder blocks as well as

Table 4.1 Production efficiency index (August 1950 to August 1957)

	For personnel at all plants (%)	For personnel in manufacturing departments (%)	Production of cars (%)	Conversion of car production to standard cars (%)	Man-hours per standard car (%)
August 1950	100	100	100	100	100
August 1951	95	94	118	136	70
August 1952	93	88	130	142	62
August 1953	93	87	101	112	58
August 1954	93	88	175	186	39
August 1955	92	92	183	219	40
August 1956	93	100	442	429	29
August 1957	106	124	712	605	24

August 1950 taken as 100%
Source Kishimoto (1959, p. 86)

[1]The "standard car" was used to give a precise picture of production growth, regardless of the types of vehicles produced. The man-hours for any type of car were converted into man-hours for a standard car. The man-hours for the standard car were the same if nothing changed in the production conditions. As Toyota began to produce many types of cars, the production figures converted into the standard car excluded the effect of any alteration in the designs of actual cars.

a standard car were reduced. Indeed, these studies show that the reduction of man-hours occurred over several years. However, the researchers stayed in the company to investigate over a few days. This suggests that the company willingly offered the data. In particular, given that the man-hour data on a "standard car" were different from the data on the actual production volume, the researchers would not have obtained such data without the company's cooperation. In other words, Toyota systematically acquired the trend of labor productivity after 1950 by using data based on "standard cars" derived from processing the data on actual car production (see Table 4.1). Toyota made an amazing transformation considering that it faced difficulty in acquiring the information on the shop floors even after the organizational reform in 1944.

Did Toyota change the method of determination of "piece rate of part" after World War II? As Toyota abolished employing contract workers after the war, the situation of butty gangs determining the piece rate of part based on the detailed data of work processes no longer existed. How did Toyota change its wage system, and its shop floors after the war? We discuss this point next.

4.2.3 Revival of Efficiency Wages

Facing the economic conditions after the war, Toyota changed its wage system. In January 1946, Toyota began to pay wages linked to cost-of-living as a measure to cope with postwar inflation. Under the new wage system, the payment comprised a basic wage, a supplemental payment, and a family allowance. The basic wage varied according to age, and the minimum of the basic wage was determined according to each age group. Therefore, Toyota suspended its efficiency rate plan for workers. Furthermore, Toyota decided to adjust the supplemental payment to price level in April 1947. The postwar democratic reform in Japan eliminated the status distinctions between office workers and shop-floor workers in Japanese companies. In February 1949, Toyota unified the wages of both types of employees under a daily basis monthly salary plan. Before this unification, Toyota revived the efficiency pay system and introduced "production allowance" (productivity bonuses) in July 1948.

This revived efficiency pay system was not the same as the prewar efficiency pay system at Toyota. In the revived efficiency system, the efficiency was defined as production allowance (productivity bonus) rate based on the collective efficiency of the direct manufacturing departments. It was defined by the following formula:

$$\text{Production allowance rate} = \frac{\text{Standard time} \times \text{Completed volume} + \text{Waiting hours and hours off the job}}{\text{Total actual working hours}} \tag{4.5}$$

This production allowance rate was calculated just on the efficiency of the directly involved departments, that is, the efficiency of each group of workers (department or plant) involved directly in manufacturing operations. Nevertheless, this rate determined the production allowance (productivity bonuses) not just for the employees in the production departments but also for the administrative and technical staff as follows:

$$\begin{aligned}&\text{Production allowance for direct departments}\\&= \text{Dailywage} \times \text{Man} - \text{hours} \times \text{Production allowance rate}\end{aligned} \tag{4.6}$$

$$\begin{aligned}&\text{Production allowance for indirect departments}\\&= \text{Dailywage} \times \text{Man} - \text{hours}\\&\times \text{Average production allowance rate at all direct departments}\\&\times \text{Factor for regular employees}\end{aligned} \tag{4.7}$$

$$\begin{aligned}&\text{Production allowance for administrative and technical staff}\\&= \text{Monthly salary}\\&\times \text{Average production allowance rate at all direct departments}\\&\times \text{Factor for office staff}\end{aligned} \tag{4.8}$$

In this resurgent efficiency pay system, the production allowance rate had a galvanizing effect on the wages of all employees at Toyota. The efficiency of the production departments basically determined the production allowance rate, which in turn decided the wages of employees in other departments and the salaries of office staff.

The disparity between two efficiency pay systems at Toyota shows how efficiency was counted. Under the revived efficiency pay system after the war, the production allowance rate was calculated based on the information of working hours such as total actual working hours, waiting times, and so on. This calculation would be possible only by precisely confirming whether the workers were actually working. This was quite different from the previous efficiency pay system: under the previous system, the piece rate was not calculated based on the difficulty of work, and the company also collected information on working time just through checking the time-clock cards of shop-floor workers (see Sect. 4.1.1).

4.3 Transforming the Control of Shop Floors

4.3.1 When Did Toyota Begin to Acquire Data on the Shop Floors?

Two external researchers revealed that Toyota considerably reduced the man-hours required for making a cylinder block as well as for a standardized car by the end of the 1950s, based on data collected over a long term (see Sect. 4.2.2). Such data would have been unavailable unless the company had willingly provided it. As the earliest data on this external research showed the situation after August 1950, it is apparent that Toyota was in possession of such data by 1950. In addition, under the efficiency pay system that Toyota revived after the war, the collective efficiency of direct manufacturing departments was calculated based on the data showing what workers did and how they did their work on the shop floors (see Sect. 4.2.3). Toyota revived its efficiency pay system in July of 1948. Under this system, it was essential to obtain the information of actual working time as well as non-working time including waiting time (see formula 4.5 in Sect. 4.2.3). Without obtaining detailed information on the work processes on the shop floors, Toyota could not introduce the revised efficiency pay system. Therefore, Toyota seems to have obtained detailed information on the production processes on shop floors, at the latest by 1948.

When did Toyota begin to collect such detailed information? In this regard, Toyota's official company history reads as follows:

> In 1947, the standard time for machining parts was calculated based on the average of the actual time for machining each part for about half a year. That was revised in September 1950 (Toyota Jidōsha Kōgyō Kabushiki Kaisha 1958, p. 494).

Furthermore, in a book titled *The Practices of Merit Pay Plans* for practical persons published in 1966, a personnel division manager at Toyota contributed an article titled "The Production Allowance System at Toyota Motor Co., Ltd." The merit pay plans or the efficiency pay system would generally use the standard time as the basis of measuring the efficiency. This article explained how Toyota set the standard time: after the company created the documentation section in the Engineering Department in 1947, Toyota began to analyze the past performance of machining processes, and calculated the standard time (Makino 1966, p. 156).

In 1947, Toyota began to accumulate data on production processes on the shop floors, precisely the data on each machining process. Based on such accumulated data, Toyota revived the efficiency pay system in 1948. Without the data on standard times, hours off-the-job, actual working hours, and so on, the production allowance rate could not have been calculated (see formula 4.5). The introduction of the production allowance system did not simply mean that Toyota revived the efficiency rate payment system, but rather that it actively acquired data on the actual working processes on the shop floors.

4.3.2 The Origin and Activities of Ohno Lines

Taiichi Ohno is well known as the author of *Toyota Production System* (Ohno 1978, 1988). Ohno received an instruction from Shōichi Saitō, Director of Toyota, in July 1948 when the efficiency pay system was revived. On the instruction and the subsequent action, Toyota's official history reads as follows:

> Considering the preparation for the approaching free competition, Director Shōichi Saitō wanted to acquire accurate information of each plant in terms of material consumption and costs, and to contribute such information to the business administration. Then in July 1948, he ordered the General Manager of the powertrain plant, Taiichi Ohno, to rationalize its plant to serve as a good model for the rationalization of the whole company. (Toyota Jidōsha Kōgyō Kabushiki Kaisha 1958, p. 289)

After July 1948, Taiichi Ohno directed the acquisition and analysis of data on the shop floors. However, the mere acquisition and analysis of data was not the main purpose, but rather to apply the data in the production lines. Such lines were often called the "Ohno lines." The Ohno lines began at the powertrain plant, but they were gradually widened to the other plants in the company. In August 1949, Toyota integrated the engine plant and the powertrain plant under the machining division of the Koromo Plant. Taiichi Ohno was appointed as General Manager of the machining division and carried forward the rationalization of all machining plants (Toyota Jidōsha Kōgyō Kabushiki Kaisha 1958, p. 290). As Ohno widened his span of supervision, the Ohno lines correspondingly widened the company's activities.

In responding to a request from the Director, the powertrain plant reordered different kinds of written reports. Until then, each group of workers at the plant had submitted at least eight major reports, but the number of reports was reduced just to two: daily work reports and daily inspection reports. Through these two reports, the powertrain plant intended to collect the data on actual production (see Fig. 4.1). This became operative in November 1948.

The data on each specific operation's man-hours were collected and aggregated based on the "Daily Labor Report" submitted from shop floors. The "Monthly Report on Man-Hours" began to be circulated within Toyota in May 1949 (Toyota Jidōsha Kōgyō Kabushiki Kaisha 1958, p. 846). Through this monthly report, management became aware of the man-hours required for operations. This would largely contribute to an understanding of the actual working hours on the shop floors. The company's official history reads as follows:

> We [Toyota] collected and analyzed the materials and calculated the actual working time required for machining automobile parts. Then while comparing this with the standard time, we measured the efficiency of each working group. Using the efficiency as a guide, each working group engaged in improving the work on the shop floors step by step (Toyota Jidōsha Kōgyō Kabushiki Kaisha 1958, pp. 289–290).

Continuous comparison of the actual working time with the standard time allowed the company to revise the production allowance rate. This also sparked a hostile reaction from some of the workers because they tended to lose their vested interests: in the prewar period, the standard processing times for parts were greater than the

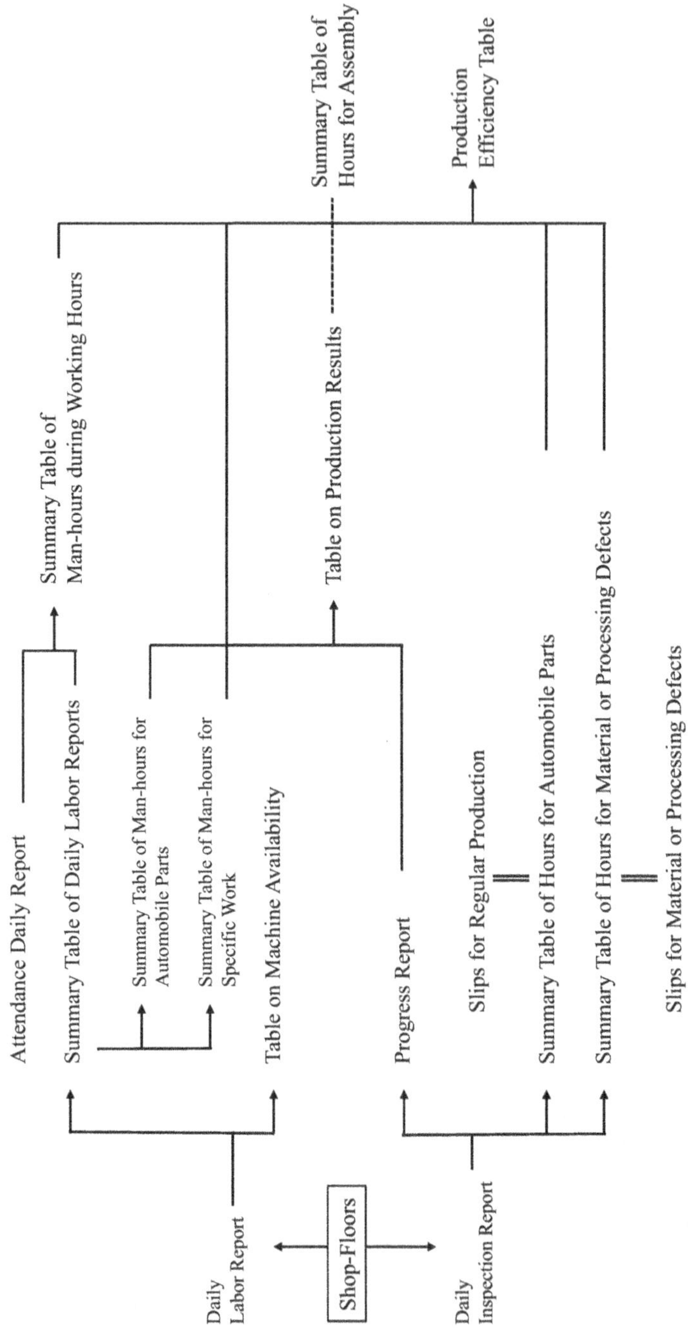

Fig. 4.1 Method of data collection on actual production. *Source* Toyota Jidōsha Kōgyō Kabushiki Kaisha (1958, p. 290)

actual processing times. However, frequent review of work data meant that this time difference gradually diminished.

Toyota's management were highly appreciative of the achievements based on data collection at the powertrain plant. In summer 1949, Ohno was promoted to General Manager at the newly established machining division of the Koromo Plant, which integrated both the engine and powertrain plants. Furthermore, the management placed administrative assistant managers in all plants at the Koromo Plant with the intention of spreading the data collection method of the powertrain plant to all other plants. This move was intended to "consolidate on-site affairs such as personnel matters, handling of work in progress, and calculating of man-hours for processes under the administrative assistant managers" (Toyota Jidōsha Kōgyō Kabushiki Kaisha 1958, p. 290). To spread this data collection method at the powertrain plant over the whole Koromo Plant, in July 1949, the management considered the enforcement of "Official Provision for the Calculation of Man-Hours at Koromo Plant" (Toyota Jidōsha Kōgyō Kabushiki Kaisha 1967, p. 379). All these changes happened within the year before the labor struggle at Toyota in 1950.

Toyota also began to enforce the central regrinding system for cutting tools in December 1950 (Toyota Jidōsha Kōgyō Kabushiki Kaisha 1958, p. 282). This began in the midst of a management crisis: Toyota's management and labor union agreed to "lower the average wage base of employees by 10% after November of 1950" (Toyota Jidōsha Kōgyō Kabushiki Kaisha 1967, p. 294). As noted earlier, Toyota had attempted to implement the central regrinding system of cutting tools during the war, but it had failed because of workers' resistance (see Sect. 4.1.2). Moreover, Toyota not only tried to have regrinding of cutting tools performed centrally, but also demanded that one worker handle several machines, possibly of the same type or other types of machine. Indeed, when one worker became efficient in handling several machines, it would be necessary to specialize and regrind the cutting tools centrally (Toyota Jidōsha Kōgyō Kabushiki Kaisha 1958, p. 282). Consequently, a part of the machining division of the Koromo Plant introduced the central regrinding system for cutting tools. Thus, by the end of 1949, precise data was not only collected for calculating the man-hours for each process, but also for the working practices of multi-machine handling and the central regrinding system for cutting tools. Both these working practices were quite different from traditional working practices, and workers began to raise concerns (Gijutsu no Tomo 1954, p. 21).

The implementation of the central regrinding system for cutting tools did not proceed promptly because it encountered many difficulties such as chattering vibration in cutting tools, or the chipping of cutting edges while regrinding (Okano 1977, pp. 209–210). Finally, in November 1951, Toyota "completed implementing the central regrinding system of cutting tools over the machining division of the Koromo Plant," one year of after the labor struggle at Toyota (Toyota Jidōsha Kōgyō Kabushiki Kaisha 1958, p. 282).

This situation summarizes the impact of the Ohno lines in about 1950. We should recall the report on the machining line for the 1,000 cc engine cylinder block by Shōwa Dōjinkai (see Sect. 4.2.2). In their report, the actual man-hours of the line after January 1949 had been indexed and were shown. The company provided such data because the Ohno lines placed a person on the shop floors to record the actual work situation.

Director Shōichi Saitō instructed Ohno "to acquire a more accurate situation of each plant in terms of material consumption and costs" (Toyota Jidōsha Kōgyō Kabushiki Kaisha 1958, p. 289). Then, what did Ohno think about this instruction? On this, Ohno admitted as a conclusion of roundtable talks with Toyota employees in June 1954. Considering that many of the references to the Ohno lines are written based on this statement, even in Toyota's official history, we would quote his detailed view here:

> I contemplated the idea of how Toyota would be recovering under the free economy after World War II. The automobile industry is the specialty of the USA, a victorious nation. In the USA, the automobile industry was the most advanced. In contrast, Japan produced only a small number of automobiles in small factories. How could we compete with the efficiency of the advanced country's automobile industry? […] If we could find a suitable way for small production volume, we would certainly survive. If we could not find it, we would just ruin ourselves. However, nobody showed us how to do it, so I devised in my mind that Toyota's people had to create a way within Toyota. In short, the ultimate goal could be summed up as the rationalization of work. However, this was no easy task. […] At the outset, I prepared to raise the production per capita; by any means, to accustom workers to move around; to move workers and let them individually handle from one machine to two or three machines to increase the volume of production. Traditionally, we referred to workers such as a lathe worker or a milling machine worker, and thus workers could not leave machines that they handled. In our factory's production method, workers should be able to handle a few kinds of machines. Therefore, names such as lathe worker became obsolete. Our workers should have abilities to handle many different machines. […] We achieved this. Then, we faced another problem: if one worker would operate many machines, he had to leave a machine to handle another machine without having to worry about its operation. To ensure this situation, it became necessary to install automatic feed equipment and automatic stop devices. It was also required to realize the homogeneity of the quality of materials. […]
>
> When proceeding with this policy, the company had to be restructured in 1950. Then some people strongly opposed our attempts, saying "Crushing down the Ōno line." If our line was to collapse, I believe that the automobile industry with its small volume production, such as in Japan, would be reduced to ashes. However, the people that remained [after the labor struggle of 1950s] cooperated with my way of thinking. Thereafter, the efficiency improvement in Toyota by rationalization became considerable (Gijutsu no Tomo 1954, pp. 21–22).

Ohno told himself that "The ultimate goal is just one word of rationalizing work" (Gijutsu no Tomo 1954, p. 21). Ohno lines spread throughout the company with the support of the management team. To this point, our discussion has focused on change on the shop floors (especially data collection on shop floors). In the next section, we evaluate the significance of movement on shop floors from the relationship with Toyota's overall movement.

4.3.3 The Rationalization Movement at Toyota

To acquire data that accurately reflected the situation on the shop floors, Toyota reformed its organization in spring 1944, setting up the Manufacturing Department.

The company's official history reads: "President Kiichiro Toyoda *strongly* ordered to improve all factories with this scheme (emphasis added)" (see Sect. 4.1.2, Toyota Jidōsha Kōgyō Kabushiki Kaisha 1958, p. 193). Indeed, Kiichiro Toyoda aggressively supported data collection on the manufacturing site. However, he had good reason for doing this. When Kiichiro Toyoda became involved in the management of a spinning company, it was extremely difficult for him to know the actual condition of labor at the factory. However, he fortunately learned "not only how to handle the machines but also how to maintain control over and run the entire spinning mill" from the engineers of Whitin Machine Works, an American textile machine company (Wada and Yui 2002, p. 171). Then, he understood the importance of getting information from the shop floors and standardizing the working processes.

Now, we consider how Toyota tried to acquire data on the working process on the shop floors using the organizational structure of the company. After deciding to continue the automobile business after the war, the management had to urgently restore the physical production facilities. However, once that was completed, the management had to turn their interest toward the broader issue of manufacturing and corporate management. In July 1947, a few months after the dissolution of the postwar extraordinary restoration office, Toyota established the Management Research Committee under direct supervision by the executive office—Toyota's highest deliberative and decision-making body (Toyota Jidosha Kōgyō Kabushiki Kaisha 1958, p. 253). Under this Management Research Committee, Toyota established three subcommittees—one of which was the Control Subcommittee. The activities of this subcommittee oversaw changing of business forms, improving the flow of administrative work, applying actual man-hours for cost control, and so on (Toyota Jidōsha Kōgyō Kabushiki Kaisha 1967, p. 270). This subcommittee was a top management organization with the task of embodying what President Kiichiro Toyoda "strongly ordered" in the spring of 1944 after the war.

In August 1948, the secretariat of this subcommittee, which was initially the Management Research Division in the General Affairs Department, became the staff organization in the executive office, and its name was changed to "Management Research Office" (Toyota Jidōsha Kōgyō Kabushiki Kaisha 1967, p. 271). This was more than just renaming. The Management Research Office was not only separated from the General Affairs Department but was also "strengthened by bringing personnel from one division of the Manufacturing Department" (Toyota Jidosha Kōgyō Kabushiki Kaisha 1958, p. 255). The division handled the basic materials for wage calculation and cost accounting after the Manufacturing Department was newly established in spring 1944. Then, the management research office formulated the first long-term plan at Toyota, "the Facility Modernization Five-Year Plan," which was officially adopted as company policy in January 1948 (Toyota Jidōsha Kōgyō Kabushiki Kaisha 1967, p. 284). By summer 1948, the Management Research Office was firmly established as the staff organization of the executive office.

In response to the sudden change in the postwar economic situation, the organization was further changed. The Management Research Committee was reorganized as the "Management Rationalization Committee," in which the executive members of the labor union became the official members (Toyota Jidōsha Kōgyō Kabushiki

Kaisha 1967, p. 271). Toyota expected further financial difficulties, and feared that its business would fall into a money-losing situation. In response, Toyota began to devise countermeasures, resulting in the establishment of the Management Rationalization Committee, in which managing directors were appointed as chairman and vice-chairman of the committee. Furthermore, the members of the committee consisted of directors, an accounting manager, a production engineering manager, and the executive chairman of the labor union. By November 1948, Toyota expanded its management rationalization campaign with the labor union throughout the company. Toyota implemented the campaign from November 1 to 30 as the first period, and from December 1 to 30 as the second period (Toyota Jidōsha Kōgyō Kabushiki Kaisha 1967, p. 830).

Against these company-wide changes, we consider the activities of the Ohno lines. In July 1948, Toyota reviewed the efficiency wage. During the same month, Director Shōichi Saito ordered "the general manager of the powertrain plant, Taichi Ohno, to rationalize its plant serving as a good model for the rationalization of the whole plant" (Toyota Jidosha Kōgyō Kabushiki Kaisha 1958, p. 290). However, it was on November 1, 1948, when Ohno actually began to gather the data on shop floors through two kinds of daily reports: daily work reports and daily inspection reports. On this same day, Toyota began its management rationalization campaign, involving the labor union, on a company-wide basis. Ohno himself was also a member of the subcommittee of the Management Rationalization Committee. Indeed, the activity of Ohno lines became fully fledged with the development of the management rationalization campaign at Toyota, because it received company-wide support.

4.3.4 Enterprise Rationalization Promotion Committee and Labor Disputes

Toyota's management rationalization movement further changed its nature. When the company's financial situation deteriorated due to the implementation of the so-called Dodge Line, the Management Rationalization Committee was renamed as the Enterprise Rationalization Promotion Committee in August 1949. Under the Management Rationalization Committee, the company tried to promote rationalization through cooperation with the labor union. However, the Enterprise Promotion Committee considered the rationalization goals such as improving production efficiency and striving to achieve such goals through the company's official organization. That is, the company sought workers' involvement in rationalization by administrative orders. Hence, the company changed its organization "to give a stronger driving force to the existing rationalization movement." However, the Management Research Office still remained responsible for the entire rationalization movement (Toyota Jidosha Kōgyō Kabushiki Kaisha 1958, p. 303).

The move "to give a stronger driving force to the existing rationalization movement" was not the only organization reform. On July 16, 1949, the "Official Provision for the Calculation of Man-Hours at Koromo Plant" was enacted (Toyota Jidōsha Kōgyō Kabushiki Kaisha 1967, p. 379), which aimed to expand the method of measuring the man-hours of each operation on Ohno lines on a company-wide basis (see Sect. 4.3.2). Furthermore, according to the organization table dated August 1, 1948, Ohno was appointed as General Manager at the newly established machining division of the Koromo Plant. In addition, a Secretariat Chief was placed in all plants of the Koromo Plant, with the intention of spreading the data collection method to all plants (Toyota Jidosha Kōgyō Kabushiki Kaisha 1958, p. 748). The establishment of the Enterprise Rationalization Promotion Committee brought about the company-wide implementation of the Ohno line.

In situations where the Rationalization Promotion Committee was established, Toyota entered into labor disputes in 1950. When Toyota's financial situation fell into a more critical situation, the company signed a memorandum with the labor union in January 1949. Both parties confirmed the rationalization plan drawn up by the Enterprise Rationalization Promotion Committee since September 1949. Furthermore, both parties agreed to reduce the average wage by 10% from January 1949. The company then guaranteed not to implement cutbacks in personnel as a means of overcoming the crisis (Toyota Jidōsha Kōgyō Kabushiki Kaisha 1967, p. 294). However, despite promising in the memorandum that the company would pay on the prescribed day without fail, the company could not completely pay employee salaries (Toyota Jidōsha Kōgyō Kabushiki Kaisha 1967, pp. 294, 298). Thus, labor disputes began at Toyota on April 7, 1950.

From summer 1949, Ohno lines expanded all over the company and labor disputes occurred in such circumstances, so some workers turned the point of attack to the Ohno lines. The company's official history notes as follows:

> In 1954, disputes between labor and management occurred over the rebuilding of the company, but at this time some people rebelled, saying, "Stop the Ohno lines." However, if this method [the Ohno lines] collapsed, it would deny the existence of Toyota Motor Corporation. Therefore, the company stuck to this method, and with the cooperation of many people striving for the reconstruction of Toyota, it gradually bore fruit. (Toyota Jidosha Kōgyō Kabushiki Kaisha 1958, pp. 282–283)

The Ohno lines were not merely collecting data on work processes on the shop floors; they had become a symbol of the rationalization movement at Toyota. For some workers, the Ohno lines became a target of protest, while the company considered them as key to its survival.

How did the company respond to these disputes? We briefly consider this point in relation to the rationalization movement at Toyota to conclude this section.

The company presented its restructuring plan in collective bargaining on April 22, 1950. The company decided to recruit volunteers who wished to retire in the plan. For those who remained in the company, the company requested to "reform the salary system and make a 10% wage reduction," and "to make personnel relocate and to renew the organization at the working place" (Toyota Jidōsha Kōgyō Kabushiki Kaisha 1967, p. 299). In addition to the reduction of wages due to a lack of funds, the company sought the transformation of institutions and its operation that would have long-term effects. The person who explained the company's rebuilding plan on behalf of the company in collective bargaining was Shūji Ohno, Managing Director, who was in charge of the Management Research Office. Announcing that the company would reform the salary system, the relocation of personnel, and the reorganization of shop floors even under the management crisis, he declared that the company would not stop the movement of "rationalization."

The labor dispute ended in June 1950. On June 5, 1950, "leaving behind Shūji Ohno, Kiichiro Toyoda [and all other managing directors] retired from office taking management responsibility for the crisis" (Toyota Jidōsha Kōgyō Kabushiki Kaisha 1967, p. 302). After the top management retired, the number of employees who wished to leave the company increased rapidly. The labor disputes that lasted for two months ended on June 10.

4.3.5 Why Did Toyota Pursue Rationalization?

Toyota consistently pursued rationalization from the time of defeat until labor dispute—and even after the labor dispute. What was the purpose of this "management rationalization" (later "enterprise rationalization")?

After the war, the Japanese government encouraged rationalization for "reducing production costs of various products to be at par with the international level," setting the goal of "restoring the international competitiveness of Japanese industry" (Sangyō Gōrika Shingikai and Tsūshō Sangyōshō Kigyōkyoku 1952, p. 9). It is likely that Toyota simply responded to the Industrial Rationalization Council established in December 1949 and the Corporate Rationalization Promotion Act established in 1952. However, as the position of the automobile industry in Japan was insignificant at that time, the main concern of policymakers remained with the spinning and textiles industry and others. Furthermore, Toyota initiated its rationalization campaign before Japanese policymakers took steps to rationalize industries and corporations. Certainly, Toyota's rationalization campaign featured many characteristics that were being pursued in postwar Japan, such as "reducing production costs to international standards." Unless the production costs of international standards could be achieved, it would be impossible for the automobile industry to continue in Japan. Those engaged in the automobile business in Japan were strongly aware of this.

After the war, Kiichiro Toyoda also frequently considered the differences between Japanese cars and foreign cars. For example, in November 1949, he wrote:

> In terms of quality and price, we must compete with foreign cars. If it is impossible, this would mean the death of management in the automobile industry. (Toyoda 1949; Wada 1999, p. 522)

After deciding to continue the automobile business, Kiichiro Toyoda had no choice but to be conscious of the differences with foreign cars "in terms of quality and price." In a short period, Toyota had to remove these differences. Toyota's management team was strongly conscious of the "death of management" unless the differences with foreign cars were addressed in terms of quality and price. In this sense, Toyota's rationalization movement was broadly in line with the rationalization movement developed in postwar Japan.

4.4 Introduction of Historical Organization at the Work Place

4.4.1 Historical Organization

When the labor dispute in 1950 came to an end, Toyota did "renew the workplace by promotion, departure, dismissal, etc." (Toyota Jidōsha Kōgyō Kabushiki Kaisha 1967, p. 299). Many journalists or scholars have investigated the details of the labor disputes but have paid little attention to this "historical organization" or what happened within the company. However, during Toyota's 20th anniversary in July 1950, the company announced itself as a "historical organization at the working place for rebuilding Toyota" (Toyota Jidosha Kōgyō Kabushiki Kaisha 1958, p. 290). Why did Toyota's 20th anniversary history refer to this organizational change as "historical organization"? Many readers might consider this statement an exaggeration.

Indeed, Toyota's 30th anniversary history made an assessment on its reorganization as "simplifying the organization by reducing the number of departments and plants to 18, while expanding and strengthening the existing management research office" (Toyota Jidōsha Kōgyō Kabushiki Kaisha 1967, p. 290). However, did Toyota's 20th anniversary really consider "simplifying the organization" and "expanding and strengthening the management research office" as "historical organization"? Here, we focus on Toyota's 20th anniversary where it documented itself as undergoing "historical organization" as follows:

> As a management theme in plants, we often talk about whether decentralized or centralized management is appropriate. If we want to implement centralized management in the true sense, setting aside the adoption of centralized management with formality, it is certainly necessary that each plant should be adequately managed. (Toyota Jidōsha Kōgyō Kabushiki Kaisha 1958, p. 291)

Many readers might be wondering whether there is any connection to the discussion of "historical organization" and topics of decentralized management and centralized management. Toyota's 20th anniversary history documented in its chronological table that the company "adopted the decentralized management system of manufacturing" in July 1950 (Toyota Jidōsha Kōgyō Kabushiki Kaisha 1958, p. 848). In other words, Toyota's 20th anniversary history identified "historical organization" with "the decentralized management system." Although both referred to the same reforms, it would be difficult for an outsider to understand what the "decentralized management system" specifically implied. However, for those engaged in Japanese manufacturing sites during the 1950s, the implications of decentralized or centralized management would have been clear. In the early 1950s, centralized management meant the control method using slips or tags, while decentralized management referred to the work-center method promoted by the Japan Management Association (JMA) to Japanese manufacturing companies after the war. The work-center method conveyed an image of non-centralized control: conventionally, the Production Control Department at the head office assumed control over production management, but in the work-center method, the work-centers on the shop floors gained power over production control. One book published in 1951 characterized these two control methods as follows:

> Progress staff and inspectors placed in the work-centers traditionally formed groups in the respective departments. They were placed on the shop floors. Thus [by adopting the work-center method], conventional production control [the control method using slips or tags] changed into the method based on the shop floors. [...] Conventional production control was centralized on the Production Control Department, and production control was not carried out based on current conditions of the shop floors, so production control often tended to become detached from current activities on the shop floors (Murai 1951, pp. 95–96).

Tetsuro Nakaoka, who had been focusing on the historical importance of the work-center method, also pointed out its characteristics as "decentralized":

> Notably, the work-center method did not centralize its control through any specialized department at the central office of the company, but decentralized it on the basis of many work units on the shop floors. (Nakaoka 1981, p. 47)

In 1950, Toyota adopted "the decentralized management system of manufacturing," which was the work-center method promoted by JMA, and the official company history referred to this as "historical organization." JMA was trying to implement inventory management, production management, and control of actual production data through the work-center method. In particular, JMA recommended acquiring actual production data through two kinds of daily reports: daily inspection reports and daily work reports. Before the labor disputes, the Ohno line began to collect data on work processes on the shop floors through the same kinds of reports. Under the "historical organization" after the disputes, Toyota extended the method of calculating the actual man-hours on each operation through the two daily reports to all plants. To achieve this, Toyota established a new engineering works section at the body plant, a man-hours section at the casting plant and the machining division, and a general administration division at every plant. Toyota's historical organization did not officially announce the adoption of the work-center method, but their actions to introduce decentralized management and acquire actual man-hours data on every working process through two daily reports followed the work-center method.

4.4.2 *What Did Toyota Do Under Historical Organization?*

During the labor disputes, the company maintained an uncompromising attitude to reform its salary plan. After the disputes, the company obtained data on man-hours and used it to reform the compensation plan and introduced the "production allowance system" in November 1950. Furthermore, the company abolished its age-related payment system in June 1951. However, Toyota had already introduced its "production allowance" in July 1948 when the company revived the efficiency pay system after the war. How was this existing "production allowance" different from the newly introduced method?

Toyota's efficiency pay system was introduced in 1948 with the aim to achieve productivity gains at each shop or plant. However, it did not stimulate productivity gains at the administrative level or in departments not directly related to production areas. After the disputes, the labor union objected to the existing production allowance because the group efficiency of the Manufacturing Department determined the salary for all employees. As most employees still wanted to receive a living wage, the union held negotiations to raise wages based on employees' work experience, as well as summer bonuses. After protracted negotiation, Toyota came into a dispute again. This labor dispute lasted 55 days until it concluded on August 5, 1953.

Thus, despite workers' resistance, Toyota introduced the production allowance system. This was also the culmination of the "management rationalization movement" that was pursued at Toyota after the war. Therefore, the company never made any concessions to establish a wage system based on "monthly production efficiency." Toyota's 20th anniversary history reads:

> Comparing to foreign cars, domestically produced passenger cars were said to be "poor in performance and high in price." To overcome such bad reputation, we made untiring efforts. Moreover, with the aim of cost reduction, we tried to modernize facilities and improve production efficiency. (Toyota Jidōsha Kōgyō Kabushiki Kaisha 1958, p. 447)

The company faced "the death of management" unless it could catch up with foreign cars in terms of quality and price. Under such a situation, the company had no intention to make concessions, and had no room for compromise.

Under the "historical organization," Toyota adopted a new production allowance system, for which the calculation of man-hours was indispensable. Data on the shop floors was gradually accumulated during and after the war, and under the historical organization, Toyota began to analyze such data systematically. The adoption of the efficiency pay system and the new production allowance system stimulated the operating efficiency. Eventually, Toyota signed the "Joint Declaration of Labor and Management" with its labor union in 1962, in which both parties accepted that the company's prosperity and labor conditions would be enhanced through the improvement of productivity (Yamamoto and Tanaka 1982, pp. 53–54). With this joint declaration, Toyota put an end to the great turmoil of workplace relations that followed the war.

4.4.3 Outline of the Production Allowance System at Toyota

The efficiency pay system introduced by Toyota in October 1950 covered all employees: "Non-applicable persons were both senior management officials above the level of division chief and apprentices employed less than six months" (Makino 1966, p. 163). However, this does not necessarily treat all employees equally. The company divided all employees into four categories as shown in Table 4.2 and decided the production allowance payment rate for each category. These categories were maintained at Toyota until at least the early 1980s.

Under the efficiency pay system, employees were paid based on the production allowance rate. This rate was the same as the payment system introduced in 1948 but the method of calculating the rate was different. The rate was different for each department as shown in Table 4.3, based on the four indicators of efficiency coefficient,

Table 4.2 Classification of calculating the production allowance pay rates

Classification	Description of duties
Department A (direct)	Belongs to a manufacturing plant and engages in work where the working time is monitored (e.g, line work department)
Department B (auxiliary)	Belongs to a manufacturing plant and is mainly engaged in specific work and indirect work (e.g., manufacturing, repairing, and transporting of molds, jigs, and tools).
Department C (indirect)	Belongs to a manufacturing plant and is engaged in indirect or specific work. The nature of the work is similar to Department B, but considering the degree of contribution to direct production and the degree of relevance, it is distinguished from Department B (e.g., workers related to power and machinery)
Department D (administrative)	Engaged in administrative, technical, or special duties

Source Makino (1966, pp. 164–165)

Table 4.3 Calculation formula for production allowance payment rate by department

Department	Calculation formula for production allowance payment rate
Department A (direct)	(Efficiency coefficient × 2/3 + Complete coefficient × 1/3) × Production allowance basic coefficient
Department B (auxiliary)	(Efficiency coefficient × 2/3 + Complete coefficient × 1/3) × Production allowance basic coefficient
Department C (indirect)	(Efficiency coefficient × 1/2 + Complete coefficient × 1/2) × Quota coefficient of Department C × Production allowance basic coefficient
Department D (administrative)	(Efficiency coefficient× 1/3 + Complete coefficient × 3/2) × Quota coefficient of Department D × Production allowance basic coefficient

Source Makino (1966, p. 171)

completion coefficient, the capacity coefficient, and the production allowance basic coefficient. In effect, the ratio of these indicators was different for each department (see Table 4.3).

First, we consider how Toyota determined the first three of these indicators. The remaining factor (production allowance basic coefficient) is considered in the next section (see Sect. 4.4.4).

(a) Efficiency coefficient

The efficiency coefficient was defined as follows:

$$\text{Efficiency coefficient} = \frac{\text{Total production time}}{\text{Total working time}} \tag{4.9}$$

The total production time formula 4.9 equals the sum of the number of vehicles that passed inspections multiplied by the standard time per vehicle, and the waiting time for work. The total working time is the actual working time, including the time that employees left the workplace due to waiting time or official use, and the time that employees could not work due to breakdown of equipment or other situations, despite their willingness to work, as defined in the following formula:

$$\begin{aligned}\text{Total production time} = {} & \text{Standard time} \times \text{Number of vehicles passed inspection} \\ & + \text{Working time for quasiregular production} \\ & + \text{Specific working time} + \text{Waiting time}\end{aligned} \tag{4.10}$$

The efficiency coefficient was not purely determined by the number of produced vehicles per certain time, but also considered time lost to equipment breakdowns, and other problems. "The figure of the efficiency coefficient is automatically adjusted for compensating to employees" (Makino 1966, p. 167).

(b) Completion coefficient

The completion coefficient was defined as follows:

$$\begin{aligned}&\text{Completion coefficient} = 1.25 \\ &\times \frac{\text{Number of vehicles produced for the month in the whole company (converted to time)}}{\text{Total working hours of the month in the whole company}}\end{aligned} \tag{4.11}$$

In formula 4.11, the constant of 1.25 is obtained by dividing the actual working hours by the production volume (converted to time) in the spring of 1949. The "number of vehicles produced for the month" in this formula was also converted into time using the "standard time" of Toyota, which was the ideal time required to manufacture a product obtained by time studies. At Toyota, the method of converting production volume into time, known as "the conversion time of products," was calculated by the following formula:

$$\begin{aligned}&\text{Conversion time of product}\\&= \Sigma(\text{Standard time per vehicle by car type}\\&\times \text{Number of vehicles by car type lined off in the current month})\\&+ \text{Time conversion of service parts}\end{aligned} \tag{4.12}$$

In formula 4.12, the "conversion time of service parts" was obtained as follows: first, the total volume of service parts would be converted to the number of large and small trucks based on prices; second, the conversion time was obtained by multiplying that number of large and small trucks by the standard time of one large and small truck.

(c) Quota coefficient

The quota coefficient was defined as follows:

$$\text{Quota coefficient} = \sqrt{\frac{\text{7hours} \times \text{Prescribed working days for current month} \times \text{Quota}}{\text{Total actual working hours at administrative department or indirect department for current month}}} \tag{4.13}$$

Essentially, if the same amount of work was performed in less working time, the quota coefficient would increase. Therefore, Toyota's 20th anniversary history notes that the quota coefficient was introduced to "stimulate the efficiency at the administrative and the indirect departments" (Toyota Jidōsha Kōgyō Kabushiki Kaisha 1958, p. 358).

4.4.4 *Did the Production Allowance System Function?*

Both the efficiency coefficient and the completion coefficient affected the calculation of the production allowance pay rate. The calculation of both coefficients was mainly done based on "standard time." That is, setting the data to standard time affected both coefficients, and, in turn, greatly affected the production allowance payment rate. Toyota spent significant effort to acquire information of working processes on the shop floors, collecting information on man-hours for individual operations, and then calculating the standard time. If Toyota were to operate this production allowance system literally, the company would have to revise the standard time every month or more often, and accordingly revise the efficiency and completion coefficients. Based on these revisions, "the production allowance pay rate is to be calculated according to monthly production efficiency (Article 10 Sect. 4.2 of Toyota's wage regulation)" (Yamamoto and Tanaka 1982, p. 48). However, the policy toward the calculation of the standard time was explained by Mr. Makino, who was a personnel division manager at Toyota:

> The company follows a method that does not affect the efficiency payment even if the standard time is revised. In other words, it is assumed that the standard time would be revised every (accounting) term [for six months], but the production efficiency [which determines the amount of wages in the efficiency payment system] would not be devaluated by this revision. This means that the efficiency of the company would be constant for a long time. In other words, this efficiency encompassed both an increase in productivity due to efforts of employees and an increase in efficiency resulting from rationalization through improvement of facilities since 1950 when the production allowance pay system began.
>
> The efficiency pay system, in a true sense, should reward workers' efficiency improvement with wages. However, in practice, it is almost impossible to distinguish the efficiency improvement by workers from the ones by company's efforts. One way to solve this problem is to reasonably modify the coefficients based on the efficiency improvement of the whole company, and to increase the workers' wages based on the modified coefficients. (Makino 1966, p. 168)

This is a strange explanation because Toyota's terms of payment for production allowance stipulates: "the production allowance will be paid based on monthly production efficiency" (Makino 1966, p. 181). Despite this provision and even though the production efficiency measurement was specified in detail, even if Toyota revised the standard time, the company did not reflect its revision in the efficiency pay (i.e., production allowance). Then, was there any meaning to measuring and setting the standard time, or to measuring the production efficiency in the first place?

In addition, the "Production Allowance Basic Factor" is listed in the calculation formula for the production allowance pay rate (see Table 4.3). On this factor, Makino explained as follows:

> The production allowance basic factor is a coefficient that modifies the production allowance payment rate to an appropriate level, preventing the wage system of the company from losing its balance, because the changes in each coefficient would cause the rise in the production allowance pay rate, and eventually in the production allowance payment. Although the production allowance basic factor went through minor changes at each pay revision, the present number has been maintained as 0.369 since January 1954. (Makino 1966, p. 171)

This is also an odd explanation. Despite having decided the efficiency and the completion coefficients based on the standard time, "a coefficient that modifies the production allowance pay rate to an appropriate level," (i.e., the production allowance basic factor) has been newly introduced. If so, there would be no need to bother calculating the coefficients. In addition, why has this basic factor been fixed from 1954 onwards? Is it not to "lose the balance of the wage system" after 1954?

Furthermore, looking at changes in the production allowance pay rate, we find this situation strange (see Fig. 4.2, which shows biennial data). This rate had risen until 1953, then plummeted in 1955, was followed by a sharp rise, and then followed by a moderate rise. Why did these changes occur? To understand this, it is necessary to consider how the production allowance system actually operated.

In the production allowance pay system, "when equipment improvement or operating improvement is done, the standard time should be constantly revised based on the degree of the improvement" (Makino 1966, p. 174). Once the standard time is revised, the production allowance pay rate should also be changed accordingly, after

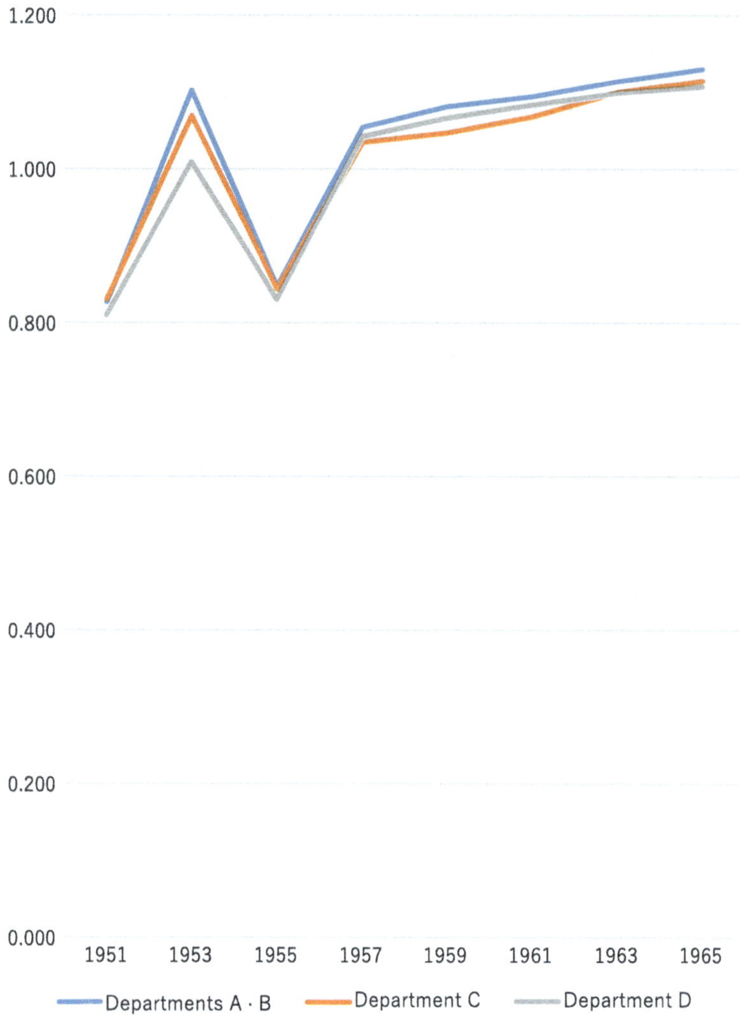

Fig. 4.2 Fluctuation in the production allowance payment rate at Toyota (1951–1965). *Source* Makino (1966, p. 171)

which the production allowance payment should be adjusted along with the revision of the production allowance pay rate. This is the whole idea of the production allowance pay system. However, Toyota "did not make these revisions after 1950. [...] The confusion of standard time became worse, as its revision had not been properly done" (Makino 1966, p. 174). It was in 1955 that the standard time was substantially revised (see Fig. 4.2; Makino 1966, p. 174).

Until 1955, Toyota did not pay wages to employees according to the production allowance (productivity bonuses) rate, although Toyota introduced the method after the labor disputes in 1950. Thus, Toyota's production allowance pay system did not function in accordance with its production allowance rate system.

4.5 Why Did Toyota Leave the Production Allowance Rate System in a Dysfunctional Setting?

Why did Toyota leave the production allowance rate system in a dysfunctional setting? This immediately reminds us about the relationship with the labor union. As the cost of living rose further after 1950, Toyota paid the increased amount of living cost as a supplemental payment until the labor disputes in 1953. Because the union remained wedded to the principle of subsistence pay, Toyota might have avoided the implementation of the production allowance pay system in December 1953. In fact, Toyota and the union decided to include the supplement payment into base salary (Toyota Jidōsha Kōgyō Kabushiki Kaisha 1958, p. 689). Consequently, Toyota officially introduced the annual regular raises in wages for the first time after World War II. In other words, "the increase in wages at Toyota was supported by the rise in base salary and in production allowance" after 1954 (Yamamoto and Tanaka 1982, p. 174). Furthermore, without changing the standard time, Toyota "paid back the results of improvement in both equipment and operation to the employees as allowance" after 1951 (Makino 1966, p. 174). This left the production allowance system in a dysfunctional setting and induced the sharp rise in production allowance rate from 1951 to 1953 (see Fig. 4.2).

Frequent changes in the standard time would be necessary for true implementation of the production allowance rate system. Frequent changes in the standard time would require personnel trained and knowledgeable in time studies. In the case of changing the standard time for work processes at the Koromo Plant, Toyota would require many people for time studies. However, "the [instability of] labor relations often prevented training workers in time studies in many Japanese companies" after the war (Ono 1957, p. 80). In fact, Toyota set the standard time in 1947, before the company implemented the production allowance pay system, based on the average data of actual working time for the previous six months (Toyota Jidōsha Kōgyō Kabushiki Kaisha 1958, p. 494). Then, Toyota did not change the standard time until 1955 (Toyota Jidōsha Kōgyō Kabushiki Kaisha 1958, p. 494).

As late as in 1955, Toyota began to train workers in full-time camps for a month in motion studies, time studies, standard time setting, and so on (Yokose 1964, p. 109). However, if the company were to implement the production allowance pay system in a true sense, Toyota would require many workers with extensive familiarity with the standard time setting and so on. This being the case, why did Toyota not train workers much earlier?

The standard time for making parts was conventionally assessed at each shop. The production allowance significantly raised the proportion of monthly income: 33.3% in 1951, 38.6% in 1954, and 42.7% in 1957 (Makino 1966, p. 162). As the standard time was an important element in determining the production allowance, the revision of the standard time increasingly influenced workers' income. Even if production equipment at one shop was renewed or modernized more than at another shop, the revision of the standard time at just one shop might prompt complaints about the inequality of income among the whole plant. Thus, the manager in charge of revising the standard time became hesitant to revise it even if production equipment was changed (Toyota Jidōsha Kōgyō Kabushiki Kaisha 1958, p. 494). As a result, "the standard time divorced from reality on the shop floors" (Tsukiyama 1959, p. 3). In the end, Toyota "paid back the results of improvement in both equipment and operation to the employees as allowance" without changing the standard time (Makino 1966, p. 174).

As Toyota began to collect data on each production process, its shop floors began to change to some extent. In fact, Toyota managed to prevent workers from manufacturing particular items at their discretion. Yet, Toyota could not immediately perceive productivity growth on shop floors to any accurate extent in the early 1950s. At this point, realization of the purpose of the production allowance pay system was in danger of remaining unfulfilled as a pie-in-the-sky vision.

Nevertheless, in the late 1950 s Toyota greatly changed the operation of the production allowance pay system. Furthermore, the company began to implement frequent changes to its standard times. Based on data for work processes, Toyota began operating the whole plant towards realizing smooth production flow. The next chapter explores how these changes were brought about at Toyota.

References

Gijutsu no Tomo (Friends of Technology). (1954). 'Kikai kōjō no konjaku wo kataru' (Talking about the machining plants' past) Gijutsu no Tomo (Friends of Technology), no.14. Toyota: Toyota Jidōsha Kogyō Kabushiki Kaisha (Toyo-ta Motor Co., Ltd).

Kishimoto, E. (1959). *Nihon sangyō to ōtoēshon* (The Japanese industry and automation). Tokyo: Tōyō Keizai Shinpōsha.

Makino, A. (1966). 'Toyota jidōsha no seisan teate seido' (The production allowance system at Toyota Motor Co., Ltd). In Rōdō Hōrei Kyōkai (The association of laws and regulations in Japan). *Gyōsekikyū seido no jissai* (The practices of merit pay plans). Tokyo: Rōdōb Hōrei Kyōkai.

Murai, I. (1951). *Kigyō gōrika no tame no seisan gijutsu* (Production technology for rationalization of business). Tōkyō: Koronasha.

Nakaoka, T. (1981). 'Senchū-sengo no kagaku teki kannri undō: Ni-hon nōritsu kyōkai to Nikka giren no katsudō ni sotte (2)' (Scientific management movement during and after the war: On the basis of activities by JMA and the union of Japanese scientists and engineers) (2). *Keizaigaku Zasshi [Osaka shiritu daigaku]* (Economics Magazine of Osaka City University) vol. 2, no. 3.

Okano, T. (1954). 'Sessaku kōgu no shūchū kenma ni tsuite' (On the central regrinding system of cutting tools). *Gijutsu no Tomo* (Friends of Technology), no. 5. Toyota: Toyota Jidōsha Kogyō Kabushiki Kaisha (Toyota Motor Co., Ltd).

Okano, T. (1977). 'Kikai kakō gijutsu no shinpo' (Advances in Machining Technology). In Toyota Gijutsu Kai (Society of Engineers at Toyota) ed. *Asu ni mukatte: Toyota Gijutus Kai sōritsu 30 shūnen kinen gō* (Towards Tomorrow: Special Issue for 30 Years Anniversary of the Society of Engineers at Toyota). Toyota-shi: Toyota Gijutsu Kai.

Ohno, T. (1978). *Toyota Seisan Hōshiki: Datsu Kibo no Keiei wo Mezashite* (Toyota Production System: Beyond Large-Scale Production). Tokyo: Daiyamondosha.

Ohno, Taiichi. (1988). *Toyota production system: Beyond large-scale production*. Cambridge, Mass: Productivity Press.

Ono, T. (1957). 'Saikin no jikan kenkyū' (Recent time studies). *Nihon Kikai Gakkaishi* (Mechanical Engineering Journal), *60*(461). Tokyo: Nihon Kikai Gakkai (The Japan Society of Mechanical Engineers).

Sangyō Gōrika Shingikai (Industrial Rationalization Deliberation Bureau) and Tsūshō Sangyōshō Kigyōkyoku (Business Bureau under the Ministry of International Trade and Industry). (1952). *Wagakuni sangyō no gōrika ni tsuite* (On rationalization of Japanese industry). Tokyo: Tsūshō Sangyōshō Kigyōkyoku.

Shōwa, D. (1958). *Setsubi kindaika to sono keizai kōka: Jittai chōsa hōkokusho* (Modernization in facility and its economic effect: Report of the field survey). Tokyo: Shōwa Dōjinkai.

Toyoda, K. (1946a). *Jidōsha kōgyō no genjō to Toyota Jidōsha no shinro* (The Current Condition of the Automobile Industry and the Direction of Toyota Motor Co. Ltd). Aichi-ken: Toyota Jidōsha Kōgyō Kabushiki Kaisha (Toyota Motor Co., Ltd), Reprinted in Wada (1999).

Toyoda, K. (1946b). 'Kongo no gijutsusha no tachiba' (Situation of engieers in the futrure) [A lecture to a private gathering of company engineers]. Reprinted in Wada (1999).

Toyoda, K. (1949). 'Jiyū keizai-ka no idōsha gijutu' (Automobile Technology in a Free Economy). In *Jidōsha Gijutsu* (Automobile Technology), *3*(3). Reprinted in Wada (1999).

Toyota Jidōsha Kōgyō Kabushiki Kaisha (Toyota Motor Co., Ltd). (1958). *Toyota Jidōsha 20-nenshi* (The 20th Anniversary History of Toyota Motor Co). Koromo-shi: Toyota Jidōsha Kogyō Kabushiki Kaisha (Toyota Motor Co., Ltd).

Toyota Jidōsha Kōgyō Kabushiki Kaisha (Toyota Motor Co., Ltd). (1967). *Toyota Jidōsha 30-nenshi* (The 30th Anniversary History of Toyota Motor Co). Toyota-shi: Toyota Jidōsha Kogyō Kabushiki Kaisha (Toyota Motor Co., Ltd).

Tsukiyama, Y. (1959). 'Kijun jikan no kanri' (Managing the standard time). In *Toyota Manejiment* (Toyota Management). Toyota-shi: Toyota Jidōsha Kogyō Kabushiki Kaisha (Toyota Motor Co., Ltd).

Wada, Kazuo comp. (1999). *Toyoda Kiichiro Monjo Shūsei* (Corpus of Kiichiro Toyoda's Documents). Nagoya: Nagoya Daigaku Shuppankai (Nagoya University Press).

Wada, Kazuo, & Yui, Tsunehiko. (2002). *Courage and Change: The Life of Kiichiro Toyoda*. Toyota City: Toyota Motor Corp.

Yamamoto, K., & Tanaka, H. (1982). 'Nihon teki koyōkankō wo kizuita hitobito (2) moto Toyota Kōgyō senmu torishimariyaku Yamamoto Keimei shi ni kiku (1)' ('People Laid the Japanese Employment Practices (2) Listen to Mr. Keimei Yamamoto, Toyota Motor Co's Ex-Senior Managing Director'). Tokyo: Nihon Rōdō Kyokai zassi (The Monthly Journal of the Japan Institute of Labour).

Yokose, T. (1964). 'Toyota jidōsha kōgyō no kanri kantokusha kyōiku' (Training supervisors at Toyota Motor Company). In Rōdō Hōrei Kyōkai (The association of laws and regulations in Japan). *Kanri kantokusha kunren no jissai* (The practices of training supervisors). Tokyo: Rōdōb Hōrei Kyōkai.

Chapter 5
Findings of Two Toyota Executives

5.1 Why Did Two Toyota Executives Go to the USA?

Eiji Toyoda, Director of Toyota, embarked on an inspection of the automobile industry in the USA on July 11, 1950, about a month after Toyota settled the labor disputes on June 10, 1950. Regarding the reasons behind the trip, Eiji Toyoda stated:

> The purpose of my visit to the US was to gauge the future prospects of the auto industry and to explore the possibility of arranging for technical cooperation of some sort from the US manufacturers. Having decided that it would be in our best interest to establish ties with American automakers, we sent a proposal to Ford, with whom we had previously entered into negotiations (Toyoda 1987, p. 106).

He returned home on October 20, 1950 (Toyota Jidōsha Kōgyō Kabushiki Kaisha 1967, p. 834). Toyota's 30th anniversary history stated that Eiji Toyoda "stayed at Ford's River Rouge Plant in Detroit for a long time and took a close look at its production and manufacturing technology" (Toyota Jidōsha Kōgyō Kabushiki Kaisha 1967, p. 327). Furthermore, the anniversary history quoted Eiji Toyoda's text from the October 1950 issue of magazine *Ryusen-kei* (*Streamline Shape*) as follows:

> This [River Rouge Plant] is the largest factory of Ford. I am surprised by the huge amount of equipment, its organization and everything else. First of all, the building area is 15 million square feet, nearly ten times as large as Toyota's Koromo Plant. Within the area, there are self-sufficient integrated facilities for producing automobiles such as blast furnaces, glass plants, docks, machining plants, assembly plants, and cupolas. There are 70,000 employees at Ford. As they recently started working in two or three shifts due to the Korean War, Ford quickened its production pace to 7,000 units per day. About 10% of the total production, 700 units, are assembled as finished vehicles in River Rouge Plant. The remaining 90% are sent to assembly plants located in various parts of the US as Ford's assembly parts.
>
> So how do they implement the mass-production of automobiles? As mentioned earlier, the Rouge Plant is the largest among the Ford's plants, but the largeness of plants does not ensure perfection in automobile production. From our point of view, it still seems to have some room for improvement as an organization of production. But, the most interesting thing is material

K. Wada, *The Evolution of the Toyota Production System*,
Studies in Economic History,
https://doi.org/10.1007/978-981-15-4928-1_5

> handling. Ford uses, particularly, advanced conveyors for material handling, and the 120 miles-long conveyors are extended throughout the plant. In other words, all the various raw materials and parts for automobile production are connected by conveyor lines, and they are gradually completed and undoubtedly absorbed and coupled to the last one assembly line (Toyota Jidōsha Kōgyō Kabushiki Kaisha 1967, p. 327).

During his stay in the USA, Eiji Toyoda was promoted to a managing director of Toyota at an extraordinary meeting of shareholders on July 18, 1950. In addition, Shōichi Saitō was also promoted to the position of managing director of Toyota at the same meeting. Saitō accompanied Eiji Toyoda to the USA for the industry survey and, upon his return, published the book titled *Jidōsha no kuni Amerika* (The Country of Automobiles, America).

Shōtarō Kamiya, who later became the chairman of Toyota Sales Company, had visited the USA prior to Toyoda and Saitō. The aim of Kamiya's visit was "to open up talks and arrange for simple technical guidance" with Ford; however, he added, "on the eve of my [Eiji Toyoda's] departure, the Korean War broke out" (Toyoda 1987, p. 106). Ford was supposed to send some engineers to Toyota as part of the planned agreement, but "the US government issued an injunction forbidding valuable technical personnel from leaving the country" (Toyoda 1987, p. 106). Consequently, the Ford engineers did not visit Toyota. However, as recalled by Eiji Toyoda, "Ford agreed to receive trainees from Toyota," (Toyoda 1987, p. 106). As a result, Eiji Toyoda and Shōichi Saitō visited the Ford facilities as trainees from Toyota.

5.2 Discovery of Mixed Production: Introducing Good Equipment at Toyota

5.2.1 Discovery of Mixed Production in the USA

Eiji Toyoda and Shōichi Saitō were interviewed by a Japanese trade journal, titled *Jidōsha Gijutsu* (Automobile Technology), in 1951 after their return to Japan. When the interviewer asked about the assembling of cars at Ford, Eiji Toyoda replied:

> It is interesting. Actually, a large variety of cars queue to assemble on just one conveyor line. There are cars in diverse colors; the tires come in three sizes; some cars have radios and heaters, but some do not. A wide variety of cars are assembled (Jidōsha Gijutsu 1951, p. 80).

Shōichi Saitō also described a similar practice in his book:

> Each part and assembled part converge at the final assembly plant [of River Rouge Plant] and are stored in constant quantities along the conveyor line. With the moving of the conveyor, parts and assembled parts are assembled. Cars of various colors and styles are lined-off (assembled). One car is assembled every 50 to 55 seconds (Saitō 1952, p. 77).

Both directors focused on the fact that Ford assembled cars of various colors and styles on one line—a practice they referred to as "mixed production."

Mixed production was also noticed by other Japanese representatives sent on productivity missions to foreign countries, particularly to the USA, and some of them noted and wrote about mixed production in their reports. For example, representatives of the electrical industries left Japan in October 1955 on a productivity mission and took a two-day tour of Ford's assembly plant in Chicago over November 16 and 17, 1955. Their report noted:

> Ford produces trucks and three different types of passenger cars at this assembly plant. Cars of different colors are assembled at this plant. Each type and color of car are assembled one after another in one assembly line at this plant.
>
> In this way, as each model and each color car is produced at a rate of 64 cars per hour, the production process is planned every second (Nihon Seisansei Honbu 1956, pp. 138–139).

Representatives on a third productivity mission focused on material handling management, and visited Ford's assembly plant at San Jose in 1961. They reported:

> The most interesting thing at this plant is the fact that five different types of cars and 16 different colors of car body are assembled one after another in no particular order on one final assembly line.
>
> […] The situation wherein painted items, such as wheels and body parts, seats, and other items are supplied with precision, at a pitch of about one minute, is absolutely spectacular (Nihon Seisansei Honbu 1962, p. 161).

Thus, the practice of mixed production astounded many Japanese industry representatives, including Toyota's directors, who visited Ford plants in the 1950s and early 1960s. Eiji Toyoda and Shōichi Saitō were also interested to see how changes were made and how and the overall mixed flow production was controlled on the assembly line. Indeed, the interviewer at *Jidōsha Gijutsu* was also intrigued by this matter and asked both directors how Ford controlled the mixed production. On this, Eiji Toyoda responded as follows:

> This worked well with the [production] order. The [production control] center gave instructions. [When giving instructions from the center], when the men at the center wrote down letters, characters came out at each station. [After this, the interviewer suggested that might be fax machines, but Toyoda did not comment, and continued as follows.]
>
> If you wrote letters on a metal plate by hand, these characters would come out. I would like to use this instrument over teletypes. With this [instrument], the control center gave instructions about aspects such as gear ratio and fender, and the work was done as per these instructions. After receiving instructions, the operator discarded the hand-written sheet of instructions. Dodge [automobile company's] plant used teletypes for this purpose. However, this indeed is a good mechanism indeed (Jidōsha Gijutsu 1951, p. 80).

What was the instrument that captured Eiji Toyoda's attention? After interpreting his remarks, it becomes apparent that the device was not a fax machine or a teletype, but rather a telautograph. A description of the telautograph from an English dictionary states:

> ... used for a facsimile telegraph for reproducing graph matter by means of transmitter in which motions of a pencil are communicated by levers to two rotary shafts that produce variations in current in two separate circuits, and by means of a receiver in which these variations are utilized by electromagnetic devices and levers to move a pen as the pencil moves (Gove 1976, p. 2349).

This product was advertised in *Automotive Industries* on March 15, 1954. The advertisement read: "Ford coordinates assembling at huge Edgewater plant ... with TelAutograph" (Automotive Industries 1954, p. 519). In addition to this, other literature describes the use of a telautograph for controlling assembly lines as early as 1937 (Scoville 1937, p. 368). Although Eiji Toyoda described the telautograph as being "a good mechanism" for carrying out mixed production, Toyota did not immediately introduce it, and did it finally when the Motomachi Plant started production in August 1959. Toyota's company history notes this as follows:

> For improving the achievement rate of the production plan while maintaining the inventory quantity to the minimum, our company [Toyota] tried to synchronize both all the plants and the main lines at each plant with the vehicle assembly plant at its center, first using machines such as interphones, Interwriter, and TelAutograph etc., according to the instructions of the production control room [emphasis supplied] (Toyota 1967, p. 425).

The telautograph device was certainly useful for giving detailed instructions from a central control room to hubs on a large assembly line. Despite the apparent benefits of the device, Toyota did not introduce it following the return of the two directors to Japan. Even if the organization had found the device to be useful for production control, it may not have divulged details about its usefulness in the interview published in *Jidōsha Gijutsu*. Unlike others in the trade, Toyota had a rare opportunity to get an inside view of the Ford plant in the early 1950s. As shrewd businesspeople do not disclose critical information pertaining to their businesses, Eiji Toyoda's remarks regarding the device should be interpreted with care.

Apart from the telautograph, what other technologies or processes used in the US plants were considered transferrable to Toyota operations? Regarding mixed production at Ford's Chicago plant, the report said, "the production process [of mixed production] is planned every second" (Nihon Seisansei Honbu 1956, pp. 138–139) with the following explanation:

> Specifically, the production process [of mixed production] is controlled through the teletype instructions issued by the control room, which is located at the center of the assembly line, to the workplace. These instructions are based on the orders received from car dealers, which are punched IBM cards (Nihon Seisansei Honbu 1956, p. 139).

The productivity mission report described IBM cards as the foundation of production process planning (Nihon Seisansei Honbu 1956, p. 139). Furthermore, the report added more information about IBM cards, in response to the intent of electrical industry personnel to know more about them.

Toyota's official history writes about this as follows:

> When Eiji Toyoda and Shōichi Saitō, both directors coming with engineering backgrounds, inspected the automobile industry in the United States, they realized that mechanization was remarkably progressing even in the field of clerical work. Specifically, they recognized that

> by extensively using excellent statistical and accounting machines, the paperwork can be processed quickly and accurately.
>
> Immediately after both executives returned to Japan, they directed the management research office to inquire about the introduction of statistical accounting machines such as those of IBM and Remington Rand at Toyota. In July 1954, we contracted two sets of IBM machines including two new accounting machines that were rarely used at that time in Japan (Toyota Jidōsha Kōgyō Kabushiki Kaisha 1958, p. 348).

In fact, Toyota decided to introduce IBM machines soon after the two directors returned to Japan. According to the above quotation, however, Toyota introduced the machines for paperwork rather than for production control. Nevertheless, the management research office, which was the core of Toyota's rationalization movement after the war, was not merely responsible for clerical paperwork.

When a few IBM accounting machines arrived at Toyota in December 1953, "the company decided to deal with paperwork on stock transactions. Subsequently, it started researching how to handle the complicated machines and prepared for the mechanization of clerical works" (Toyota Jidōsha Kōgyō Kabushiki Kaisha 1958, p. 348). However, did two directors with engineering backgrounds decide to introduce the machines just for handling the paperwork on stocks? If the IBM machine was primarily used to handle paperwork on stocks, then the company would have terminated the use of IBM machines after outsourcing company operations on stocks in August 1956 (Toyota Jidōsha Kōgyō Kabushiki Kaisha 1958, pp. 798, 806). However, the company continued to use the machines.

Next, we examine why Toyota actually used the IBM machines.

5.2.2 *Why Did Toyota Use IBM Machines?*

Besides the paperwork on stocks, the company history documented another use of the machine as follows:

> In June 1954, one of two new accounting machines that had already arrived was installed and mechanization through the use of IBM machines started in full swing. […] In the same year, the company succeeded in mechanizing, one after another, the following items: cost accounting of materials and parts, calculation of fixed assets, personnel statistics, calculation of wage increases and bonus payments, and *calculation of working times* […] (emphasis added; Toyota Jidōsha Kōgyō Kabushiki Kaisha 1958, p. 442).

The above quotation reveals that Toyota used the IBM machines to calculate work hours. In 1955, Toyota began to calculate standard times for parts as well as for vehicles (Toyota Jidōsha Kōgyō Kabushiki Kaisha 1958, p. 442). The daily labor report on the turnaround time of processes was punched on the card each day, and, at the end of each month, the company processed the cards through the machine and calculated the total working time and real man-hours for each work process, among others. Thus, the data on working hours for vehicles and parts were calculated on a monthly basis (Toyota Jidōsha Kōgyō Kabushiki Kaisha 1958, p. 803). Consequently, in 1955, "the standard times for manufacturing parts and vehicles were calculated" (Toyota Jidōsha Kōgyō Kabushiki Kaisha 1958, p. 442). In 1958, the company calculated the load of every machine (Toyota Jidōsha Kōgyō Kabushiki Kaisha 1958, p. 799). In this way, Toyota used the IBM machines for production control.

Before the two executives went to the USA, Toyota faced issues regarding the management of the production allowance system. To operate this system smoothly, it was necessary to calculate the standard times for parts, among others, and to promptly revise the times (see Chap. 4). In this sense, the introduction of the IBM machines contributed toward solving the company's management problem. The setting and revision of standard times was essential for the operation of the production allowance system. The setting of the standard times gave an opportunity to set standard prices. A book titled *Cost Accounting: Cost Accounting as Management Accounting*, which was preferred for learning standard cost accounting in Japan around the 1950s, reads: "It was G. Charter Harrison who built standard cost accounting, which was just after the European war" (Yamabe 1961, p. 272). Harrison's book not only illustrated a number of diagrams showing the flow of administrative procedures, but it also illustrated the use of punched cards (e.g., see Harrison 1921, Fig. 1). Furthermore, Harrison emphasized the benefits of using punched cards in his books as follows:

> The outstanding advantage of the punched card method of compiling information is its extreme flexibility, whereas in the case of the compilation of written data, any rearrangement of the information requires an entirely new written tabulation; by the use of punched cards, any desired combination of information can be obtained merely by resorting and retabulating the cards (Harrison 1921, p. 103).

If anyone were interested in standard cost accounting, then it would not have been inconceivable to think of using the punched card system in Japan in the 1950s. Unlike Japan, the use of the punched card system was popular in factories and offices in the USA.

With their engineering backgrounds, it is not surprising that Eiji Toyoda and Shōichi Saitō showed particular interest in the punched card system. Eiji Toyoda was aware of the work of Joseph Geschelin through his frequent publications in the American journal *Automotive Industries*. However, it is likely that the third edition of *Work Routing, Scheduling and Dispatching in Production* (Younger and Geschelin 1947) was of particular interest to Eiji Toyoda because it specifically described production control using the punched card system. While earlier editions of this book (Younger 1930) did not cover the use of punched card systems, the third edition gave an example of Dodge's truck manufacturing department under Chrysler's affiliation and explained about production control using punched cards:

> Consider the practice in scheduling Dodge truck production. This is done by cooperative action of the sales and production departments, the sales department being responsible for advance planning which enables the manufacturing department to adjust tentative production

schedules some months in advance. Such advance planning enables the purchasing department to schedule the flow of parts and raw materials from outside vendors. Assembly lines are scheduled eight days in advance, tentatively, and are given firm schedules daily.

Owing to the lead time required for body production, bodies are scheduled three days in advance of the assembly line.

Scheduling is done by teletype from a central office called a broadcasting department. The system starts with punched cards […] issued from the sales department, giving the detailed specifications for each individual vehicle. The card shows chassis model, wheelbase, color, tire size, axle type and ratio, and, in addition, special items such as auxiliary springs, governor, oil filter, brake booster, shock absorbers, bumpers, and other parts (Younger and Geschelin 1947, p. 133).

Although Eiji Toyoda was aware of Geschelin's work, as evident from his reference to the Geschelin's work in the *Automotive Industries* magazine, Eiji Toyoda did not specifically mention the punched card system (Toyoda 1940, p. 682; Geschelin 1940).

Before Eiji Toyoda and Shōichi Saitō left Japan to visit the USA, Toyota was unable to achieve smooth operation of the production allowance system. During Toyota's rationalization movement, the company had created a mechanism to acquire detailed data on work times on the shop floors. Toyota intended to operate the production allowance system based on the standard time for producing each part, but this data was not effectively utilized in implementation of the production allowance system. As a result, the standard times increasingly deviated from the reality of the shop floors (see Chap. 4.5), and the production allowance system did not efficiently contribute to the bonus system.

Toyota used IBM machines to set the standard times, as noted its official history:

Each element required for controlling the standard time are recorded on the IBM [punched] cards, and their calculation is done by IBM machines. The standard time so far was based on the man-hours measured on the workers' group, but now it is possible to set the machining time per machine unit. In making a production plan, the required man-hours and the load on the machinery and equipment are easily calculated by IBM machines. This is very useful for production control (Toyota Jidōsha Kōgyō Kabushiki Kaisha 1958, pp. 494–495).

In August 1956, Toyota handled the calculation of the monthly man-hours for the manufacturing department by using IBM machines. Furthermore, based on its production plan, Toyota began to calculate the necessary machining time per machine unit and the required man-hours (Toyota Jidōsha Kōgyō Kabushiki Kaisha 1958, pp. 803–804). Toyota then began to use this information to calculate the costs of parts or vehicles in 1956. As a result, Toyota used the IBM machines to calculate the production allowance rate as well as the wages of each worker by the late 1950s (see Fig. 5.1).

Despite this obvious progress, the setting of standard times in machining shops took more time than in other workshops. This was caused by the significant changes in the shops that were implemented after the two directors returned from the USA. The next section considers the changes that were motivated by the visit to the USA and the effects on Toyota's operations.

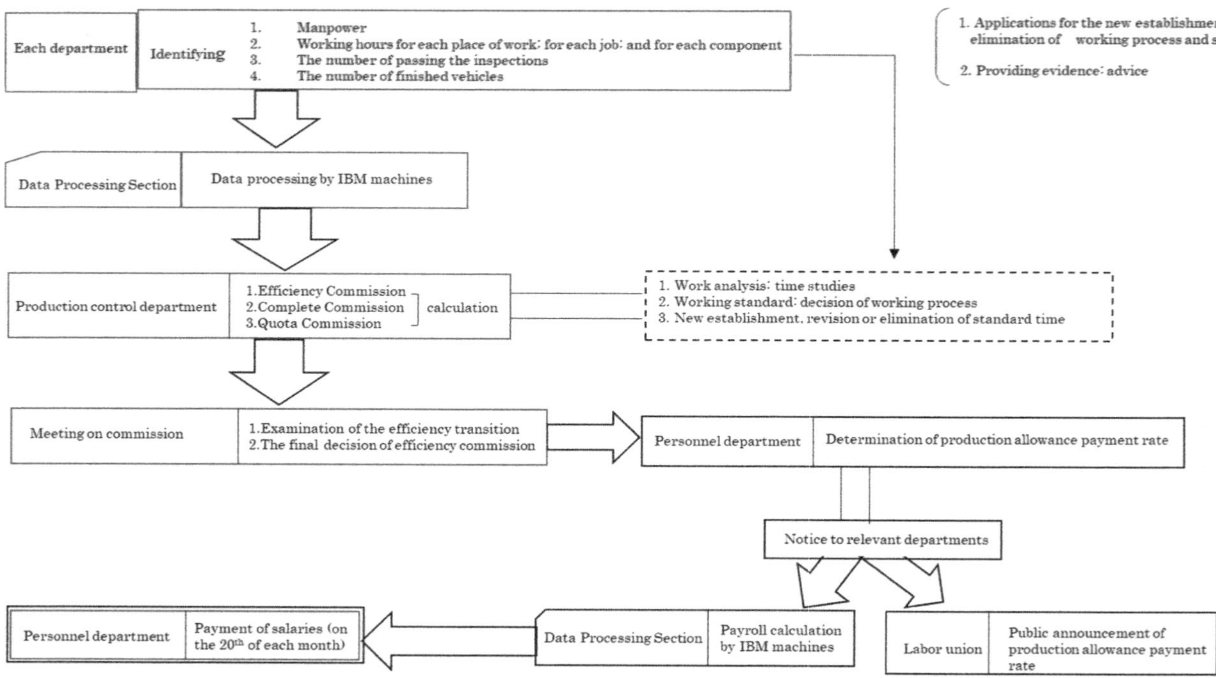

Fig. 5.1 Method for calculating the production allowance rate

5.3 Recognizing the Importance of Materials Handling

5.3.1 Two Directors Recognize the Significance of Materials Handling

During their visit to Ford, in addition to mixed production, Toyota's two directors were also impressed with the material handling practices at the American factories. Saitō emphasized the importance of materials handling in his book as follows:

> It is surprising how improving the material handling methods help to devaluate costs and contribute to an increase in mass production.
>
> The factories in the US, at present, are paying 40% of their wages for materials handling that does not make any contribution to the value of the product. Even some factories are spending over 60% of total wages for materials handling. [...] Ford examined packing methods, transportation, and facilities by investigating, researching, and analyzing costs. In the last few years, Ford has spent millions of dollars and has facilitated modernization. Among cost centers, the most expensive were batch loading and container loading. Successful integration of the forklift truck and the standard steel container with the existing facilities, conveyors, and arrangements in the factory increased the efficiency. [...] Research on materials handling in the US is the basis of the whole factory management. We should not easily avoid this because the labor cost is high in the US, and we also need to deal with safety and sanitation standpoints. In fact, the results of these studies have identified a wasteful three-dimensional flow of work at the River Rouge Plant (Saitō 1952, pp. 88–91).

Japanese businessmen became more interested in materials handling from the mid-1950s. The Japan Productivity Center issued 170 reports based on the field surveys of productivity missions to foreign countries over the 12 years after 1955. However, only three of these reports focused specifically on materials handling. In fact, the first mission on this topic, which was sent in 1956, was tasked with describing how the term of materials handling was defined in the USA. However, the second mission, in 1958, pointed out more specific differences in terms of materials handling between the USA and Japan:

> Looking at the materials handling in the United States, the thing that really struck us was *the good condition of the road surface and working floor* [in the factories]. *This was most terribly different from Japan.*
>
> In order not to hinder the operation of handcarts, the factory's road surface was flattened—there were no obstacles such as door grooves, thresholds, and steps. Furthermore, platforms, cars, and cargo were connected by a crossover board (Emphasis in original; Nihon Seisansei Honbu 1959, p. 31).

After the third productivity mission on materials handling, the Japanese understanding of the topic gradually improved. Of course, the fact that equipment for materials handling was installed at some Japanese factories also contributed to improved awareness. The report from the third mission on materials handling confidently reassured Japanese industrialists:

> Materials handling in the US is not particularly different as an individual method, compared to the method in Japan. Indeed, the capabilities of individual machines are excellent, and the

> amount handled is large in the US. However, there is nothing we never knew about materials handling methods in the US. The difference between the two countries is that the devices are more popular in the US, and they are familiar with their smooth operation (Nihon Seisansei Honbu 1962, p. 60).

However, the third mission also revealed the stark difference between the factories of the two countries:

> In Japan, there are a lot of wooden factory buildings… and in many cases, small buildings will be built one after another in the factory… Except for some new factories, the factory often builds a lot of small buildings on a site without a solid plan. This complicates both the transportation routes and the working processes, and as a result, increases the materials handling cost… This is often pointed out by American specialists on materials handling who came to Japan.
>
> In factories in the United States, except for the case of special factory conditions even in the case of a small wooden factory, most of them are unexceptionally single-story, and still huge buildings (Nihon Seisansei Honbu 1962, p. 60).

From the mid-1950s, the productivity missions prompted the gradual introduction of individual equipment for careful handling of materials.

Toyota sent its employees on the second and third productivity missions on materials handling. Other Japanese automobile assemblers also sent employees to the second and third productivity missions, but no other manufacturer sent their delegates twice. This fact and the recognition of the two directors of the importance of materials handling in 1950 show that Toyota placed much emphasis on materials handling, at least when compared with other car assemblers. So, how did this actually affect Toyota's factory? This point is discussed in the next section.

5.3.2 Extension and Renovation of Koromo Assembly Plant

After Eiji Toyoda and Shōichi Saitō returned to Japan from the USA, materials handling at Toyota changed significantly. As the committee chairman, Saitō decided to formulate a policy on materials handling, and then set about implementing it. Through gradual improvements that were overseen by the committee, Toyota improved its material handling practices. Toyota had installed various types of conveyors in all plants by 1958, whereas only the required number of conveyors had been installed up until the end of the war (see Table 5.1). The most significant change was the introduction of the "unit load system," which standardized pallets and pallet boxes. Furthermore, Toyota implemented widespread use of forklift trucks instead of trucks. When using trucks, work was often interrupted due to loading and unloading, and product damage occurred more frequently as the number of loading–unloading cycles increased (Toyota Jidōsha Kōgyō Kabushiki Kaisha 1958, p. 340). From 1953 onwards, Toyota significantly increased the use of such materials handling equipment (see Table 5.2).

In the late 1950s, Toyota built a new plant not far from the Koromo Plant; it was named the Motomachi Plant and began operation in 1959. At this time, the materials

Table 5.1 Number of conveying equipment pieces at Toyota by end of August 1958

Type of conveying equipment	Number of pieces installed		
	Production department	Non-production department	Total
Hoists	398	232	630
Cranes	83	27	110
Conveyors	154	16	170
Total	635	275	910

Source Toyota Jidōsha Kōgyō Kabushiki Kaisha (1958, p.662)

Table 5.2 Type and capacity of materials handling equipment at Toyota in late 1950s

Type of materials handling equipment	Capacity (tons)	Year		
		1953	1955	1957
Trailers for heavy-duty trucks	4–7	2	2	6
Trailers for heavy-duty trucks	0.75–4	58	65	88
Forklift trucks	0.5–3	18	31	55
Packet lift trucks	1.35–2	2	3	4
Battery-powered forklifts	0.3–1	1	1	5
Trailers	0.5–2.6	–	–	278
Tow trucks		–	–	12
Total		81	102	448

Source Shōwa Dōjinkai (1958, p. 29)

handling equipment was also replaced and renovated in the Koromo Plant. Toyota's in-house newsletter, *Toyota Shimbun*, reported this as follows:

> We renewed our equipment to state of the art based on the rationalization program. Along with this, we renewed the facility of the assembly plant from the beginning of this year [1954]. This work will be complete by next spring and will cover buildings, lighting, various materials handling equipment, contact and communication facilities and tools (Toyota Shimbun 1954, p. 1).

This renovation of the Koromo Plant was carried out to allow the production of new models, the Toyopet Crown and Toyopet Master, which were labeled as '"purely domestic-made cars," despite the fact that other domestic automakers were forming technical ties with foreign automakers (Toyota Motor Corporation 1988, p. 134). In expanding the plant, not only was new materials handling equipment installed, but it was also designed so that it could be easily moved inside the plant. Fluorescent lighting was also installed throughout, following the trends observed in American plants.

After the expansion and renovation, how did the Koromo Plant perform? Notes on its operation in the spring of 1959 (before the Motomachi Plant started operation) were recorded as follows:

> In this plant, five vehicles of the same model and same specification are regarded as one unit, and every unit flowed through the assembly line in accordance with a pre-determined assembly schedule. … All instructions are controlled by the central control room. … Assembly lines are controlled and adjusted precisely and quickly, almost without performing conventional paperwork. This automation is being carried out not only within this plant but also between this plant and the Toyota Auto Body, a body manufacturing company located in Kariya, 18 km away from the plant. Based on Toyota's assembly schedule, the cab and truck for the truck made by Toyota Auto Body are loaded on several long trailer trucks according to the scheduled operation plan, and timely put on Toyota's total assembly line (Kishimoto 1959, p. 87).

Two points mentioned in this quote are noteworthy. First, as Kishimoto observed, Toyota had begun assembling a large number of vehicle types and specifications by changing the vehicle type and specification every "five vehicles of the same model and same specification." Second, the cab and truck for the truck loaded on the trailer truck was operating between the Toyota Auto Body and Toyota, which were 16 km apart. This situation showed that materials handling only inside the Koromo Plant did not entirely address the problem of materials handling. Moreover, Toyota's official history explains the reason why even trailer trucks were operated according to the scheduled plan as follows:

> By setting the operating schedule of the trailer, we can feed the necessary products correctly to the necessary places, when necessary. This will make production management smoother and the dead stock will also decrease (Toyota Jidōsha Kōgyō Kabushiki Kaisha 1958, p. 340).

The third productivity mission on the control of materials handling also pointed out the relationship between materials handling and inventory volume as follows:

> Changes in inventory in the plant always have an impact on work. Too much stock will require extra storage space, the travel distance will be longer, and in many cases the distance from the outside will also increase. If the amount of inventory in hand is insufficient, you will have to function in an irregular way to supply the missing items to the assembly line, and the smooth flow of things will be damaged.
>
> Poor inventory control means an increased transportation expenses, warehouse costs, staircase carriage and management expenses (Nihon Seisansei Honbu 1962, p. 83).

This mission's report not only mentioned that inventory quantity at Ford's San Jose plant was higher than in Japan's plants, but it also stated about another company, "generally, stock seemed to be more than in Japan in order to decrease the manpower" (Nihon Seisansei Honbu 1962, p. 160). Until this time, the productivity missions on the control of materials handling generally considered what the mission had learned in the USA, and often praised the American methods. By the early 1960s, however, the productivity missions provided some criticism of the current state of practices in the USA, especially on inventory reduction.

After the labor disputes ended in 1950, Toyota made significant efforts to reform the Koromo Plant and its operations. Significant gains were made by introducing practices observed in American plants (especially from Ford). In the late 1950s, however, Toyota began to add its own ingenuity to plant management and operations. In the next chapter, we consider the activities of Toyota in the late 1950s.

References

Automotive Industries. (1954). Advertisement of TelAutograph. *Automotive Industries*, v. 110, March 15, 1954, p. 519. Philadelphia: Chilton Co.

Geschelin, J. (1940). Following Ford tractors down the line. *Automotive Industries*, *83*(1), 4–11.

Gove, P. B. (Ed.). (1976). *Webster's third new international dictionary of the English language, unabridged*. Springfield, Mass: G. & C. Merriam.

Harrison, G. C. (1921). *Cost accounting to aid production: A practical study of scientific cost accounting*. New York: Engineering Magazine Co.

Jidōsha gijutsu (Journal of Society of Automotive Engineers of Japan). (1951). 'Ford jidōsha kōjō no kichō shisatsu dan' (Discourse after returning to Japan on visit to Ford automobile plant). Jidōsha gijutsu (Automotive technology), vol 5, nos. 3–4. Tokyo: Jidōsha gijutsu kai(Society of Automotive Engineers of Japan).

Kishimoto, E. ed. (1959). *Nihon sangyō to ōtomēshon* (Japanese industry and the automation). Tokyo: Tōyō Keizai Shinpōsha.

Nihon Seisansei Honbu (Japan Productivity Center). (1956). *Denki kōgyō: Nihon denki kōgyō seisansei shisatsudan hōkokusho (Electric Industry: Report of productivity mission by Japan electrical industry)*. Tokyo: Nihon Seisansei Honbu.

Nihon Seisansei Honbu (Japan Productivity Center). (1959). Unpan: Dai 2-ji unpan kanri senmon shisatsudan hōko-kusho *(Materials handling: The report of the second productivity mission on the conrol of materials handling)*. Tokyo: Nihon Seisansei Honbu.

Nihon Seisansei Honbu (Japan Productivity Center). (1962). *Unpan: Dai 3ji unpan kanri senmon shisatsudan hōkokusho (Materials handling: Report of the third productivity mission on the control of materials handling)*. Tokyo: Nihon Seisansei Honbu.

Saitō, S. (1952). *Jidōsha no kuni America* (The Country of Automobiles, America). Tokyo: Seibundō Shinkōsha.

Scoville, J. W. (1937). Production control: Some methods of organization in the American industry. In *The Automobile Engineer*, Vol. 37 (October 1937), pp 365–368. London: Iliffe and Sons.

Shōwa Dōjinkai. (1958). *Setsubi kindaika to sono keizai kōka: Jittai chōsa hōkokusho* (Modernization in facility and its economic effect: Report of the field survey). Tokyo: Shōwa Dōjinkai.

Toyoda, E. (1940). "Ford torakutā no seidsan kōtei ni tsuite" (On the production process of Ford tractors), in *Kikai Gakkai-shi* (*Journal of the Society of Mechanical Engineers*), vol. 43, no. 285, p. 682. Tokyo: Nihon Kikai Gakkai.

Toyoda, E. (1987). *Toyota: fifty years in motion: An autobiography by the chairman*. Tokyo: Kodansha International.

Toyota Jidōsha Kōgyō Kabushiki Kaisha (Toyota Motor Co., Ltd). (1958). Toyota Jidōsha 20-nenshi (The 20th Anniversary History of Toyota Motor Co). Koromo-shi: Toyo-ta Jidōsha Kogyō Kabushiki Kaisha (Toyota Motor Co., Ltd).

Toyota Jidōsha Kōgyō Kabushiki Kaisha (Toyota Motor Co., Ltd). (1967). *Toyota Jidōsha 30-nenshi* (The 30th Anniversary History of Toyota Motor Co). Toyota-shi: Toyota Jidōsha Kogyō Kabushiki Kaisha (Toyota Motor Co., Ltd).

Toyota Motor Corporation. (1988). *Toyota: a history of the first 50-years*. Toyota City: Toyota Motor Corporation.

Toyota Shimbun [Toyota Newspaper]. (1954). 'Risōteki-na nagare sagyo: nihon de hajimete' (Ideal flow production: for the first time in Japan) in *Toyota Shimbun* [Toyota Newspaper], no. 160 (October 12, 1954). Toyota-shi: Toyota Jidōsha Kogyō Kabushiki Kaisha (Toyota Motor Co., Ltd).

Yamabe, R. (1961). *Genka keisanron: Kanri kaikei to shiteno genka keisan*. (Cost accoounting: Cost accounting as management accounting). Tokyo: Chikurashobō.

Younger, J. (1930). *Work routing in production, including scheduling and dispatching*. New York: Ronald Press Co.

Younger, J., & Geschelin, J. (1947). *Work routing, scheduling and dispatching in production*. New York: The Ronald press company.

Chapter 6
The Emergence of Flow Production at Toyota

Toyota managed to establish the small-volume production system for automobiles during the war years. However, the company did not achieve smooth production workflow. The 20th anniversary publication documenting Toyota's history explains how the organization resolved this situation:

> Despite adopting the methods to achieve a smooth production flow at our company, semi-finished and finished products accumulated at the start and end of the production line in each plant. Several work processes were scattered across the production line. Although such a scenario gives an impression of an active workplace, it is actually indicative of inefficient management. The factory site used for wasteful or useless materials, and an unnecessary increase in the working capital leads to a high-cost situation. The supermarket system has been adopted to overcome this situation (Toyota Jidōsha Kōgyō Kabushiki Kaisha 1958, p. 490).

Indeed, much literature has focused on addressing the problem of production flow. While these studies have emphasized the role of the "supermarket system" in shaping Toyota's production system, they have ignored the work in other Japanese industries to increase productivity in the mid-1950s. This chapter examines the introduction of the "supermarket system" in Toyota while emphasizing the impact of reforms in other sectors of Japanese industry in the 1950s.

6.1 Operating Trailers as Per Diagram: The Propagation of Just-in-Time

6.1.1 Driving Coal Wagons as Per Diagram at a Coal Mine

The importance of materials handling was well recognized in Japan after the war, partly because of its fundamental impact on manufacturing, but also because of the productivity missions to the USA. In Japan, representatives of several industries

K. Wada, *The Evolution of the Toyota Production System*,
Studies in Economic History,
https://doi.org/10.1007/978-981-15-4928-1_6

believed that transportation management of materials (i.e., materials handling) played a crucial role in increasing production efficiency, and hence they implemented ideas to improve materials handling on work sites. This was particularly noticeable in coal mining; as fuel shortages became a serious problem in postwar Japan, the ability to increase coal production was seen as an urgent issue.

After the war, many Japanese engineers involved in production control during the war joined various private companies. Among them, some accepted consultancy roles at the Japan Management Association (JMA). The JMA provided consultancy services to diverse industries and dispatched consultants to assist companies when deemed appropriate. As Japan sought to increase energy security after the war, consultants were sent to Japanese coal mines to contribute toward increased coal production (Nihon Nōritsu Kyōkai 1982, p. 52).

Their achievements in coal mines were described in an article titled "Operation based on diagram and its management," which was published in *The Management.* The article described the achievements of consultants at the Mukaiyama Coal Mine located in the Kyushu region (Hamanaka 1952). In coal mining operations, "the transportation of coal is more than just an auxiliary process" (Sumiya 1968, p. 376). This is because the working faces in coal mines shift as coal extraction is performed. Given this context, as mining progressed after the war, the distances over which coal had to be transferred from the working faces to the surface of the earth became larger. As a result, managers and production supervisors at coal mines continually faced issues relating to the handling and transport of coal.

Mukaiyama Coal Mine along with "twelve investigators [of JMA] conducted a work and process flow study in order to comprehend the actual situation of transportation and to improve it" (Hamanaka 1952, p. 35). Based on this study, the coal mine decided to determine the coal wagon schedule in advance, similar to a train's operation model, and tried to manage the coal output in a planned way. This practice became known as "operation as per diagram," and significantly reduced the time spent waiting for the arrival of coal wagons to transport the extracted coal. As a consequence, the mine was able to more than double its output (Hamanaka 1952, p. 38).

This case drew much attention in Japan at the time, because its details were also described in a book edited by the Council for Industrial Rationalization under the Ministry of International Trade and Industry (Sangyō Gōrika Shingikai 1953). Furthermore, JMA circulated the progress of the consulting service within JMA. In fact, the journal edited by JMA showed interest in this case and published an article with the following content:

> Isn't it possible to arrange transportation in the factory as per diagram? As coal wagons were possible to drive as per diagram, it must be carried out somewhere. That's why we contacted Japanese National Railways (JNR); we found out that it was carried out at Kokura Plant and making great achievements (Tomonaga 1953, p. 48).

The Kokura Plant was involved in the repair of railroad vehicles. About half of all the work at the plant involved the movement of goods from one place to another. Therefore, the plant underwent a rationalization program based on the belief that improvements in materials handling would improve plant operations. Specifically, the plant obtained 30 trailers in May 1952 (and an additional 20 in August), and established two routes in the plant that connected all warehouses in the workplace. Subsequently, the trains of trailers ran the routes based on schedules prepared in advance, that is, as per the diagram or timetable (Tomonaga 1953, p. 48).

This leads to the question of what was changed by the introduction of this new transportation method at the Kokura Plant. The manager of the plant commented:

> Based on the transportation by trailers, we could see the flow of goods in a consistent manner. Hence, this gave us a general view of the working process. As a result, we could control the schedule generally. This was an unexpected benefit (Tomonaga 1953, p. 48).

The operation of trailers as per diagram not only organized work processes and materials used during these processes, but also clarified the operation route of trailers. Consequently, production personnel developed a better understanding of the connections between processes and the flow of work processes in the entire plant.

By the mid-1950s, Japanese companies were beginning to recognize the importance of materials handling. This may be attributed to the efforts of consultancies in emphasizing the significance of operating trailers as per diagram. However, at the same time, without reflecting on the implications of materials handling, some companies installed materials handling equipment, such as conveyors, and were content with mere installation. At this time, rationalization and mechanization of transportation was booming in Japan.

> Aside from the case of "carrying out underground minerals to the surface of the ground" in mines and coal mines, it is necessary to thoroughly consider that transportation itself is always a negative phenomenon in the case of production by comprising several work processes. This is similar to the case of transportation at mines and coal mines. This is because "short-distance transportation, from the underground to the surface is just necessary" and any additional transportation exerts a negative effect on management (Shingō 1956, p. 60).

This quotation gives mines or coal mines as examples to argue that driving trailers as per diagram in mines led to recognizing the importance of transportation or materials handling at that time in Japan. Against the trend, Shigeo Shingō warned not to exaggerate its importance because the transportation itself does not produce any value—it is only meaningful to cut the cost and time involved (Shingō 1956, p. 60).

6.1.2 Operating Trailers as Per Diagram at Toyota

In postwar Japan, the operation of coal wagons as per diagram was replicated in industrial plants. This application was well known at the time. The Japanese terms "*Daiya (shiki) unten*," which means driving trains or trailers as per diagram, and "*Teiji (sei) unten*" or "*Teiji (sei) unpan*," which means driving trains or trailers (or more generally transporting something) regularly based on time schedule, became buzzwords in management journals at that time.

Considering this situation, the fact that trailer trucks operated on a prearranged schedule between Toyota and Toyota Auto Body was not unusual (see Sect. 5.3.2). However, the following two points should be considered regarding operation of the trailer trucks: why did Toyota Auto Body collaborate with Toyota on the operation of trailer trucks? What was the influence of this operation on Toyota's production?

Toyota Auto Body was established in August 1945 as an independent company, but in December 1945 the company changed its name to Kariya Auto Body. It was renamed again as Toyota Auto Body in June 1953. We consistently refer to this company as Toyota Auto Body.

After the war, Toyota Auto Body faced challenges when manufacturing the all-metal cab. Until the end of the war, truck cabs were made with wooden frames in Japan. After the war, there was a shift to steel cabs. Subsequently, when Toyota planned to sell a truck chassis with a cab, this would discontinue the practice of selling them separately, and Toyota Auto Body would face threats to it existence. Until then, Toyota Auto Body manufactured the wooden frame cab and sold it to regional dealers. When Toyota manufactured and sold a chassis with a cab, orders for cab production at Toyota Auto Body declined. As a result, Toyota Auto Body had to transition to the production of all-steel cabs to survive as a body maker. The company had the experience of creating only wooden frame cabs and had no metal-processing technology. However, it "made a bet-the-company decision," embarking on all-steel cab production. After two-months of negotiations with Toyota, the company succeeded in receiving orders for steel cabs from Toyota (Toyota Shatai Kabushiki Gaisha 1975, pp. 58–59; Toyota Shatai Kabushiki Gaisha 1965, pp. 107–109).

Toyota Auto Body started producing all-steel cabs in June 1951. Initially, Toyota transported the chassis to Toyota Auto Body and mounted the cab at Toyota Auto Body. However, after changing the design in March 1953, the cab was transported from Toyota Auto Body to Toyota, and the cab was mounted on the chassis in the Toyota plant. As a result, the production lines at Toyota and Toyota Auto Body became directly connected. This is exactly what Kishimoto observed; that is, Toyota Auto Body's long trailer trucks were used for carrying cabs and loading them onto Toyota's total assembly line (see Sect. 5.3.2).

In addition, Toyota Auto Body transformed its materials handling inside the company when it began transporting cabs to Toyota on trailers. A business magazine, at that time, reported as follows:

> In the past, miscellaneous material handling methods, such as delivery by hand, handling by rear cars or hand barrow, battery cars, and forklifts, were used without order. In the new method, the company implemented production flow based on takt time. Then the trailers started supplying parts according to the takt time. In other words, the trailers, operating from the warehouse and parts processing hubs *according to the predetermined time schedule,* evenly supplied necessary parts, as many as necessary, at the necessary times.
>
> As a result, the assembly work continued according to the takt time without interruption. Waiting time due to a lack of goods or delay in goods procurement was eliminated; the workers themselves no longer carried the goods. In addition, the amount of work-in-process was significantly decreased, and the well-organized workplace environment witnessed a significant improvement [emphasis supplied] (Manegimento 1957, p. 60).

The phrase "according to the predetermined time schedule" mentioned in this quotation implied the operation of trailers as per diagram—a concept that originated from materials handling in coal mines. The article cited above also carried a photograph of this operation with a caption reading, "running trailers on time." Considering that Toyota Auto Body invited some engineers from JMA in July 1949 and introduced process control based on the work-center method (see Sect. 4.4.1), it appears likely that the company introduced the operation of "running trailers on time" by learning about the operation of coal wagons or trailers as per diagram as advocated by the JMA (Toyota Shatai Kabushiki Gaisha 1965, p. 117).

Furthermore, the official history of Toyota Auto Body claimed in its section entitled "The launching of just-in-time method":

> The transporting method of "just-in-time," launched in 1956 just before we established a new IB plant at Kariya, was so unique that it attracted attention from outside the company, and a specialized magazine covered it. The study group on materials handling publicly disclosed it; many visitors came to inspect it (Toyota Shatai Kabushiki Gaisha 1975, p. 197).

What was this "just-in-time method"? Certainly, the company official history called it "just-in-time," but this was compiled in the mid-1970s, long after the events of the mid-1950s. When the method was implemented in the mid-1950s, was it so-called at that time? To answer these questions, we can examine the materials written in the mid-1950s. The in-house newsletter of Toyota Auto Body at that time described as follows:

> From August 1st [of 1957], electrical parts components were delivered directly to our manufacturing site by lifts from Nippon Denso, which is adjacent to our company. Nippon Denso carries parts such as radiators … twice a day by regularly scheduled lift trucks with trailers. As a result, the two companies benefited enormously, and the *just-in-time method* helped to save space because it did not need extra components in hand as they were supplied as necessary, helping to rationalize in various ways [emphasis supplied] (Toyota Bodei 1957, p. 1).

Toyota Auto Body started transporting parts by running trailers on a schedule between the company and Nippon Denso (now Denso). Based on this operation, the in-house journal of Toyota Auto Body referred to this operation as the "just-in-time method." Although the term of "just-in-time" was originally expressed by Kiichiro Toyoda (Wada and Yui 2002, p. 279), it has rarely been used in the documents issued by Toyota or its affiliates. In the mid-1950s, the operation of running trailers to a schedule led to the term "just-in-time." The use of this term was not a one-off, but became used by business magazines and visitors, among others (Suzuki and Kawada 1958, p. 45).

To increase the productivity of Japanese coal mines after the war, engineers at JMA conceived the operation of coal wagons as per diagram. When they disseminated this idea across the manufacturing industry, the idea came to be known as "running trailers *on time*" because trailers would run based on a prescheduled timetable. Subsequently, Toyota Auto Body, whose production control was improved by the engineers from **JMA**, introduced the operation of running trailers *on time* to transport the cabs and decks of trucks between the company and Toyota and for transporting parts and components between the company and Nippon Denso. Over time, this transport method came to be known as the "just-in-time method," named after the term closely connected with Kiichiro Toyoda. Subsequently, the just-in-time method gained prevalence as the method of operating trailers in manufacturing plants.

6.2 Introducing the Supermarket Method

6.2.1 Explaining the Supermarket Method

Discussion to this point leads us to question Toyota's mechanism for production control following its acceptance of cabs and decks from Toyota Auto Body.

In the spring of 1954, *The Daily Automobile Newspaper* reported that the Lockheed Marietta plant saved $250,000 per year by implementing a method along the lines of operating a supermarket. Looking back at the years of introducing the supermarket method, Yukio Arima, Toyota's plant manager, insisted that this report inspired the introduction of Toyota's supermarket method (Arima 1960, p. 93). However, because this newspaper is not stored in the public library of Japan, detailed information on this report is not available. Nevertheless, Yukio Arima, who was deeply involved in the conception of the "supermarket method" at Toyota, wrote as follows:

> The Toyota-type supermarket method is by no means a copy of Lockheed Airlines' method. It was not possible for us to grasp from the newspaper article what kind of method the company employed. We just wondered what the company would have adopted (Arima 1960, p. 93).

If this statement is true, then it would also make sense to follow the thinking process of the parties involved.

Most of the descriptions on the supermarket method at Toyota, such as the company's official histories are based on Arima's article (but without citing a source). Furthermore, as Arima's argument has been shortened and rearranged, it is difficult to understand the thought process of the parties involved from the description. By examining the discussion of Arima, we consider how Toyota mangers thought and created the "Toyota-type supermarket method" at that time. Arima clarified their rationale behind applying the operation of supermarket to Toyota's manufacturing setting as follows:

> At supermarkets, customers can get the number of items they want at any point of time whenever they want. Additionally, a customer goes to a supermarket to make a purchase. In the case of assembly work at a machine shop, we should assume that machined parts are items in the [super]market and workers are consumers. If this way of thinking were applied to the shop floor, workers would no longer crouch over many parts at the assembly shop. So, we applied this way of thinking to *the transportation method inside the machining plant*, as well as *between the machining plant and the final assembly plant*. In other words, from the

> standpoint of the final assembly plant, the machining plant is the [super]market. Therefore, we decided *to go and collect the necessary items* and *transport them from the following process to the prior process* [emphasis supplied] (Arima 1960, p. 93).

Furthermore, Arima continued:

> All items require preparation in the case of a supermarket. In the same company, however, it should be known *in advance* what particular type of items the assembly plant requires. Then, such items should be prepared *in advance*. Therefore, according to the order of the assembly schedule, by the type of automobiles in the final assembly plant, the machining plant should assemble the required items *in advance*. Then, necessary automobiles can be assembled in the order of the predetermined assembling schedule. Also, according to the assembling order in the assembly plant, workers from the assembly plant should go and collect the necessary parts and components in the machining plant, which is assumed to be the supermarket. This is the principle of the Toyota-type supermarket method [emphasis supplied] (Arima 1960, p. 93).

Accordingly, the Toyota-type supermarket system can be summarized as follows: first, necessary items are collected and transported from the next process to the preceding process. Second, within the same company, the preceding process should *produce the necessary parts in advance* according to the information on the production plan for the following process. In doing so, it would be essential to prepare a form or memo listing the items to be collected and their location; the term *"Kanban"* was coined based on this need.

Considering the above explanation alone, it is not clear why Toyota applied "the supermarket method" to the transportation method. Above all, it was not explained how they specifically applied this method to the *transportation* method. Management books on Toyota as well as Toyota's official histories have ignored these points. In particular, if someone tried to imitate the Toyota-type supermarket method, or attempted to understand it precisely, then it would be crucial to know how to specifically apply it to the transportation method. Any explanation on this point has been completely lacking. However, Arima gave some detail as follows:

> The company proceeded to produce just as many cars as required by the customers according to its daily schedule. In addition, at that time, trailers were delivered to the company. [...] Then, the company started carrying only the necessary parts, just the required number, at the required time by trailers' *teiji sei unten* [emphasis supplied] (Arima 1960, p. 93).

The term "*teiji sei unten*" was a buzzword in management journals at that time (see Sect. 6.1.2) and was often used in Japan in the mid-1950s. Although the *Handbook on Process Control* published in 1960 listed this term with the English translation of "diagram handling system," the English translation failed to capture the meaning of the original term. Nevertheless, the *Handbook* explains this term simply and clearly as follows:

> This is a method not to drive by car every time something to be carried is produced, but to collect and distribute goods regularly based on *a diagram*. This not only reduces driving without loading, but also increases the average load capacity of the car, and reduces waiting time as time is forecasted [emphasis supplied] (Kōtei Kanri Benran Henshū Iinkai 1960, p. 672).

Essentially, "*teiji sei unten*" was derived from the operation of running coal wagons as per diagram; that is, according to a predetermined schedule. This contributed towards improving the production efficiency of postwar Japanese coal mines. This practice was then applied to plants or factories for driving trailers as per diagram, and led to coinage of the term "on-time operation." This explains why Toyota Auto Body started referring to this system as a just-in-time system.

In the process of introducing efficient materials handling, whose significance was captured by the management team in its US tour, Toyota introduced trailers and other transport equipment (see Sect. 5.3.2). By utilizing such equipment, Toyota began to implement *teiji sei unten*, where the trailer or other transport equipment was used to collect necessary items and transport them from the preceding process to the following process.

Toyota then added another condition to the operation of this practice. On this matter, Arima wrote as follows:

> The company [Toyota] aimed to produce as many cars as needed, according to the daily plan. Also, at that time, the trailers were also delivered to our company, and the necessary number of units was five because of the "towing capacity" of the tow truck and the "ease of calculation".
>
> In other words, it was a trailer's *teiji sei unten* transport system, in which only the necessary parts were transported at the required time. Of course, in this case, the engine, the front, the rear, the propeller, and the steering are "set" and transported for five automobile units each (Arima 1960, p. 93).

Here, Arima explains that the trailer carries five units at one time because of "towing capacity" and "ease of calculation." While the trailer towing capacity is dictated by the limitations of the trailer or the towing vehicle, it is unclear how the restriction to five units relates to "ease of calculation." Certainly, it may be assumed that the collection and alignment of parts for only five vehicles will keep calculations to a simple level. However, does Arima refer to the "ease of calculation" in this sense? In this method, the final assembly line selects the parts required for the type of automobiles from the preceding process, such as machine shops, and then transports them to the final assembly line. The requirement to produce parts is signaled from one process to the previous process. Later, this approach was known as the "pull system." Arima was focusing on the adoption of this system for every process in the plant. In other words, carrying the necessary parts in multiples of five implies that each of the five vehicles running through the final assembly line will have the same shape, specification, and color. In the late 1950s, Toyota began assembling a large number of vehicle types and specifications by changing the vehicle type and specification of each of the "five vehicles of the same model and same specification" (Kishimoto 1959, p. 87). In order to achieve production leveling, it is essential to produce each vehicle in different types and colors. This operation requires complex calculations. According to a retrospective study at the end of the 1960s, Toyota began formulating computerized production plans from around 1966; earlier, the plans were developed manually, that is, by human calculation (Mizuno 1969). This means that the determination of the assembly schedule, that is, the order of the type of automobiles in the final assembly plant in the supermarket method, was based on manual or human calculation. In this case, the formulation of a production schedule that has units of five vehicles would significantly contribute to "ease of calculation."

Arima described "set production" as a method of transporting the necessary parts of five automobile units as a single unit. This "set production" was performed as follows:

> For set production, when coming to the machining plant from the final assembly plant, if the requirement for each assembly of parts does not meet the need for five automobile units, then we do not transport the five automobile units of assembled parts (Arima 1960, p. 93).

Why did Arima insist on carrying assemblies of parts for five automobiles as a set? If assemblies of parts for five automobiles fall short, then the following production process would be interrupted. Arima explained the reason behind emphasizing "set production" as follows:

> [If five automobile units of assembled parts are not transported,] the line of the final assembly plant will stop. However, the purpose of the practice was not to shut down the final assembly plant, but to encourage workers in the workplace to drive the urgency to address the problem promptly. At the same time, …in the consistent flow of automobile production, the impact would be large where there were a problem in any place: the workers should recognize and feel responsible for this by themselves. Also, if a group of workers can produce 10 parts for one set, it would be much better to be able to produce 10 parts in 95% of sets, rather than producing 9 parts on schedule and just one part in half because of absenteeism—the [set production] method aimed to make workers understand this (Arima 1960, pp. 93–94).

The Toyota-type supermarket system carried out *teiji sei unpan* and "set production" in order to realize "just-in-time production." To achieve smooth operation, information on the production plan was sent not only to the final assembly line but also to the relevant workplaces in advance. This is the "supermarket" method introduced by Toyota, and it differs significantly from the explanation provided in the company history and literature written for the general public (e.g., see Ohno 1988, p. 5).

6.2.2 *Towards the Reformation of Progress Management at the Koromo Plant*

The Koromo Plant was composed of several shops and factories (see Fig. 3.3). Owing to this situation, Kiichiro Toyoda had issued circulars urging "the tempo of work to be coordinated in all the shops and factories and to make sure one shop or factory does not get far ahead of the others." The circular even permitted the workers "who have produced their target figure for the day to return home" (Toyoda 1939; Wada and Yui 2002, pp. 288–289). Such circulars were some of the attempts to keep the working time of each shop or factory constant and to coordinate the "flow production" direction of the entire plant, ensuring that individual working time was not recognized. However, these attempts did not organize the "flow production" of the entire plant. By introducing the supermarket method, Toyota began to organize flow production at the Koromo Plant. This leads to the question of how Toyota managed its production, particularly the automobile production progress at the Koromo Plant, before the implementation of the supermarket method.

Before establishing the Koromo Plant, Toyota produced automobiles at the Kariya Plant. Concerning Kariya Plant's management practices, Toyota's 20th anniversary history noted:

> Every site of work had an office, where all clerical jobs related to production, personal affairs at shops or factories, or even the supply goods and maintenance services for the plant were carried out. Additionally, all the shop-floor operations were conducted under contract systems. Each shop or factory (main factory and assembly shop) determined its progress management, considering its own standard for the volume of work-in-progress (Toyota Jidōsha Kōgyō Kabushiki Kaisha 1958, p. 87).

At the Kariya plant, each shop or factory managed its own production activities, among other management tasks.

In the given context, we examine how Toyota managed its production after the commencement of operations at the Koromo Plant. As explained earlier, Toyota introduced *Gōguchi* production control during the war years. Under the *Gōguchi* production control system, some units of automobiles, say 10 or 20 units of final products, were regarded as a unit of lot. Every part comprising the same unit of lot was allocated the same serial number. Subsequently, the information on the progress of parts production was easily obtained (see Sect. 3.4; Toyota Jidōsha Kōgyō Kabushiki Kaisha 1958, p. 87). Thus, the Koromo Plant attempted to control the production progress of every process by using a serial number for the final products. However, this did not necessarily exert control over the progress of production for individual parts—it was unclear which departments played a role in determining the production plan.

In 1954, when Toyota's total annual volume of production surpassed 20,000 vehicles for the first time, the Koromo Plant controlled its progress of production as follows:

> For internally manufactured products at the casting, forging, and autobody plant, the engineering work department in the engineering division provides production direction to each plant, instructing how many particular items should be produced monthly. Based on the production directions, each plant made its own daily production plan and controls the volume of work-in-progress. This same method was applied even in the general [final] assembly plants, except in the case of assembly work, the painting or plating plants, and the machining plants (Toyota Jidōsha Kōgyō Kabushiki Kaisha 1958, p. 87).

The Koromo Plant did not change the method of controlling the progress of production at the Kariya Plant—the volume of monthly production stipulated for each plant. However, each plant decided the detailed daily schedule of production comprising manufacturing, operation, and control. The engineering division or any other division did not play a role in the operation and management of this daily schedule.

In the previous quotation, the monthly production volume was stipulated for "general [final] assembly plants, except in the case of assembly work, the painting or plating plants and the machining plants" (Toyota Jidōsha Kōgyō Kabushiki Kaisha 1958, p. 87). Although the plating plant did not appear on the layout of the Koromo Plant just after completion, the plating plant was located in the final assembly plant in the figure of the Koromo Plant in 1958 (Toyota Jidōsha Kōgyō Kabushiki Kaisha 1958, pp. 658–659).

This leads to the question of why production direction was not given on a monthly basis for the assembly process in the final assembly plant. After 1951, Toyota modernized production facilities by implementing a five-year plan for modernization (see Sect. 4.2.2). Many conveyor lines were installed and expanded in the final assembly plant as well as in the machining plant. However, the conveyor lines did not move completely without interruption. In 1954, a Toyota employee asked, "although the sound of a buzzer is often heard [inside the machining plants at Toyota], is this a proper way of running the conveyor system?" In response to this question, Taiichi Ohno replied, "this is a so-called takt system from Germany, that is assembling work is intermittently done while using conveyor lines" (Gijutsu no Tomo 1954, p. 18). Furthermore, more generally, at the Koromo Plant the conveyor did not move constantly at regular intervals (Toyota Jidōsha Kōgyō Kabushiki Kaisha 1958, p. 461). Why didn't Toyota give production directions on a monthly basis to the assembly process in the final assembly plant? The reason is not attributed to materials handling. If the company had confirmed the volume of shipments, not on monthly basis, but on a daily or weekly basis, then it would have been rational for this assembly process to receive production instructions on a daily basis instead of on a monthly basis.

At the Koromo Plant, every item produced in the machining plants was transported to the assembly process in the final assembly plant (Toyota Jidōsha Kōgyō Kabushiki Kaisha 1958, pp. 658–659). In other words, the machining plants were situated at the process preceding that in the final assembly plant. The production instruction to the preceding process, that is, the machining plant, was made on a monthly basis, and the production instruction to the following process, the assembly process, was not given on a monthly basis. Furthermore, Toyota conducted trials for implementation of the supermarket method in the machining plants, which consisted of *teiji sei unpan* and *set production* (see Sect. 6.2). Therefore, we investigate how the machining plants operated, as well as the relationships between the final assembly plant and the machining plants before the supermarket method was implemented.

On this matter, Arima describes the situation of the machining plant around 1953/1954, just before implementation of the supermarket method:

> In the machining plant at that time, all machined parts were transported to the final assembly plant by the group of workers assigned to transportation with a slip of one item per leaf. This meant a method of "carrying items from the preceding process to the following process." Furthermore, all the finished items were sent without giving adequate thought to inconvenience of the other party [the final assembly plant]. There were many machine failures at each group of machining because preventive maintenance of the machines was not conducted; production based on the standard worksheet was also not well controlled. As a result, it was impossible to expect that a stable number of parts could be transported to the following process (Arima 1960, p. 91).

Hence, following processes had to cope with a scenario wherein the required number of parts did not come from the previous process. As a result, "the assembly plant occupied much more area for parts storage than the area required for assembly" (Arima 1960, p. 91).

The priority for the person in charge of the production was to execute smooth production at the plant. For this purpose, more parts than necessary were stored in the plant. The consequences of these actions on the whole company were ignored. It can be assumed that the person in charge of production faced penalties if the plant produced less than the scheduled volume of production. However, if the planned quantity is achieved even when more than the necessary number of parts is stored, then nobody would receive any penalty. Therefore, they considered their own plant first rather than the whole company. In other words, their behavior was directed toward partial optimization rather than total optimization for the whole company.

To complete a car, it is necessary to load various parts in the assembly line. Before Toyota began to implement set production, Arima described the situation of the work site as follows:

> By observing which model could be assembled while observing the parts in stock, the assembly plant began its assembling work. But the following situation often happened: there was no part A for the front section and there were no B and C parts at the rear section; concerning the parts for this car model, all in-house products were in stock, but outsourced items were unavailable. As a result, the assembly of the parts was interrupted and put it in another place; only parts in stock were assembled and the remaining parts were temporarily removed. So, the working time for assembly work on the conveyor was curtailed. Especially, in the beginning of the month, when all parts are not aligned, only about half volume of the production schedule could be assembled. ... In terms of managing production, it was in a pre-management state (Arima 1960, p. 91).

The number and type of parts required for completing an automobile are fixed. An assembly is produced by assembling parts, and an automobile is completed by assembling several types of assemblies. However, at the stage of producing assemblies, necessary parts were frequently missing. This often happened inside the machining plant. If completed assemblies remain inside the plant, then this would lead to space restrictions, but unfinished assemblies, which are caused by a lack of necessary parts, must remain inside the plant and contribute further to reducing the working space.

Under these circumstances, after assembling the parts, the person in charge of production at the machining plant would try to transport them to the final assembly plant immediately. Even if the final assembly plant did not need such assemblies, the person's priority would have been to secure the working space in the machining plant. As a result, the following occurred:

> The assemblies assembled in the machining plant were piled up on a heavy-duty truck like a mountain and carried to the line side of the final assembly plant. The final assembly plant did not take active part in assembling as many automobiles as the planned-type and volume. The final assembly plant would assemble any type of automobiles if all assembles were in place—in assembling heavy-duty trucks, if outsourced parts and engines and so on were in place, but only 10 units of assemblies were available for the front section, then the final assembly plant would assemble only 10 heavy-duty trucks. When assembling light trucks, if the outsourced parts and the assemblies made in the machining plant were available in

> scheduled quantities, but only 12 automobile frames were in stock, then the final assembly plant would assemble only 12 light trucks. At that time, there were some problems with many parts. It was difficult to proceed with assembling automobiles according to the daily production schedule until the middle of the month. In addition, many workers in charge of production progress had to investigate the number of parts in kind and then send a prompt for parts (Arima 1960, p. 91).

According to the above quotation, Toyota had "many workers in charge of production progress" at that time. It could be interpreted as if many subdivided production units were located throughout the whole plant and each unit had a worker in charge of production progress; this implied that the work-center method was fully adopted. In fact, after the labor disputes in 1950, Toyota emphasized having, at least, a trait in common with the work-center method for measuring the man-hours of each production process (see Sect. 4.4.1). The work-center method tried to organize the whole process flow by subdividing the work site and carrying out work management, inspection, and progress carefully. This initiative emerged from a reflection on the management of production during the war. The work-center method aimed at solving "the end of month" problem, in which the actual amount of production would surge during the last several days of the month to achieve the target production volume for the month (see Sect. 2.3.1). Under the work-center method, the progress manager assigned at each work-center would carefully monitor the progress of production. However, as this method placed many work-centers in the whole factory and required many personnel to achieve its objective, some companies would abandon the method when labor costs started rising, even though they recognized the advantages of the method.

In the mid-1950s, Toyota did not achieve leveled production despite assigning several personnel to oversee production progress in the plant. One of the departments achieved smooth progress in production by sending personnel to the previous process to find the necessary parts and bring them back to their own department, or at least urge the production of the necessary parts. Thus, the department would secure the necessary parts because the parts would be preferentially produced without specifications from other departments. In this situation, each department put more priority on their own matters and the production plan for the whole plant would be given a low priority. In other words, just partial optimization was pursued, and total optimization for the whole plant was not considered. Because this would promote confusion in the plant, many workers in charge of production progress rushed around the production site to find necessary parts or "investigated the number of parts and lobbied for parts" (Arima 1960, p. 91). Despite the efforts of these people, in the machining plant "many unfinished or finished products were piled up at the ends of lines or the beginning of lines; to make things worse, piles of work-in-progress also existed" (Toyota Jidōsha Kōgyō Kabushiki Kaisha 1958, p. 490).

Even during the war, Toyota tried to measure the standard time for each working process. After the labor disputes of 1950, the company managed to establish a production allowance system through the use of an IBM machine. Nonetheless, the company still knew the monthly man-hours, and each plant was provided only with the monthly production volume. As a result, this caused problems similar to those observed by the aircraft companies in the war years: "the actual amount of production would tend to surge during the last several days of the month to achieve the target production volume for the month" (see Sect. 2.3.1). Arima clearly admitted that this happened at Toyota in the mid-1950s as follows:

> There is no longer anyone who talks about this term (the end-of-the-month problem) in Toyota's production. However, five to six years ago, this word was used, without any doubts, and we unquestioningly accepted it.
>
> At the end of the month, we managed to assemble the parts and handed over the assembly plant. Of course, some assemblies produced the required volume at the end of the month, but some were not produced because parts were missing. Contrastingly, there were not enough parts to assemble. At the result, we did not reach the planned daily production. … The same situation was repeated every month (Arima 1960, p. 91).

The way to solve this problem was to use "set production." If the assemblies required for one car were transported as a set, the final assembly plant will continue production without interruption. However, the question is whether there were problems in other departments. One solution would be that every factory would produce according to the final assembly line production sequence. Instead of monthly production instructions, the final assembly line production order would be the production order that each factory had to follow.

6.2.3 *Was Set Production Toyota's Original Idea?*

Toyota initiated "set production" to confront the end-of-month production. This idea of transporting the necessary items for producing a final product to the final assembly plant was well known as "kit marshalling." Even in Japan, the *Handbook on Process Control* in 1960 introduced "kit-based assembly preparation" as follows:

> In a factory that produces a large number of standard products or special specification products close to this …, the focus of process control for the final stage of the assembly plant is to have all the parts. In other words, it is not preferable to send various parts to the assembly place individually because it takes time and effort to arrange parts and to prompt for shortages. For this purpose, the pre-assembly worksite … or parts warehouse should be in charge of the parts assortment work; they should supply it as so-called kit, comprising all parts and subassemblies required for assembly (Kōtei Kanri Benran Henshū Iinkai 1960, p. 272).

This did not describe how this idea was created. However, it was well known that kit marshalling was created in the British aircraft industry during World War II. The method was evaluated as follows:

> Yet at a time when the industry was facing an acute shortage of supervisory staff, kit marshalling reduced the managerial effort required to maintain the flow of work and guarded against shortages of particular supplies. Labour efficiency improved considerably during the war as a result of such measures (Ritchie 1997, p. 244).

When Toyota introduced "set production," this was a good way to meet the goals the company wanted to achieve. Kit marshalling has similar characteristics to set production.

In the UK, kit marshalling was used during World War II. It may be speculated that Nissan, which was aligned with Austin, a British auto company, in the postwar period, might have wanted to introduce this in Japan. Nissan's 30th anniversary history documented that the "Marshalling method was adopted at the Yokohama First Factory's Assembly Section" in October 1955 (Nissan Jidōsha Kabushiki Gaisha Sōmubu Chōsaka 1965, p. 330). However, Nissan could not achieve rational plant placement on a large site because the site of the original plant was small. Furthermore, achieving rational factory placement on a large site was not achieved even in the mid-1950s, due to condemnation by the US military (Nissan Jidōsha Kabushiki Gaisha Sōmubu Chōsaka 1965, pp. 316–317). Nissan's entire plant was repeatedly relocated, and plant placement and machine placement could not be fixed. In such a situation, Nissan's production managers were trying to achieve normal work by kit marshalling at the assembly plant alone, although kit marshalling required space for reworking parts into a kit. In fact, kit marshalling tended "to rebuild the cushion of parts and components" and, in normal situations, "this would have been uneconomic in terms of finance" and "factory capacity (because of the additional storage space)" (Ritchie 1997, p. 244).

Toyota's set production was quite similar to kit marshalling. Nevertheless, Toyota was simultaneously working to reduce the cushion of parts and components—driving trailers as per diagram.

6.2.4 The Need to Rewrite the Standardized Worksheet

In the mid-1950s, Toyota began to implement the supermarket method. However, it took many years for Toyota's supermarket system to take root. To realize set production, it would be ideal to produce parts in small lots—just making parts for five cars, at every process. However, achieving small-lot production was not an easy task in any process, and it sometimes took time to achieve. Furthermore, as many processes changed in the production process, it was necessary to formulate a standard worksheet and put it up so that the work would be the same for all the workers involved in the process. Arima commented on this situation:

> If the number of production items changes, and the number of items to be produced at a fixed time changes, it would naturally be necessary to recreate the standard worksheet. This would become one of the important tasks as a supervisor, as well as management ability. It became one of the qualifications as a supervisor. (Arima 1960, p. 92).

To realize set production smoothly, it would be necessary to know the standard time of each process. Work should be done based on a standard worksheet for each work process. If there were a change in any work process, it would be immediately reflected in the standard worksheet. To smoothly carry out the work, as well as to properly measure the cost, the company had to be aware of changes in working times due to changes on the standard worksheets.

To create a standard worksheet and to revise it, trained personnel were required. For training, although the method of on-site management in the USA, such as "Training Within Industry" was also implemented at Toyota, the production workshop achieved great results at Toyota. About this production workshop, participants at that time stated:

> The 17th production technology workshop (abbreviated "P Workshop") sponsored by the JMA (Japan Management Association) was held at our company (Toyota), and 12 factory engineers from our company and 10 engineers from related associated company factories participated. This was the first P Workshop. From that time to this year (1964), we trained 366 factory and chief engineers by holding P Workshops 14 times. As a result, for production technology, company-wide intention unification was carried out including associated factories. Furthermore, rationalization of the production line made great progress. The P Workshop conducted research on movement analysis, time research, operation analysis, fatigue research, standard time setting, and process research, among others, in close contact with the production site thorough on-site training and research methods. This was a one-month full-time training camp. In the daytime, on-site observation, investigation, arrangement, and preparation of presentation materials were conducted after returning to the dormitory at night, so it was hard training to be performed every night at 9 o'clock, 10 o'clock, and sometimes all night (Yokose 1964, p. 109).

Although this P Workshop ran at full capacity after 1959, the number of trainees including those from other training courses increased from the late 1950s. Toyota's need for such human resources was also related to changing production instructions. On this topic, Toyota's company history reads:

> The Material Section of the Planning Division (independent as the Inspection Division in May 1955) began to investigate plant capacity and to issue production instructions after adjusting the capacity and load. In the past, the company had a rough idea of how many cars each plant could produce in a month. From this time on, the company came to examine the capabilities of each plant by their respective manufacturing sector. And in 1957, the company came to grasp the production capacity of each machine in the pressing and forging sector (Toyota Jidōsha Kōgyō Kabushiki Kaisha 1958, p. 452).

With an accumulation of trained personnel, Toyota set and revised standard work, standard worksheets, and standard times at manufacturing sites. Furthermore, the company was able to set up the production plan for the entire plant based on precise information on the production capacity and load of each plant. At this time, not only standard time, but data such as load factors for each machine were recorded sequentially with punch cards on IBM machine, and various calculations were mechanized (Toyota Jidōsha Kōgyō Kabushiki Kaisha 1958, pp. 803–804). In fact, the payment rate of the production allowance system, which was based on the calculation of standard times and other data, was stabilized after 1957 (see Fig. 4.2).

The company could give precise instructions to each plant based on detailed information by obtaining the data and processing it on IBM machines. By around 1960, Toyota was able to move towards flow production. However, Toyota produced "five vehicles of the same model and the same specification in what was regarded as one unit" (Kishimoto 1959, p. 87). Thus, Toyota had not yet achieved complete flow production in the sense of leveling production as a whole.

References

Arima, Y. (1960). "Toyota shiki sūpah maketto houshiki ni yoru kannri" (The control by Toyota type supermarket method) in *Gijutsu no Tomo* (Friends of Technolo-gy), vol. 11, no. 28. Toyota: Toyota Jidōsha Kogyō Kabushiki Kaisha (Toyota Motor Co., Ltd).

Gijutsu no Tomo (Friends of Technology). (1954). "Kikai Kōjō no Konjaku wo Kataru" (Talking about Machining Plants" History) in *Gijutsu no Tomo* (Friends of Technolo-gy), no. 14. Toyota: Toyota Jidōsha Kogyō Kabushiki Kaisha (Toyota Motor Co., Ltd).

Hamanaka, K. (1952). "Daiya unten to sono kanri" (Operation based on diagram and its management) in *Manegimento (The Management),* vol. 11, no. 7. Tokyo: Nihon Nōritsu Kyōkai.

Kishimoto, E. ed. (1959). *Nihon sangyō to ōtomēshon* (Japanese industry and the automation). Tokyo: Tōyō Keizai Shinpōsha.

Kōtei Kanri Benran Henshū Iinkai (Handbook on Process Control editorial committee). (1960). *Kōtei kanri benran* (Handbook on Process Control). Tokyo: Nikkan Kōgyō shinbunsha.

Manegimento (The Management). (1957). "Sagyō kaizen no arubamu: Toyota Shatai" (The album of work improvement: Toyota Auto Body Co.) in *Manegimento (The Management),* vol. 16, no. 9. Tokyo: Nihon Nōritsu Kyōkai.

Mizuno, T. (1969). "Purodukushion kontorōru" (Production control) in *Hinshitsu Kanri* (The statis-cal qualty control), vol. 20, no. 3. Tokyo: Nihon Kagaku Gijutsu Renmei (Japanese Union of Scientists and Engineers).

Nihon Nōritsu Kyōkai (Japan Management Association). (1982). *Keiei to tomoni: Nihon Nōritsu Kyōkai konsarutingu gijutsu 40-nen (With management: Japan Management Association con-sulting technology 40 years).* Tokyo: Nihon Nōritsu Kyōkai.

Nissan Jidōsha Kabushiki Gaisha Sōmubu Chōsaka (The Research Section of General Affairs Department at Nissan Motor Corporation) ed. (1965). Nissan jidōsha sanjūnenshi: shōwa hachi-nen shōwa sanjūhachinen (Nissan 30th anniversary history: from 1933 to 1963). Nissan Motor Corporation.

Ohno, T. (1988). *Toyota production system: Beyond large-scale production.* Cambridge, Mass: Productivity Press.

Ritchie, Sebastian. (1997). *Industry and air power: The expansion of British aircraft production, 1935–41.* London: Frank Cass.

Sangyō Gōrika Shingikai (Industrial rationalization Council). (1953). *Unpan kanri (Transport management).* Tokyo: Nikkan Kōgyō Shinbunsha.

Shingō, S. (1956). "Kaizen wa dare ni mo dekiru: seisann no kaizen sono 2" (Anyone improve it: improving production part 2) in *Manegimento (The Management),* vol. 15, no. 6. Tokyo: Nihon Nōritsu Kyōkai.

Sumiya, M. (1968). *Nihon sekitan sangyō bunseki (The Analysis of Japan coal industry).* Tokyo: Iwanami Shoten.

Suzuki, Z., & Kawada, Y. (1958). "Gaichū kannri no jissaiteki na yarikata•kanngaekata" (The practical way and the way of thinking about outsourcing management) in *Manegimento (The Management),* vol. 17, no. 2. Tokyo: Nihon Nōritsu Kyōkai.

Tomonaga, M. (1953). "Daiya unten no saiyo kara jisshimade" (From adoption of driving trailers as per the diagram to its implementation) in *Manegimento (The Management)*, vol. 12, no. 7. Tokyo: Nihon Nōritsu Kyōkai.

Toyoda, K. (1939). "Tsūtatsu roku"(Circular), No. 8 [typescript]. Koromo-shi: Toyota Jidōsha Kōgyō Kabushiki Kaisha (Toyota Motor Co., Ltd).

Toyota Bodei (Toyota Body). (1957). "Densō → Shatai: Chokutsū unten hajimaru" (From Denso to Toyota Auto Bdoy: The beginning of direct transporting) in *Toyota Bodei (Toyota Body)* no. 8. Kariya: Toyota Auto Body.

Toyota Jidōsha Kōgyō Kabushiki Kaisha (Toyota Motor Co., Ltd). (1958). *Toyota Jidōsha 20-nenshi* (The 20th Anni-versary History of Toyota Motor Co). Koromo-shi: Toyo-ta Jidōsha Kogyō Kabushiki Kaisha (Toyota Motor Co., Ltd).

Toyota Shatai Kabushiki Gaisha (Toyota Auto Body Co., Ltd). (1965). Toyota shatai 20-nenshi (The 20th Anniversary History of Toyota Auto Body Co). Kariya: Toyota Shatai Kabushiki Gaisha.

Toyota Shatai Kabushiki Gaisha (Toyota Auto Body Co., Ltd). (1975). Toyota shatai 30-nenshi (The 30th Anniversary History of Toyota Auto Body Co). Kariya: Toyota Shatai Kabushiki Gaisha.

Yokose, T. (1964). "Toyota jidōsha kōgyō no kanri kantokusha kyōiku"(The education for management supervisors at Toyota Motor Corporation) in Rōdō Hōrei Kyōkai ed., *Kanri kantokusha kunren no jissai* (The practice of eduction for management supervisors). Tokyo: Rōdō Hōrei Kyōkai.

Wada, K., & Yui, T. (2002). *Courage and Change: The Life of Kiichiro Toyoda*. Toyota City: Toyota Motor Corp.

Chapter 7
Quality and Its Assurance

7.1 Introducing Quality Control

7.1.1 Diffusing Quality Control Among Suppliers

Shortly after the end of World War II, Kiichiro Toyoda claimed that if Japanese automobiles could not compete with foreign counterparts in terms of cost and quality, this meant "the death of the management of the [Japanese] automobile industry" (Wada 1999, p. 522). Once Toyota somehow managed to produce the automobile, the issue of automobile quality was recognized as an important management issue.

An automobile is composed of many parts. Toyota used not only its own parts but also numerous parts from external suppliers. Therefore, it was necessary to improve the quality of the parts that come from suppliers as well, without which the quality and reliability of the automobile could not be guaranteed. However, it was difficult to enforce high quality levels on suppliers when Toyota itself did not maintain those levels in-house.

First, we will consider Toyota's commitment to quality. Toyota had its own quality philosophy or control activity called "audit improvement" since its foundation (Wada 1999, pp. 297–298). Once faulty parts were found, the company would find the root causes, and "put them into a chart so that everyone clearly saw how much progress was made" (Wada and Yui 2002, p. 287). This was particularly effective in eliminating the number of defects in its early years, but the need for statistical quality control increased as the number of cars produced continued to rise.

Toyota started learning statistical quality control methods only after the war, just like many other Japanese companies. In 1949, the company began to learn statistical quality control through books or external training sessions. In 1950, Toyota experimentally introduced the control chart method at the machine shop. The company found this method effective in understanding the characteristics of the process. Therefore, Toyota began to promote the use of this method in every process of the company. In 1953, Toyota even conducted in-house training sessions on quality

K. Wada, *The Evolution of the Toyota Production System*,
Studies in Economic History,
https://doi.org/10.1007/978-981-15-4928-1_7

control (Toyota Jidōsha Kōgyō Kabushiki Kaisha 1958, pp. 341–343). In 1955, Toyota decided to collect data on quality at its Inspection Division. Furthermore, in 1956 Toyota collected the inspection data for every process and processed it with IBM machines (Toyota Jidōsha Kōgyō Kabushiki Kaisha 1958, p. 804). Indeed, Toyota had learned about statistical quality control, but focused on maintaining quality through post-production inspections.

Toyota did not immediately promote the idea of quality control among its suppliers. The company had an extreme shortage of personnel that could advise the management of suppliers or provide technical guidance. Indeed, Toyota rarely provided guidance on the manufacturing processes of suppliers. In addition, Toyota itself was faced with instability in management. However, Toyota began instructing and intervening in the management and technical aspects of suppliers after a "*keiretsu* diagnosis" conducted in 1952/1953 (see Wada 1992). The *keiretsu* diagnosis was conducted not by Toyota, but by the Small and Medium Enterprise Agency.

Toyota and 21 suppliers were subjected to a *keiretsu* diagnosis. The summary of the *keiretsu* diagnosis urged Toyota to strengthen its Purchasing Department, where 40 people were in direct contact with suppliers. It was considered that the Purchasing Department was too small to administer the plethora of transactions between Toyota and its suppliers. Although the suppliers were eager to receive technical guidance from Toyota, only three people were authorized to offer such technical guidance, and they spent most of their time making design changes to parts. As a result, Toyota had essentially nobody in charge of providing technical guidance to suppliers (Wada 1992, pp. 30–33). However, Toyota was able to learn how to audit factories and assess enterprises.

After the *keiretsu* diagnosis, Toyota changed its ordering method and began placing orders to suppliers in advance. It also sought to determine the unit price of parts from suppliers through cost calculation based on standard work times (Toyota Jidōsha Kōgyō Kabushiki Kaisha 1967a, p. 395). Given that standard work times were used to determine in-house costs, Toyota tried the same method for outsourcing parts (see Chap. 4).

Toyota established a quality control committee in October 1953 and intended to introduce quality control across the entire manufacturing process after the *keiretsu* diagnosis (Toyota Jidōsha Kōgyō Kabushiki Kaisha 1958, pp. 438, 854). Toyota tried to rationalize the inspections of parts that were outsourced from suppliers. To achieve this, Shōichi Saitō recommended introducing quality control at suppliers' facilities and rationalizing the inspection of parts. By sending its engineers to suppliers, Toyota investigated the advent of quality control at each supplier and aimed to train the relevant people by providing on-the-job instructions. After 1953, Toyota forced suppliers to submit a control chart of the production process with the supplied parts (Yamada 1961, p. 39). Thus, Toyota became actively involved in the suppliers' production processes. Toyota's effort in quality control focused on rationalizing the inspection process by using control charts until the late 1950s.

For some time, Toyota did not expect suppliers to adopt its inspection-oriented approach and actively engage in quality control. However, in 1959, seven years after the suppliers first submitted control charts for inspection, Toyota planned to implement and promote quality control for suppliers. Then Toyota realized that "there was a considerable gap in understanding and implementation in terms of quality control among the suppliers, and for that reason the plan had to be delayed" (Yamada 1961, p. 39). Although Toyota was able to obtain information about the management of the suppliers and exert some influence, it was far from changing the attitude of suppliers fundamentally, at least with regard to quality control issues.

7.1.2 American Impacts Through the Special Procurement from APA

From the late 1950s, Toyota became directly involved in special procurement work from the Army Procurement Agency (APA). The allied forces stationed in Japan required supplies for military use. The US Government entered into contracts with individual Japanese manufacturers for supplies, which ensured a huge demand in Japan. Among them, the APA was the procurement department for the US Army. In 1958, the APA decided to purchase vehicles as relief items for South-East Asia, and it sought competing bids from manufacturers. Toyota and Shin-Mitsubishi (now Mitsubishi Motors) were awarded contracts. In 1959, the APA requested further bids, and Toyota made a successful bid, except for quarter-ton trucks, for which Shin Mitsubishi received the contract. Toyota supplied a total of 51,273 trucks to the APA up until 1962 (Toyota Jidōsha Kōgyō Kabushiki Kaisha 1967a, p. 463). The total value of such orders was about $155 million (about 6% of Toyota's total sales for the period). Furthermore, even after 1962, the APA ordered spare parts to the value of about $40 million until 1966 (Toyota Jidōsha Kōgyō Kabushiki Kaisha 1967a, p. 463).

The supply of trucks and spare parts to the APA contributed significantly to Toyota's business. In addition, Toyota gained valuable experience from this special procurement to the APA, particularly because other Japanese automobile manufacturers, besides Toyota and Shin-Mitsubishi, did not participate in these bids. Thus, Toyota gained significant knowledge from the APA concerning quality inspection and packaging of parts. In 1959, one article in Toyota's in-house magazine (*Toyota Management*) described the APA's inspection:

> Delivery of spare parts for the [APA's] special procurement is under extremely strict control... After inspected by Toyota and APA inspectors, spare parts are sent to the lines of rust prevention treatment and packaging; and spare parts are delivered only after these rust prevention and packaging inspections. This rust prevention and packaging is also instructed in detail for the contract, and the quality of rust prevention oil as well as the material of the woodchip used for packaging are strictly specified (Kuroda 1959, p. 28).

About 100 inspectors from the US Army were posted at inspection stations for major processes. The inspectors verified whether the product conformed to the detailed standards, which the US Army created for general vehicles. This was the first experience for Toyota in performing inspections based on such detailed standards (Toyota Jidōsha Kōgyō Kabushiki Kaisha 1967b, pp. 468–469). Toyota's company history (but not publicly disclosed) described in detail the lessons learned from this APA special procurement.

> A valuable study for export was packing of spare parts. … The common thought at that time was that rust prevention, packaging, and packing work were not very important. Most believed that it would be enough if it were packed. When we started packing the spare parts for the APA, it became clear that the US military standards were unexpectedly strict, and the specifications and standards were standardized to every detail. When the US military supplied military weapons and parts during the Second World War, it suffered significant damage, both strategically and economically, because they were rusted or damaged during transportation. Based on that bitter experience, everything from washing, preserving, packaging, and secondary materials used in military standards was carefully examined and standardized. Military standards were more than 50 types. Our company started by researching and understanding the contracted specifications and standards. However, we were not able to fully do this, and could not apply many of the military standards to spare parts in the beginning (Toyota Jidōsha Kōgyō Kabushiki Kaisha 1967b, pp. 468–469).

Toyota learned inspection methods whereby US military standards were used for packaging and so on. Toyota also gained this knowledge especially considering that Toyota's exports shifted towards mainly knockdown exports from the late 1950s to the early 1960s.

The special procurement production for the APA could not be met by Toyota alone: Toyota produced the chassis, but Toyota Auto Body handled the bodywork, and Toyota Auto Loom (now Toyota Industries) was in charge of vehicle inspection (Toyota Jidōsha Kōgyō Kabushiki Kaisha 1967a, p. 464). This prompted Toyota and its affiliated companies to move toward the automobile business. Even Toyota Auto Loom, which had been at the heart of the Toyota group's textile manufacturing business, found its potential in automobiles by participating in this special procurement production (Toyota Gurūpu 2005, p. 105). This special procurement production was a turning point for Toyota and its group companies to work together on automobile production.

Toyota realized that its inspection method was ineffective as per American standards and was surprised at the extent to which the inspection alone was specified and standardized. Toyota's people viewed it as a strict inspection, and that was exactly the difference in quality control between the USA and Toyota.

7.2 Steps to Mass Production and Its Setback

7.2.1 Production Growth and Facing Problems

In 1952, the then company president, Taizō Ishida, stated in the Diet that Toyota's target production level was to produce 500 vehicles a month (Sangiin 1952, p. 2). In other words, an annual production of 6,000 vehicles was Toyota's goal. However, production volume increased significantly beyond expectations. Toyota rapidly increased its production after 1960. In 1959, its production was about 100,000 vehicles, and it jumped to about 155,000 vehicles in 1960, and over 400,000 in 1964. Even if only passenger cars are considered (except for trucks that account for the majority of production), annual production exceeded 7,400 cars in 1955, reaching about 42,000 cars in 1960, and in 1964 it was about 182,000 cars.

In August 1959, Toyota began operations at the Motomachi Plant, which specialized in passenger cars. This supported the growth in production, particularly in the production of passenger cars. Now, Toyota had two assembly plants: the Honsha Plant, formerly called the Koromo Plant, and the Motomachi Plant.

In 1960, Toyota launched the Corona PT20, which was expected to sell well. However, "the model change had been made hurriedly, and design changes aimed at reducing costs were being carried out right up until the time the car was put on sale. This resulted in problems such as difficulties in fitting the doors properly and with the suspension… Breakdowns were especially frequent with Coronas that were being used as taxis" (Toyota Motor Corporation 1988, p. 138). These experiences resulted in a poor reputation for this car, and poor sales followed.

Even before launching the Corona PT20, Toyota was faced with managerial problems. Toyota's official history notes that inter-departmental collaboration no longer functioned smoothly. In fact, as Toyota's production grew, the number of employees also expanded: about 5,900 in 1958, about 7,500 in 1960, and about 12,000 in 1963 (Toyota Jidōsha Kōgyō Kabushiki Kaisha 1967a, p. 673). An external investigator also wrote that Toyota's middle management was dissatisfied, saying that "the clerical work cannot keep up with the growth in production" (Nihon Jinbun Kagakkai 1963, p. 58). One of the attendees at the roundtable discussion "Rationalization of Purchasing" also made the following remarks, which were published in *Toyota Management*, Toyota's internal magazine:

> Many people complain that they cannot handle their job because the clerical work has increased so much. Looking at statistics, the amount of work at the end of last year [in 1958] had increased by 230% compared with March of 1958. Although we have improved the form design and rationalized the clerical work itself, we are still too busy to concentrate on the job (Toyota Manejiment 1959, pp. 14–15).

In 1957, the Purchasing Department changed its suppliers' contracts from three months to six months. In doing so, the department reduced the burden of price negotiation with suppliers (Toyota Jidōsha Kabushiki Kaisha 1987, p. 306).

7.2.2 Introduction of Total Quality Control at Toyota

At the time of launching the Corona PT20, Toyota also faced other problems related to the expansion of its operations. With the impending trade liberalization of passenger cars, Toyota announced the "30,000 vehicles plan," which aimed to achieve a production target of 30,000 vehicles per month within three years. To achieve this, Toyota particularly focused on "the production division between Toyota and its associated companies," "the policy of utilizing the subcontracting factories," and "the relationship between the Honsha Plant and the Motomachi Plant" (Toyota Jidōsha Kōgyō Kabushiki Kaisha 1967a, pp. 484–488). In considering its future business direction, Toyota needed to be clear about the coordination between its two assembly plants as well as its relationships with its affiliated companies and suppliers. This meant that Toyota had to review and rebuild its management system in the face of production growth and the problems related to the Corona PT20.

Toyota introduced Total Quality Control (TQC) (Nonaka 1995) at its factories in 1961. In doing so, the company envisaged that the implementation of TQC would do more than merely promoting the idea of quality control. After the end of the second "quality month" in 1961, a monthly event to promote TQC at Toyota, Vice President Eiji Toyoda contributed an article that stated "we will promote TQC as the backbone of business management" (Toyoda 1961, p. 3). The company's official history also notes that the purpose of introducing TQC was "the revolutionary renovation of business management" and "the development and production of high-quality and inexpensive products" (Toyota Jidōsha Kōgyō Kabushiki Kaisha 1967a, p. 507). In other words, Toyota decided to renew its management system, focusing on fixing the delay in quality control revealed by the APA special procurement.

In fact, Toyota underwent organizational changes with the progress of TQC. In 1961, the Quality Control Department at the head office decided to transfer the inspection of in-house parts to each assembly plant. In addition, the inspection of outsourced parts was also transferred to each assembly plant in 1963. Thus, all inspection work was carried out at each assembly plant. The Purchasing Department at the head office became solely responsible for managing the suppliers. Both the Quality Control Department and the Purchasing Department jointly held quality management workshops and provided research guidance to 68 suppliers from 1960 to 1961. Following the *keiretsu* diagnosis in the 1950s, Toyota divided the suppliers into several layers and provided specific guidance to each supplier. Not only was this necessary to reduce the number of defective parts, but it was also essential for Toyota to reduce prices in the face of liberalized trade in passenger cars. In fact, at the end of 1961, Toyota requested a substantial discount for parts at the general meeting of *Kyohōkai*, an organization of suppliers (Kyōhōkai 1967, p. 42).

Toyota also became actively involved in the activities of *Kyohōkai*. Toyota not only dispatched personnel to form study groups within suppliers but also planned a series of factory audits for suppliers and promoted cooperation among suppliers. The *Kyohokai* eventually cooperated toward the realization of Toyota's policy. For example, when Toyota was promoting mass production, product assurance, and cost reduction in 1964, the Tōkai branch of the *Kyohōkai*, the organization of suppliers located near Toyota, set up new committees to support these goals (Kyōhō Nūsu 1964a, p. 1; Kyōhō Nūsu 1964b, p. 1). This demonstrated that some suppliers started to synchronize their delivery of parts with Toyota's production lines. In fact, the *Kyohokai News* reported that a supplier would deliver all its parts to the Motomachi Plant without inspection (Kyōhō Nūsu 1965, p. 2). The other suppliers soon followed.

Toyota established the Purchasing Control Department in 1965, which had centralized control over suppliers without the involvement of the Quality Control Department. Toyota began to provide direct guidance to the suppliers through the Purchasing Control Department on the development of company policies, process improvements, and increased motivation for improvement through QC circles. Toyota structured the appropriate guidance to every supplier based on an evaluation. Toyota was involved in setting management goals and allocating management resources for its suppliers. After 1968, Toyota established the "gathering on management," where the managers of each supplier and the executives and general managers of Toyota discussed management issues. In 1969, the Toyota Quality Control Award was established as an incentive to increase the willingness of suppliers to improve their management (Toyota Jidōsha Kōgyō Kabushiki Kaisha 1978, pp. 358–360).

In the late 1960s, the relationship between Toyota and its affiliated companies grew closer. Certainly, there was gathering of presidents among Toyota and its affiliates before the 1960s, although not on a regular basis, but after the 1960s, gatherings of presidents of Toyota and seven affiliates became more regular. The aim was to make adjustments to Toyota's production plan and each company's long-term plans and to coordinate important matters. In 1962, a liaison committee on quality control was established between Toyota and its affiliated companies. As an example, this committee held a QC circle exchange meeting for each occupation among Toyota and its affiliated companies. Exchanges between Toyota and its affiliated companies progressed at various levels, not just at the top management level. Furthermore, after 1967, this committee conducted management audits for affiliated companies to understand management problems and gain a common understanding of countermeasures (Toyota Jidōsha Kōgyō Kabushiki Kaisha 1978, pp. 360–361).

Before 1960, Toyota's affiliated companies began to recognize the future of the automotive business, but Toyota and its affiliates were not close to each other. However, in the late 1960s, focusing on the quality problem, they became closely related at not just the top management level but at each level of management. Furthermore, Toyota and its affiliates even had a mechanism to push each other's management issues in the same direction.

7.3 Assurance of Reliability

When Eiji Toyoda urged Toyota employees to prepare for liberalization of automobile trade in the *Toyota Newspaper,* Toyota's in-house journal, he pointed out the importance of reliability:

> The foundation that supports mass production is reliability. Please ensure higher reliability by thorough quality control as currently being promoted company-wide (Toyota Shimbun 1969b, p. 1).

Many researchers have focused their attention on QC circles and company-wide quality control movements when it comes to Toyota quality control (see Nonaka

1995). From the above quote, it is reasonable to think that Toyota further activated a company-wide quality control movement in the late 1960s. However, Toyota's action at this time launched a new era. Specifically, it was intended to guarantee quality assurance from a different perspective than quality control on site.

From the late 1960s, passenger cars rapidly increased in popularity in Japan, and the number of cars owned also increased rapidly. The number of automobiles owned in Japan was close to 5 million in 1964, but exceeded 6.3 million in 1965, exceeded 10 million in 1967, and surpassed 15 million in 1969.

In 1969, as this motorization trend was progressing, the *Asahi Shimbun,* one of Japan's national newspapers, reported that "Japanese automakers did not disclose the defects of its cars, but secretly corrected them" (Asahi Shimbun 1969, p. 15). This so-called "recall problem" became a major issue not only for Toyota but for the entire Japanese automobile industry. For example, the company history of Tōyō Kogyo (now Mazda) also noted this "recall problem," and demonstrates the magnitude of the problem:

> In 1969, the so-called recall problem was widely reported. The *New York Times*, dated May 11 of 1969, pointed out that the imported cars, including Japanese cars, were secretly collecting defective cars without any recall campaign. This article eventually became sensational in Japan and raised public interest in car safety.... This led to an emergency measure centered on the Ministry of Transport, which stipulated the publication and notification of recalled vehicles. Furthermore, it conducted complete inspections to existing vehicles. On June 11, the representative meeting of the automobile industry was held. It decided to report on the recalled car problem and its countermeasures to the relevant government agencies. As the automobile industry as a whole, they further decided to strengthen its safety measures (Tōyō Kōgyō Kabushikigaisha 1972, pp. 447–448).

This recall problem was extremely serious for the automobile industry in Japan at the time. For Toyota's management, this was not a problem that could be ignored. Eiji Toyoda sent a message on the *Toyota Newspaper* to employees: "use as a precious experience" (Toyota Shimbun 1969a, p. 1). However, such a message alone did not solve the problem. What measures did the company take to make use of this problem as a "precious experience"?

Among Eiji Toyoda's appeals to the employees in 1969, there was a mention of achieving "management efficiency through innovating the information systems" (Toyota Shimbun 1969b, p. 1). Toyota also used information systems for quality assurance. In December 1970, an article in the *Toyota Newspaper* announced the emergence of its quality assurance:

> Recently, aiming at improving the reliability of Toyota vehicles, a new quality information system (DAS; Dynamic Assurance System) was launched. This corresponds to the recent diversification and sophistication of the quality demanded by customers. This intends to collect and analyze the quality information more quickly and reliably. The obtained results would be fed back accurately to the product planning, design and manufacturing departments, as well as to suppliers. All Toyota would work together to promote its quality improvement (Toyota Shimbun 1970, p. 1).

Toyota's official company histories do not explain DAS in detail. However, a short explanation on DAS is available in Toyota's *Sōzō kagirinaku*.

> With this system, the information on complaints about our vehicles is accumulated in the history file of individual vehicles not only in Japan but also in overseas markets. So we can use this history file not only for the settlement of claim costs but also for recall processing and technical information (Toyota Jidōsha Kabushiki Kaisha 1987, p. 529).

A more detailed explanation on DAS was provided by the *Toyota Newspaper* when DAS was introduced.

> In a nutshell, …DAS creates a register of vehicles and then processes the quality information data based on this register. In other words, the information on production, dispatch, shipping, and registration is input daily to this register of the vehicle (=history file of the vehicle). This file contains the model, specifications, line-off plant, the date of inspection pass, and registration for each vehicle. In addition, the breakdown history of the vehicle in the market is organized and filed. This history file of the vehicle is then used to check whether the claim raised matches the warranty conditions, to perform the technical analysis of customer complaints and to create a document on reliability (Toyota Shimbun 1970, p. 1).

By using the history file of a vehicle as a source, it was possible to rapidly obtain information on "when a failure occurs and how frequently" or "when a failure related to a safety part occurs or when a failure occurs that never happened in the past." More importantly, when a failure occurs, it is possible to "provide a prompt recovery instruction by computers and check whether it has been accurately withdrawn." This is because the "actual product" that caused the problem is withdrawn and the cause is investigated, without merely conducting statistical analysis of technical issues (Toyota Shimbun 1970, p. 1).

As durable consumer goods such as automobiles are used for a certain period of time after purchasing, the history file of each vehicle contributes to a prompt response to the technical troubles or defects that are reported by consumers. For example, it previously took 41 days for the information to reach Toyota via Toyota Sales after the dealer obtained the claim information, but it was shortened to 12 days once DAS went into operation (Toyota Shimbun 1970, p. 1).

The DAS established a quality assurance system based on the information system. As the DAS also collected quality information on products, Toyota could use it to elucidate the cause of failure and for future product designs.

7.4 The Information System at Toyota

In the late 1950s, Toyota significantly increased both the volume of vehicle production and the number of employees. When the Corona PT20 problem occurred in 1960, the management of Toyota regarded poor coordination between departments as one of the causes. Toyota needed organizational reform, and the company did this by pursuing company-wide quality control. In fact, while Toyota needed improvements in product quality, the management recognized that introducing TQC would not only improve product quality but also contribute to organizational reform. To enhance product quality, Toyota had to deepen its relationships with suppliers and affiliated companies.

The Corona PT20 problem also showed that employees at Toyota found it difficult to handle their usual tasks due to the increased amount of clerical work. Toyota had already made efforts to rationalize clerical work, but after 1963, it further accelerated this process (see Chap. 8.1). The rationalization of clerical work meant that Toyota would need to collaborate and coordinate with companies related to its automobile business, such as Toyota Sales and Toyota's affiliates, to reduce the necessary clerical work. This resulted not only in an increased use of information systems at Toyota but also in closer links of Toyota's information systems to affiliated companies. In the next chapter, we discuss the development of information systems at Toyota.

References

Asahi Shimbun (The Asahi Newspaper). (1969). "Kekkan naze kakusu" (Why hide defects) in *Asahi Shimbun*, the morning edition, June 1, 1969. Tokyo: Asahi Shinbun sha.

Kyōhōkai. (1967). *Kyōhōkai no ayumi* (The history of Kyōhōkai). Toyota: Kyōhōkai.

Kyōhō Nūsu (The Kyōhō News). (1964a). "Jiyūka he no ketsui mo aratani: ryū, shitsu no kakuho to kosuto teigen" (Renewing our commitment to capital liberalization: ensuring the production volume as well as the quality and reducing costs" in *Kyōhō Nūsu* (the Kyōhō News), May 5, 1964. Toyota: Tōkai Kyōhōkai.

Kyōhō Nūsu (The Kyōhō News). (1964b). "San iinkai shin hossoku: zōsan, genka, hinshitsu" (Newly establishing three committees: increasing production, cost and quality) in *Kyōhō Nūsu* (the Kyōhō News), June 5, 1964. Toyota: Tōkai Kyōhōkai.

Kyōhō Nūsu (The Kyōhō News). (1965). "Zenhinmoku mukensa ukeire kyoka!: Tōkai rika denki seisaku jo" (All items permitted without inspection! Tokai Rica Co. Ltd) in *Kyōhō Nūsu* (the Kyōhō News), July 5, 1965. Toyota: Tōkai Kyōhōkai.

Kuroda, K. (1959). "APA hokyu-you buhin no nounyu ni tsuite" (On delivery of APA's spare parts). *Toyota Manegement* (Toyota Management). Toyota: Toyota Motor Company.

Nihon Jinbun Kagakkai (Japanese Literature Society), ed. (1963). *Gijutsu kakushin no shakaiteki eikyō* (Social impact of technological innovation). Tokyo: The University of Tokyo Press.

Nonaka, I. (1995). The development of company-wide quality control and quality circles at Toyota Motor Corporation and Nissan Motor Co. Ltd. In Haruhito Shiomi and Kazuo Wada eds. (1995). *Fordism transformed: the development of production methods in the automobile industry*. Oxford: Oxford University Press.

Sangiin (The House of Councillors). (1952). *Sangiin un'yu iinkai kaigiroku: Dai 13kai kokkai* (The House of Councillors Transport Committee: The 13th session of the Diet). Tokyo: Sangiin Un'yu Iinkai Chōsashitsu.

Toyoda, E. (1961). "Hinshitsu kanri wo keiei kanri no bakkubōnni" (Quality management as the backbone of business management) in *Toyota Manejiment (Toyota Mangement)*, November 1961. Toyota: Toyota Motor Co., Ltd.

Tōyō Kōgyō Kabushikigaisha. (1972). *Tōyō Kōgyō 50 nenshi. 1920–1970: enkaku henn* (Fifty yeas history of Tōyō Kōgyō: the corporate development). Fuchūchō, Hiroshima: Tōyō Kōgyō Kabushikigaisha.

Toyota Gurūpu (Toyota Group). (2005). *Kizuna: Toyota gyōdan kara toyota gurūpu e* (The bond: from the corporate association of Toyota to Toyoa group). Nagoya: Toyota Gurūpushi Hensan Iinkai.

Toyota Jidōsha Kabushiki Kaisha (Toyota Motor Co., Ltd). (1987). *Sōzō kagirinaku: Toyota Jidōsha 50-nenshi* (Endless creation: 50-year history of Toyota). Toyota: Toyota Jidōsha Kabushiki Kaisha.

Toyota Jidōsha Kōgyō Kabushiki Kaisha (Toyota Motor Co., Ltd). (1958). *Toyota Jidōsha 20-nenshi* (The 20th Anniversary History of Toyota Motor Co). Koromo-shi: Toyo-ta Jidōsha Kogyō Kabushiki Kaisha (Toyota Motor Co., Ltd).

Toyota Jidōsha Kōgyō Kabushiki Kaisha (Toyota Motor Co., Ltd). (1967a). *Toyota Jidōsha 30-nenshi* (The 30th Anniversary History of Toyota Motor Co). Toyota: Toyota Jidōsha Kogyō Kabushiki Kaisha (Toyota Motor Co., Ltd).

Toyota Jidōsha Kōgyō Kabushiki Kaisha (Toyota Motor Co., Ltd.). (1967b). *Toyota Jidōsha 30-nenshi bekkan* (Separate volume of the 30th anniversary history of Toyota Motor Co., Ltd.). Toyota: Toyota Jidōsha Kōgyō Kabushiki Kaisha (Toyota Motor Co., Ltd.).

Toyota Jidōsha Kōgyō Kabushiki Kaisha (Toyota Motor Co., Ltd). (1978). *Toyota no ayumi: Toyota Jidōsha Kōgyō Kabushiki Kaisha sōritsu 40-shūnen kinen* (History of Toyota: 40th anniversary of Toyota Motor Co., Ltd). Toyota: Toyota Jidōsha Kōgyō Kabushiki Kaisha.

Toyota Manejiment (Toyota Mangement). (1959). "Kōbai gyōmu no gōrika" (The rationalization of purchasing job) in *Toyota Manejiment (Toyota Mangement)*, February 1959. Toyota: Toyota Motor Co., Ltd.

Toyota Motor Corporation. (1988). *Toyota: A history of first 50 years*. Toyota: Toyota Motor Coporation.

Toyota Shimbun [Toyota Newspaper]. (1969a). "Rikōru mondai:kichōna taiken toshite ikase" (Recall problem: Use it as a valuable experience) in *Toyota Shimbun* [Toyota Newspaper], July 5, 1969. Toyota: Toyota Motor Coporation.

Toyota Shimbun [Toyota Newspaper]. (1969b). "Ketsui aratani minzoku shihon tsuranuku" (Renewing our pledge as a home-grown capital) in *Toyota Shimbun* [Toyota Newspaper], October 18, 1969. Toyota: Toyota Motor Coporation.

Toyota Shimbun [Toyota Newspaper]. (1970). "Shinrai sei kōjō wo mezashi: DAS sutāto" (Aiming to improve reliability: DAS started) in *Toyota Shimbun* [Toyota Newspaper], December 19, 1970. Toyota: Toyota Motor Co., Ltd.

Wada, K. (1992). The development of tiered inter-firm relationships in the automobile industry: A case study of Toyota motor corporation. *Japanese Yearbook on Business History*, Vol. 8. Tokyo: Japan Business History Institute.

Wada, Kazuo comp. (1999). *Toyoda Kiichiro Monjo Shūsei* (Cor-pus of Kiichiro Toyoda's Documents). Nagoya: Nagoya Daigaku Shuppankai (Nagoya University Press).

Wada, K., & Yui, T. (2002). *Courage and change: The life of Kiichiro Toyoda*. Toyota City: Toyota Motor Corp.

Yamada, M. (1961). "Kyōryoku kojō no QC shidō" (QC guidance of partner factories) in *Toyota Manegement* (Toyota Management), no. 11. Toyota: Toyota Motor Company.

Chapter 8
Computerization of the Management of Toyota as a Group

8.1 From Mechanization to Digitization

8.1.1 Revising the Parts Numbering Method

In 1963, Toyota and Toyota Sales jointly revised its parts numbering method. This step was necessary to further advance mechanization through the use of punch cards and IBM machines.

With the increased number of automobiles in the market, the opportunity for repairs and replacing parts also increased (Toyota Jidōsha Hanbai Kabushiki Gaisha 1962, pp. 208–209). Toyota Sales needed to supply parts for repairs. To order parts from Toyota, it was necessary to specify the parts accurately so that Toyota and Toyota Sales could identify the parts easily. As the types of automobiles and parts were increasing, easy identification of parts was also important for the production process itself. However, Toyota basically used the same parts numbering method, which was forced upon Japanese automakers in 1944 by the Japanese Army (Koide 1949, p. 67). After the war, Toyota changed its parts numbering method several times, and further changed it significantly in 1963 for the supply of parts handled by Toyota Sales, as well as the diagram numbers on design drawings (Usami 1963, p. 88). As a result, Toyota and Toyota Sales, and Toyota's affiliates and suppliers that were engaged in the automobile business began to use the same parts numbering system.

The reason for revising the parts numbering method in 1963 was explained by a manager at the time:

> The revision of the part number leads to rationalization of allocating the part number in the technical department and facilitates *the mechanization of the work accompanied with the part number*. In addition, it saves the necessary man-hours of already *mechanized work* and ensures its accuracy [emphasis supplied] (Usami 1963, p. 93).

In the above quotation, "the mechanization of the work accompanied with the part number" and "the mechanized work" mean the use of IBM machines. For

K. Wada, *The Evolution of the Toyota Production System*,
Studies in Economic History,
https://doi.org/10.1007/978-981-15-4928-1_8

example, Toyota's 20th anniversary history notes that "in 1957, with the development of the supermarket system, IBM machines processed from the ordering of parts to its delivery" (Toyota Jidōsha Kōgyō Kabushiki Kaisha 1958, p. 494).

Until the major change in the parts numbering system in 1963, Toyota had specified parts alphanumerically (combined letters and numbers). However, the new system allowed parts to be identified by numbers alone so that it could be processed with a punch card. Before the change, Toyota changed the part number format to numeric characters to allow processing on IBM machines (Usami 1963, pp. 86–87). This required additional work. Therefore, as the amount and opportunity for processing on IBM machines increased, the incentive to change the conventional part numbers increased.

Furthermore, Toyota Sales' "parts numbering method was not suitable for mechanization due to the uneven number of digits" (Toyota Jidōsha Hanbai Kabushiki Gaisha 1980, p. 211). Toyota Sales managed its inventory with a card system called *Cardex* (Toyota Jidōsha Hanbai Kabushiki Gaisha 1962, p. 210). However, with the rapid increase in the types and quantities of parts handled, this system almost reached its limit. Therefore, in 1963, Toyota Sales collaborated with Toyota to incorporate the new parts numbering method that used a ten-digit number (Toyota Jidōsha Hanbai Kabushiki Gaisha 1980, pp. 210–211). This parts numbering method enabled Toyota Sales to introduce an inventory control system through IBM machines (Toyota Jidōsha Hanbai Kabushiki Gaisha 1980, p. 211).

The designation of parts became easier because not only Toyota, but also its associated companies in the automobile business, suppliers, and Toyota Sales, used the same parts numbers. This not only contributed to business efficiency but also created a sense of unity between Toyota and its related companies.

8.1.2 Reducing Clerical Work: Advancement in Mechanization

The Kanban method was originally used by Toyota. Kanban implies operation by the supermarket method, and it explicitly specifies part numbers that are indispensable to clarifying the exact parts that must be transported or produced.

In 1963, after adopting a new parts numbering method, Toyota officially began to use Kanban to deal with its suppliers. At the end of 1963, Toyota asked some of its suppliers to provide parts depending on Toyota's needs as the supermarket method developed. Then, Toyota newly introduced the so-called SD card (synchronized delivery), which implied delivery to be synchronized with the production line, to transactions with its suppliers. Toyota's official history mentions the following:

> After confirming the effects of the in-house Kanban method, the SD card was first applied to outsourcing. In other words, it was a Kanban system for purchased parts, and after that, it was carried out with extensive expansion since the improvement of the operation method (Toyota Jidōsha Kōgyō Kabushiki Kaisha 1967, p. 192).

The SD cards were introduced with the intention of applying the results of production-ordering Kanban used at Toyota to outsourced parts (on in-house and supplier Kanban, see Monden 1983, pp. 14–20). Initially, the SD cards were thought to be different from in-house Kanban but were eventually called supplier Kanban.

The supplier Kanban was used only for the delivery of parts that Toyota used in large quantities. For example, Kanban was not used for delivery of parts such as seats, propeller shafts, and cranks. Moreover, this delivery method was initially applied only to suppliers located near Toyota (Araki 1963, p. 54; Yamakawa and Kinoshita 1969, p. 55). In other words, if the parts used in large quantities were delivered frequently in small quantities, Toyota's inventory would decrease, but its paperwork associated with purchasing parts would increase. Toyota had to solve this problem.

In ordering and delivering parts, supplier Kanban and IBM cards moved between Toyota and suppliers. For each delivery lot, Toyota issued a supplier Kanban with two IBM cards. In delivering the parts, the supplier handed them over with a supplier Kanban and two IBM cards, one of which corresponded to the purchasing order from Toyota and the other to the acceptance certificate from Toyota (Kusaba 1967, p. 72). As the supplier Kanban moved with IBM cards, it was initially put in a plastic bag with IBM cards. In the late 1970s, the punch cards attached to supplier Kanban were replaced by barcodes (Wada 2015, p. 142). Later, this barcode was further replaced by QR codes (Kotani 2008, p. 82). However, the size of a supplier Kanban is approximately the same as that of a punch card (Kotani 2008, p. 72).

Toyota began using punch cards in dealing with suppliers in the late 1950s. Toyota's 20th anniversary history writes: "in 1957, with the development of the supermarket method, IBM machines processed from the ordering of parts to their delivery" (Toyota Jidōsha Kōgyō Kabushiki Kaisha 1958, p. 494). To be precise, Toyota mechanized "paperwork from the ordering of parts to their delivery" (Toyota Jidōsha Kōgyō Kabushiki Kaisha 1967, p. 186).

Toyota increased production, as well as the number of models throughout the 1960s and 1970s. The number of punch cards at Toyota also rapidly increased from 100,000 sets per month in 1965 to 1.5 million sets per month in 1978. In addition, as the amount of paperwork also increased due to multiple deliveries, the increase in the number of punch cards and errors in punch cards became a problem (Densōjihō 1980, p. 22; Wada 2015, p. 142). As a result, rather than attaching punch cards to a supplier Kanban, a barcode was printed on it. However, whether a barcode or, later, a QR code, the role remained the same: to reduce paperwork.

8.1.3 Why Did Toyota Mechanize Data Processing?

After Eiji Toyoda and Shōichi Saitō returned from the USA, Toyota installed IBM machines and began to process a variety of data with punch cards from the early 1950s (see Sect. 5.2). In fact, through IBM machines, Toyota collected and processed data on not only parts purchasing but also on production processes such as the production time of each process and the load factor of machines (Toyota Jidōsha Kōgyō Kabushiki Kaisha 1958, pp. 801–806). However, in the early stages, Toyota was only successful in reducing clerical works on purchasing through mechanizing data processing (see Sect. 7.3.2). Even just on parts purchasing, did Toyota ultimately aim to reduce clerical work by using IBM machines?

Looking through Toyota's in-house magazine, *Toyota Management*, one employee opened up about the company's intention and current situation when Toyota started introducing IBM machines in its purchasing operation:

> Considering the use of IBM machines in the narrow sense of parts purchasing, we achieved the goal anyway. In other words, after the company decided when, what and how many parts should be delivered, it ordered from the manufacturers and achieved it [received the parts]. This was our first goal. However, for the management, the most important thing is to determine what parts, when and how many parts are to be delivered. We treated it as if it were decided. We did not tackle it at all (Toyota Manejiment 1958, pp. 31–32).

According to the above, this employee considered that solving the administrative issues was just the first step. The most important point was to determine the part to be delivered as well as its quantity and date or time of delivery. Despite the company ordering parts from suppliers by specifying the delivery time and quantity, why did this employee say that the company "did not tackle it all"?

Another employee clarified what it meant to decide the delivery time and quantity of parts:

> Trying to link the material plan and the in-house production plan… We have to calculate the required number of single parts, and to add the number of material processing shortages. Furthermore, we have to subtract the raw material inventory, and to check the capacity and load of machine equipment. Moreover, we have to check the manning schedule. Then we can complete the in-house production plan. Furthermore, we can finally make a start in material planning… We have to subtract the amount of inventory and consider the remaining amount of purchasing contracts. Then we can determine the amount of purchasing order (Ohta 1962, p. 19).

In other words, the goal was not to order simply parts but to derive the necessary parts from the material plan and production plan of the entire company. By using IBM machines, the company tried to draw up the material plan. Calculating the necessary parts and materials from a monthly production plan required a huge amount of work. IBM machines in those days could not achieve this easily, and even if it was possible to calculate, it took several months, and it could not be used in reality (Ohta 1962, p. 19). In this situation, Toyota concentrated on reducing clerical work by using punch cards on purchasing jobs.

Toyota began ordering parts from suppliers by using supplier Kanban. However, the company did not order the quantity of parts and the time of delivery on a rational basis. It specified them by taking a seat-of-the-pants approach. Therefore, for the time being, the company concentrated on reducing office work by mechanizing purchasing jobs.

However, even then, the company was thinking about overcoming this situation; that is, it was looking at ways to make an in-house product while placing an order on a rational basis.

8.1.4 Ordering Parts Based on a Reasonable Foundation

As late as the late 1950s, Toyota did not determine the quality and date of parts purchasing in a rational way. In other words, the company did not order parts from suppliers based on the material plan, which had to reflect its production plan. Nevertheless, some employees talked about what was required for purchasing parts on a reasonable foundation.

In a roundtable discussion on the rationalization of purchasing operations, one employee in charge of purchasing revealed the king of information he wanted:

> When negotiating prices or obtaining materials, we have to explain to the other party with specific details. That is why we want a standard physical unit [that is, quantity of raw material, fuel, or time required to produce one product or a certain amount of product] that can convince the other party. For example, in the case of purchasing as an assembly [component part], the standard physical unit in a disassembled form is desired for products that are divided into rubber synthetic resin, iron plate, glass, etc. In addition, we want a standard physical unit that is classified and displayed by vehicle type (Toyota Manejiment 1959, p. 15).

The person in charge of purchasing wanted the standard physical unit of every part used by each vehicle type. The standard physical unit was a common term in Japan at that time. In fact, Toyota's official history cites data per automobile—data such as the consumption of pig iron, alloy steel, tin, coal, coke, and petroleum products. This shows the data per vehicle produced as an index, not by vehicle type, from April 1954 to May 1958 (Toyota Jidōsha Kōgyō Kabushiki Kaisha 1958, p. 646). Because the inflation rate was high, Toyota had collected not only the cost in monetary terms but also data for the physical consumption. As Toyota had collected such data at least for a period of time, the employee in charge of purchasing naturally requested it as a matter of course, and a purchaser would have requested to clarify the standard physical unit of each part be by vehicle type like the quote above.

In response to this remark, an employee from the Engineering Department who had attended the roundtable discussion said, "When you decide on the price, I think it should have been that course" (Toyota Manejiment 1959, p. 15). Furthermore, Mr. Kitō from the Purchasing Department attended this roundtable discussion and explained the current situation as follows:

> When the drawings came to our technical staff, we can know the materials used for each part and their weight, to some extent, on the basis of such drawings. However, as the company produces many vehicle models now, the personnel of our department are only capable of managing such drawings. For the time being, we just put together which parts are used in a particular vehicle model, as the need arises (Toyota Manejiment 1959, p. 15).

To supplement this, another employee from the Purchasing Department remarked:

> On examination, our company now produces 16 types of automobiles as standard models. Furthermore, we are planning to produce 42 types of vehicles. I am wondering whether we manage to organize the parts used in each vehicle type for many different types (Toyota Manejiment 1959, p. 15).

Immediately after this, Mr. Kitō from the Purchasing Department again explained the current situation:

> So, talking about it won't do anything. We can't achieve it immediately. Although we set it as the goal, we are putting together the lists of parts and the process sheets. We are planning to make it possible to create the materials [for the parts used in each vehicle type], based on those we are now arranging ones, when our company needs them. Even by arranging them, this is extremely demanding indeed (Toyota Manejiment 1959, p. 15).

If the lists of parts required for each vehicle type as well as the process sheets for manufacturing the parts are combined, the company could clarify the amount of materials required for each vehicle. Then, when determining the production plan of a particular vehicle type, the company could predict the amount of materials required to achieve the production plan. Therefore, once the company can be clear about both the process and the parts listed, it can predict the amount of materials required in advance. Furthermore, once the cost and price of materials can be predicted, the exact cost of the vehicle can be ascertained. Based on the material requirement, the company can plan the procurement of materials. Similarly, it can also decide the number of parts to be purchased externally by taking stock of its inventory. Based on a process analysis, the company can also negotiate costs with suppliers once it has determined cost estimates. Eventually, such procedures built a rational foundation for the entire purchase process.

Although not clearly stated, Toyota's employees in the Purchasing Department wanted not only the list of parts used in the final product but also the amount of raw materials and energy used. At that time, the term "bill of materials (BOM)" was not widely used. By the end of the 1980s, the *Glossary of Production Engineering* defined this term as follows:

> The materials list showing the relationship between the part names that make up the final product and the required number of parts (Namiki and Endō 1989, p. 235).

In other words, they were requesting data comparable to the BOM. More precisely, they wanted data that exceeded the BOM definition given above. They wanted the standard physical basic unit, including the amount of raw material and energy, and the lists of production process. Therefore, some employees from the Purchasing Department requested data that exceeded the BOM definition above to order parts based on a reasonable foundation.

As late as in 1966, Toyota introduced a new delivery system to its suppliers, and Toyota's 30-year history reads:

> In December 1966, the company implemented a new delivery system which would announce the required quantity for the next three months [to the supplier] and instruct the delivery schedule based on the company's required quantity for each day. As a result, the delivery method for purchased parts has greatly advanced (Toyota Jidōsha Kōgyō Kabushiki Kaisha 1967a, p. 192).

Around 1966, Toyota prepared a production plan using IBM machines. Takaharu Mizuno, later Director of Toyota, wrote the following:

> [The company] then creates a "production schedule." Previously, it was done manually, but with the increase in production volume and diversification of car models, it has been done with computers since about three years ago [1966]. …More detailed conditions such as paint

color were added for each assembly line. A plan is made for each vehicle (Mizuno 1969, p. 37).

By 1966, Toyota's production plan was prepared for every vehicle, not every five vehicles, by using computers. Nonetheless, Mizuno emphasized that Toyota still could not calculate the amount of parts required to be outsourced using the computer, even though basic data for outsourcing parts was already recorded and accumulated on punch cards by this time. In other words, despite basic data being recorded on punch cards, Toyota could not calculate the data necessary for controlling "the planning stage for a new model of car to the start of commercial mass production [through its production planning]" using computers by the mid-1960s (Mizuno 1969, p. 37).

Toyota already recorded data making up the BOM, but it could not easily calculate this using a computer. Therefore, did Toyota resolve this, and if so, how? We consider this in the next section.

8.2 Was Toyota Trying to Realize BOM?

8.2.1 Enhancing the Online Network Within the Toyota Group

In the late 1960s, Toyota had to prepare for the liberalization of automobile trade. In fact, Eiji Toyoda was appealing to employees in the *Toyota Shimbun*, the in-house newspaper as follows:

> The capital liberalization will take place [in October 1971]... As the timing of capital liberalization has been decided, we have to speed up strengthening our company. ...I would like to ask you to do the following things for two years until capital liberalization (Toyota Shimbun 1969b, p. 1).

Eiji Toyoda explained that Toyota was expanding its production capacity to achieve an annual production of two million vehicles. Then, he requested some specific points from his employees and concluded with the following remarks: "Please make full contact with affiliates, suppliers, dealers, etc. to make the best use of All Toyota" (Toyota Shimbun 1969b, p. 1). This seems to indicate general or ceremonial emphasis on strengthening the power of the Toyota Group, but it seems crucial considering what Toyota had been doing around this time.

Toyota and Toyota Sales, as well as Toyota's body and parts manufacturers, were making their business online. The following article was published in the *Toyota Shimbun* six months before Eiji Toyoda's remarks:

> On April 1 [1969], Toyota Sales began an online real-time system (immediate processing method) for allocating the Crown [Toyota's passenger car]. This system uses computers to rationalize the dispatching operation by combining orders from the dealer and the production schedule (Toyota Shimbun 1969a, p. 1).

Furthermore, the computers at Toyota and Toyota Sales were connected online in March 1970. To be precise, the computer at Toyota Sales headquarters was connected with the computer at Toyota headquarters, which was connected with the computer at the Takaoka Plant of Toyota that began its operation in 1967 (Toyota Shimbun 1970a, p. 1). As the dealers of Toyota Sales had already installed telex in September 1964, Toyota Sales collected information on car orders and could send it to Toyota immediately, which helped with the production plan and the production could proceed.

This expediting of information from receiving orders to production and dispatch was important for the Japanese automobile industry in the late 1960s. In October 1965, for example, Toyota Sales introduced the "wide selection" for the Crown. In facing sluggish demand of medium-sized cars, such as the Crown, Toyota Sales introduced a wide range options, including car shapes, to increase the demand not just for company cars but also for family cars. This stimulated demand for the car. However, it was necessary to produce the car as ordered by the dealer and arrange it quickly to be delivered to the customer. With the introduction of wide selection for the Crown, by January 1966, Toyota began making a production plan whereby an order can be closed every 10 days, while previously it closed an order every month. The rapid expansion of consumer choices was supported by such prompt production plans and the production itself (Toyota Jidōsha Hanbai Kabushiki Kaisha 1970, p. 369).

In 1970, Toyota Sales introduced the Celica, a passenger car, which boasted a "full choice" with a wider range of options. Toyota also introduced the "Daily Order System," which accepted production orders every day, and further shortened the time between receiving the order to dispatch, making the Celica's full choice possible (Toyota Shimbun 1970b, p. 1). This full choice was introduced to other passenger cars and stimulated demand. Full choice and the daily ordering system were made possible by the prompt and efficient communication of information between Toyota Sales, Toyota and its plants, and other body makers and parts manufacturers (Toyota Shimbun 1972, p. 1). This shortening of the time taken from receiving an order to dispatch was considered an important means for Toyota and Toyota Sales to protect the domestic market from foreign cars.

8.2.2 Digital Processing and Management of Product Number

For mass-producers of cars like Toyota, the company must deal with many different parts. To identify a specific part, the company generally uses a part number. By organizing the product numbers, the company must maintain a correspondence relationship between the specific part number and the part name.

In 1963, Toyota revised its product numbering method. This change made it easier for computers to handle tasks that involved the part number. As explained earlier,

Toyota mechanized, or computer processed, the processing of slips with suppliers, on which the part number was indispensable (see Sect. 7.3.1). This did not change the way in which parts from suppliers were purchased but significantly reduced the burden of document processing associated with the receipt and payment of money among Toyota and its suppliers.

After the change in the numbering method, not only did the number of models increase, producing about 25 car models in the early 1970s, but variations within each model also increased. As a result, the number of part numbers also increased rapidly. However, at the time, the company still used a paper-based system. In the other words, the product name and the part number were registered on paper. To find a specific item's part number, the employees had to perform a manual search. This situation is described in the following:

> The design management section of the Engineering Management Department [at Toyota] has about 1,100 books of part numbers (called the parts ledgers). Each parts ledger, on average, contains 300 cards on which the part number or the reserved part number is written.
>
> To register the part number formally, ... an official registration card is drafted. ...When inserting the official registration card into the parts ledger, it is checked against the reservation card [on which the reservation part number is written] and the reservation card is discarded. Until the spring of 1974, part numbers were given by this process (Matsumura 1975a, p. 60).

The author of this article was a Design Manager of the Design Management Section at Toyota's Engineering Management Department, and was deeply involved in the work described here. According to the above quotation, Toyota managed product numbers in paper form "until the spring of 1997." The company did not use computers to handle them. Moreover, the total product numbers increased rapidly after the 1960s, and by 1974 "the total number of product numbers exceeded 300,000" (Matsumura 1975a, p. 60).

The following describes the situation where the relationship between product names and product numbers is disturbed:

> Our company [Toyota] made a large-scale change of the product numbering method in July 1963, but the number of product numbers was 30,000 at that time. So, it was possible for us to have a keen eye for detail. Now, the product development period has become short, and many products are being developed. Many parts have to be numbered at one time (part numbers from 2,000 to 4,000 parts per week are required). If a careless mistake occurs, it is impossible to find the part number from among 300,000 items. The management of product names has become complicated, and it has become impossible to manage finely, although its management takes many man-hours. In addition, when the person in charge of management changes or when maintenance of information is delayed, the relationship between the basic number and the product name becomes disordered. Product names have become longer year by year, and the organization of product numbers and product names has become a problem not only in design departments but also in related departments (Matsumura 1975a, p. 60).

In response to this situation, after Toyota sorted out the product names and product numbers, it converted them into digital data for use on computers. This required substantial work. In addition, there was no excuse for failure because data was fundamental for the company. The following quote shows how hard this work was:

> As for the transition work on part number..., we decided the data input form at the end of December 1972 and began to convert the data (from parts ledger to IBM card form) in January of the following year. We finished converting all data on part numbers, product names, materials, etc. for over 270,000 parts in early May. We spent 7,000 man-hours for this conversion. The number of punch cards reached 500,000 IBM cards in March and April at a peak period. For punch many cards in a short period, we punched cards just in Japan, but also in Korea. In July and August, we employed many part-time students to check the data input to the computer. We spent about 5,000 man-hours for this job. Furthermore, we checked the component ledger card against the data in the computer twice (Matsumura 1975b, p. 49).

With such an effort, why did Toyota convert the data for part numbers and product names? Indeed, data was mired in confusion. Toyota had to get out of this situation, but it was aiming for something else; that is, "computerization of the bill of materials."

8.2.3 Computerization of BOM: Specific Management System

In December 1973, the *Toyota Newspaper* posted an article called "Computerization of BOM", which stated:

> Computerization of the bill of materials will start on some models from the end of this month. This is to move the bill of materials... from conventional distributed management by each department to centralized management using a computer, and to provide the necessary information in a timely manner. This is a revolutionary development (Toyota Shimbun 1973, p. 1).

Toyota began considering computerization of the BOM when it revised the parts numbering method in 1963 (Toyota Shimbun 1973, p. 1). In fact, the official history of Japan IBM notes that Toyota mechanized the production management tasks centered on parts management in 1965. It explained how IBM machines worked for this:

> At that time, approximately 100,000 parts were delivered to Toyota every month, but a delivery instruction program was developed to calculate the delivery date and quantity for each part using the IBM650 (Nihon Keieishi Kenkyūjo 1988, p. 173).

If this description were right, however, Toyota had difficulties "in calculating the delivery date and quantity of each part" because the BOM was not computerized. Therefore, computerization of the BOM had been a long-standing challenge for Toyota. Although there is no mention of BOM in the English version of Toyota's company history, Toyota's 40th anniversary history describes this situation as follows:

> The BOM is the core of related works in many departments inside and outside the company as technical information, but due to the progress of diversification [of cars], increase in part numbers as well as in design change, and further due to the process changes, etc., our company has no accurate bill of materials. A countermeasure was eagerly desired.
>
> Regarding the possibility of computerization, the computerization approach [of BOM] after the revision of part numbering method in 1963 has failed.
>
> It was in the fall of 1969 that we found the possibility of computerization of the BOM (Toyota Jidōsha Kōgyō Kabushiki Kaisha 1978, p. 354).

In April 1970, the Technical Management Department, Production Management Department, and Computer Department "set up a project team and made a start on the computerization of the BOM." In addition, Toyota's company history describes how the project team achieved computerization of the BOM:

> Over three years, the project team has conducted over 300 research and review meetings. It completed computerization of the bill of materials in May 1973 (Toyota Jidōsha Kōgyō Kabushiki Kaisha 1978, p. 354).

Therefore, the BOM was defined as follows: "for all parts making up the vehicle, the following are clearly specified by part numbers: (1) the relationship between the vehicle and parts; (2) the relationship between parts; (3) the manufacturing process; (4) the description of parts (the name of parts, materials, etc.)" (Toyota Jidōsha Kōgyō Kabushiki Kaisha 1978, p. 354). This explanation is not much different from the usual explanation for the BOM.

Computerization of the BOM means that the BOM would be available online, and for this purpose, the part number must be available on the computer. In other words, "the digital management of product number" (see Sect. 8.2.2) was necessary for computerization of the BOM. After referring to "computerization of the BOM" as SMS (Specifications Management System) from the beginning, the *Toyota Newspaper* reported that SMS could develop into related fields in the near future (Toyota Shimbun 1973, p. 1).

In fact, Toyota was not just computerizing the BOM—it was also expanding the role of SMS to other areas. In June 1975, the *Toyota Newspaper* reported that "as the second step of the computerization of BOM, the automatically calculated system of the necessary parts was completed and now is applied to some models of cars" (Toyota Shimbun 1975, p. 1). After determining the production plan, the necessary parts for each model have to be calculated by referring to the BOM. "The new system uses [digitized] BOM information, so the necessary number of parts is automatically created by doing the vehicle type, production process, etc." (Toyota Shimbun 1975, p. 1).

Furthermore, Toyota expanded SMS to the body makers to whom the production of Toyota cars was outsourced. The *Toyota Newspaper* reported that Toyota would disclose SMS to the body makers and share parts throughout the Toyota group:

> Toyota's parts list is disclosed to the body makers so that the modification information can be communicated quickly and promptly. Next March [in 1978], by directly connecting the computers between our company, the company plans to share the parts among all Toyota (Toyota Shimbun 1977, p. 1).

In addition, Toyota developed a computer system linked to SMS. On this, the *Toyota Newspaper* reported:

> In November 1979, the company completed the "supply parts number information management system" that had developed for a long time in collaboration with the Business Department and the Computer Department of our company. This system started full-scale operation from this month [in December 1979].
>
> This system uses computers to manage the supply form, the production process, and the suppliers of about 600,000 supply parts, including the current and old models. This information

can be retrieved at any time from all SMS terminals including Toyota Sales and the body makers, and so on (Toyota Shimbun 1979, p. 1).

The SMS was also linked to a system for creating a new car catalog in Toyota Sales. SMS has become an important system in Toyota. In other words, it was not just a parts list, but it was also used in various other ways in different departments. The system was also used by Toyota Sales and the body makers. The SMS, which was named with the intention of "establishing a comprehensive management system with product specifications (vehicle and parts specifications) as the key," actually indicated such intention from the start (Matsumura 1981, p. 65). As a result, before the merger of Toyota Sales and Toyota in 1980, the two companies had already integrated their businesses in many ways.

References

Araki, T. (1963). Tosha ni okeru buhin nōnyū keikaku shinnkō tōsei oyobi zaiko kanri [Parts delivery planning/progress control and inventory management in our company]. In *Toyota Manejiment* [Toyota Mangement]. Toyota: Toyota Motor Co. Ltd.

Densōjihō. (1980). Toyota jikō ni okeru bākōdo riyō nit suite [On the use of barcode at Toyota]. In *Densōjihō*. Kariya: Nippon Denso (now Denso).

Koide, T. (1949). Toyota ni okeru keishiki to hinban nit suite [On the model and parts number at Toyota]. In *Gijutsu no Tomo* [Friends of Technolo-gy], Vol. 1, No. 1. Toyota: Toyota Jidōsha Kogyō Kabushiki Kaisha (Toyota Motor Co. Ltd).

Kotani, S. (2008). *Riron kara shuhō made kichin to wakaru toyota seisan hōshiki: Nyūmonsho no ketteiban* [Toyota production system that can be understood from theory to method: The definitive version of the primer]. Tokyo: Nikkankōgyō shinbunsha.

Kusaba, I. (1967). Kōza: kaite•urite no kankei [The course: Relationship between buyers and sellers]. In *Hinshitu Kanri* [Statistical quality control]. Tokyo: Nihon Kagaku Gijutsu Renmei.

Matsumura, T. (1975a). Tōtaru ka wo shikō suru buhin jōhō no tōrok kannri sisutemu (1) [The registration and management system of parts information orienting to totalization (1)]. *IE*. Tokyo: Nihon Nōritsu Kyōkai.

Matsumura, T. (1975b). Tōtaru ka wo shikō suru buhin jōhō no tōrok kannri sisutemu (2) [The registration and management system of parts information orienting to totalization (2)]. *IE*. Tokyo: Nihon Nōritsu Kyōkai.

Matsumura, T. (1981). Kakudai suru SMS no bunya: sekkei gijutsu jōhō no dēta bēsu, dēta komunikēshion [Expanding the field of SMS: The database and data communication of design technological information]. In *Gijutsu no Tomo* [Friends of Technolo-gy], Vol. 33, No. 1. Toyota: Toyota Jidōsha Kogyō Kabushiki Kaisha (Toyota Motor Co. Ltd).

Mizuno, T. (1969). Purodukushion kontorōru [Production control]. In *Hinshitsu Kanri* [The statiscal qualty control], Vol. 20, No. 3. Tokyo: Nihon Kagaku Gijutsu Renmei (Japanese Union of Scientists and Engineers).

Monden, Y. (1983). *Toyota production system: Practical approach to production management.* Norcross, GA: Industrial Engineering and Management Press.

Namiki, T., & Endō, K. (1989). *Seisan Kōgaku Yōgo Jiten* [The glossary of production engineering]. Tokyo: Nikkankōgyō shinbunsha.

Nihon Keieishi Kenkyūjo (Japan Business History Institute). (1988). *Nihon Ai Bi Emu 50-nenshi* [The fifty years' history of Japan IBM]. Tokyo: IBM.

Ohta, O. (1962). Denshi keisanki dōnyū ni yoru hyōjunka [Standardization by introducing the electronic computer]. In *Toyota Manejiment (Toyota Mangement)*. Toyota: Toyota Motor Co. Ltd.

Toyota Jidōsha Hanbai Kabushiki Gaisha (Toyota Motor Sales Co., Ltd). (1962). *Toyota jidōsha hanbai kabushiki gaisha no ayumi* [The footsteps of Toyota Motor Sales Co., Ltd]. Nagoya: Toyota Jidōsha Hanbai.

Toyota Jidōsha Hanbai Kabushiki Kaisha (Toyota Motor Sales Co., Ltd). (1970). *Mōtarizeishon to tomo ni* [With motorization]. Nagoya: Toyota Motor Sales Co., Ltd.

Toyota Jidōsha Hanbai Kabushiki Gaisha (Toyota Motor Sales Co., Ltd). (1980). *Sekai e no ayumi: Toyota Jihan 30-nenshi* [Steps towards the world]. Nagoya: Toyota Motor Sales Co. Ltd.

Toyota Jidōsha Kōgyō Kabushiki Kaisha (Toyota Motor Co., Ltd). (1958). *Toyota Jidōsha 20-nenshi* [The 20th Anniversary History of Toyota Motor Co.]. Koromo-shi: Toyo-ta Jidōsha Kogyō Kabushiki Kaisha (Toyota Motor Co., Ltd).

Toyota Jidōsha Kōgyō Kabushiki Kaisha (Toyota Motor Co., Ltd.). (1967a). *Toyota Jidōsha 30-nenshi bekkan* [Separate volume of the 30th anniversary history of Toyota Motor Co. Ltd.]. Toyota: Toyota Jidōsha Kōgyō Kabushiki Kaisha (Toyota Motor Co., Ltd.).

Toyota Jidōsha Kōgyō Kabushiki Kaisha (Toyota Motor Co., Ltd). (1978). *Toyota no ayumi: Toyota Jidōsha Kōgyō Kabushiki Kaisha sōritsu 40-shūnen kinen* [History of Toyota: 40th anniversary of Toyota Motor Co. Ltd]. Toyota: Toyota Jidōsha Kōgyō Kabushiki Kaisha.

Toyota Manejiment (Toyota Mangement). (1958). Zadannkai: gennba gijuin wa kataru [Round-table talk: On-site engineers talk]. In *Toyota Manejiment (Toyota Mangement)*. Toyota: Toyota Motor Co. Ltd.

Toyota Manejiment (Toyota Mangement). (1959). Kōbai gyōmu no gōrika [The rationalization of purchasing job]. In *Toyota Manejiment (Toyota Mangement)*. Toyota: Toyota Motor Co. Ltd.

Toyota Shimbun [Toyota Newspaper]. (1969a, April 5). Keikaku hanbai wo sokushin: kuraun haisha gyōmu wo gyōkai hatsu no onrain ka [Promoting the planned sales: the dispatch operation of Crown became the first online in the industry]. *Toyota Shimbun* [Toyota Newspaper]. Toyota: Toyota Motor Corporation.

Toyota Shimbun [Toyota Newspaper]. (1969b, October 18). Ketsui aratani minzoku shihon tsuranuku [Renewing our pledge as a home-grown capital]. *Toyota Shimbun* [Toyota Newspaper]. Toyota: Toyota Motor Corporation.

Toyota Shimbun [Toyota Newspaper]. (1970a, March 7). 200 mandai taisei ni sonae kanzen onrainka wo mezasu: jihan to densanki chokketsu [Aiming at the complete online for establishing a system of two million vehicle production: Direct connection of computers with Toyota Sales]. *Toyota Shimbun* [Toyota Newspaper]. Toyota: Toyota Motor Co. Ltd.

Toyota Shimbun [Toyota Newspaper]. (1970b, December 5). Deirii ōdā sisutemu kaishi [Daily order system started]. *Toyota Shimbun* [Toyota Newspaper]. Toyota: Toyota Motor Co. Ltd.

Toyota Shimbun [Toyota Newspaper]. (1972, April 21). On Raine no nettowāku wo jujitsu [Enhanced the online network]. *Toyota Shimbun* [Toyota Newspaper]. Toyota: Toyota Motor Co. Ltd.

Toyota Shimbun [Toyota Newspaper]. (1973, December 14). Buhinhō no densanka: kazukazu no kōka kitai, hitsuyō jōhō taimuri ni [Computerization of the bill of materials: Expecting many effects, necessary information in a timely manner]. *Toyota Shimbun* [Toyota Newspaper]. Toyota: Toyota Motor Co. Ltd.

Toyota Shimbun [Toyota Newspaper]. (1975, June 20). Densanka de gyōmu no kōritsu kōjō [Computerization improves operational efficiency]. *Toyota Shimbun* [Toyota Newspaper]. Toyota: Toyota Motor Co. Ltd.

Toyota Shimbun [Toyota Newspaper]. (1977, September 9). Ōgata dennsanki wo dōnyū: SMS wo kanren geisha hemo kakudai [Introducing large computers: Expansion of SMS to affiliated companies]. *Toyota Shimbun* [Toyota Newspaper]. Toyota: Toyota Motor Co. Ltd.

Toyota Shimbun [Toyota Newspaper]. (1979, December 21). Kongetsu kara honkakuteki ni kadō kaishi: hokyū hinban jōhō sisutemu [Starting full-scale operation from this month: Supply parts number information system]. *Toyota Shimbun* [Toyota Newspaper]. Toyota: Toyota Motor Co. Ltd.

Usami, M. (1963). Hinban•hinmei no kaisei ni tsuite [Revision on parts number and name]. In *Gijutsu no Tomo* [Friends of Technolo-gy], Vol. 15, No. 1. Toyota: Toyota Jidōsha Kogyō Kabushiki Kaisha (Toyota Motor Co. Ltd).

Wada, K. (2015). Why did Toyota respond less quickly to globalization? In *Enterprises et Histoire*, no. 80. Paris: ESKA.

Yamakawa, S., & Kinoshita, K. (1969). Gaichū buhin no ryō oyobi nōki kanri nitsuite [On the quantity and delivery management of outsourced parts]. In *Toyota Manejiment (Toyota Mangement)*. Toyota: Toyota Motor Co. Ltd.

Chapter 9
Conclusion

Much literature on the production system at Toyota has dealt intensively with Kanban. Several of these sources often emphasize that Kanban is unrelated to computers. The typical view is: "Utilizing the Kanban system, workshops of Toyota no longer rely upon an electronic computer" (Sugimori et al. 1977, p. 559).

However, even with Toyota's production system, it is important to decide on a production plan, and then decide on a daily sequence schedule. A computer is used in this decision-making process. Kanban is used to manufacture the necessary parts to realize the daily sequence schedule in the final production line. Without the production plan and the daily sequence schedule, the part numbers used for Kanban or even Kanban are useless.

Even so, why would those who worked at Toyota say, "workshops of Toyota have no longer rely upon an electronic computer"? Toyota had a bitter experience as a result of using computers. After 1970, Toyota installed 52 computer terminals at the assembly plant in the Motomachi Plant. As the number of car models increased significantly, Toyota decided to provide production instructions using the computer terminals. However, the production instructions via the computer terminals caused confusion on the shop floor (Toyosaka and Mano 1978, pp. 34–35). Problems emerged because the staff "worked ahead as a result of extracting information from each computer terminal, and as a result, there were many shortcomings such as frequent assembly errors and obstruction of standardization of work" (Toyota Jidōsha Kōgyō Kabushiki Kaisha 1978, pp. 345–346). Consequently, computers are not visible on the shop floor at Toyota. This is also the reason why Sugimori et al. (1977) emphasized that the workshops of Toyota no longer relied upon electronic computers. Computers are rarely found on the shop floors or in the workshops, and work instructions are no longer issued through computer terminals on the shop floor.

Here, we pay attention to the following description in Ohno's book:

> At Toyota, we do not reject the computer, because it is essential in planning production leveling procedures and calculating the number of parts needs daily. We use the computer freely, as a tool… (Ohno 1988, pp. 47–48).

K. Wada, *The Evolution of the Toyota Production System*,
Studies in Economic History,
https://doi.org/10.1007/978-981-15-4928-1_9

The calculation capability of computers is indispensable in drawing up the production plan.

The "Toyota-style information system" was one section that Setsuo Mito, the ghost writer for the *Toyota Production System*, could not write. Fujio Cho, who later became Chairman of Toyota, rewrote this section on behalf of Mito (Wada 2015, p. 143). It should be noted that the section contained the following statement:

> In the Toyota Production System, the method of setting up this daily schedule is important. *During the last half of the previous month, each production line is informed of the daily production quantity for each product type*. At Toyota, this is called the daily level. On the other hand, the daily sequence schedule is sent only to one place—the final assembly line. This is a special characteristic of Toyota's information system (Ohno 1988, p. 49).

Work at Toyota's production sites is carried out according to Kanban. Materials used must be prepared prior to production according to Kanban. Furthermore, because Toyota obtains parts from suppliers, the company must calculate the delivery date and quantity for each part. For this, the digitalization of the bill of materials (BOM), which Toyota calls a specifications management system (SMS), is indispensable for the Toyota Production System.

The Toyota Production System dealt with in this book may be summarized as follows: while production progress on the shop floors was conducted according to Kanban, the production and material planning, and parts arrangement were performed using computers and the digitalized BOM.

In general, the Toyota Production System has not been strictly defined by most researchers that have discussed it. It is typically considered as the control of production progress according to Kanban. Hence, people understand that the Toyota Production System is an efficient production system where progress at the site is controlled with simple tools such as Kanban, without mentioning the production plan behind it. Even this production system changes significantly when it focuses on supporting systems hidden behind Kanban, such as drawing up the production plan and the daily sequence schedule, and the placing of orders with suppliers. What is characteristic of this system is that it aims to create a smooth flow throughout the production process, rather than aiming at increasing efficiency. In this sense, this system is an evolution of "flow production" that engineers sought before and during the war. Furthermore, suppliers deliver parts several times a day or monthly to Toyota. The supply of parts has evolved from being intermittent to a steady but continuous flow.

How did the staff perceive this production system? An informative article dealing with this issue was posted in *Friends of Technology*, a Toyota journal. The article, "The Production System of Toyota," was written by Fujio Cho (at that time, he was in the Production Research Department of the Production Management Department and later became Chairman) (Cho 1974). Table 9.1 shows the inventory turnover rates for Toyota and other major auto manufacturers. Cho noted that for data in the table, "larger values imply less stock and more efficient production" (Cho 1974, p. 2). The figure for Toyota is far larger than the other companies, although due to the separation of Toyota and Toyota Sales, it is large even if the number of completed vehicles on

Table 9.1 Inventory turnover ratios (sales/inventory assets) for major automobile manufacturers for 1965–1972

Year	Toyota	Nissan	Tōyō Kōgyō[a]	GM	Ford
1965	41.0	13.1	15.6	6.9	8.0
1966	57.1	12.5	11.2	6.5	7.7
1967	52.3	14.1	11.8	6.2	7.3
1968	54.9	14.0	16.3	6.6	7.5
1969	69.3	15.0	10.9	6.5	5.8
1970	65.5	12.8	8.6	4.6	5.0
1971	81.4	13.7	9.2	7.1	5.0
1972	86.8	16.0	10.9	–	–

[a]Now Mazda
Source Cho (1974, pp. 2–3)

Table 9.2 Value added per employee (1,000 yen) for major automobile manufacturers for 1965–1972

Year	Toyota	Nissan	Tōyō Kōgyō[a]	Honda	Isuzu
1965	2,878	3,129	2,729	3,722	2,927
1966	3,569	2,813	2,933	3,060	3,527
1967	4,880	2,927	3,171	2,552	3,518
1968	4,608	3,151	3,051	3,615	3,450
1969	5,685	3,614	3,199	3,965	3,540
1970	5,841	4,328	3,462	4,261	3,852
1971	6,877	4,856	3,558	4,521	3,743
1972	7,119	5,921	3,710	4,620	4,259

[a]Now Mazda
Source Cho (1974, pp. 2–3)

hand is small at Toyota. The inventory turnover ratio at Toyota has consistently increased, and the company seems to be confident in this system. Furthermore, in terms of value added per employee, Toyota surpassed the other companies after 1966 (Table 9.2). In particular, Toyota could produce more different types of vehicles than any other company on an assembly line (Table 9.3). The production system at Toyota was able to meet the diverse demands of consumers.

There seemed to be no problem with the production system at Toyota. However, Toyota's international development was delayed, and it was necessary to reform the digitalized BOM that supported its production system. Traditionally, Toyota's overseas plants used a simplified BOM, or SMS, but this had to be transformed into a consistent SMS. Toyota's SMS has not significantly changed over the years, and it has been used even though the information system itself has changed significantly. Toyota's overseas plants used a simplified BOM, but it needed to transform this into a

Table 9.3 Number of types handled per assembly line for major automobile manufacturers

Manufacturer	Number of models handled	Number of types that can be handled
Toyota	2	100,000,000
Tōyō Kōgyō[a]	2	1,600
Nissan	2	13,000
GM	2	Unknown

[a]Now Mazda
Source Cho (1974, pp. 2–3)

globally consistent SMS. In response to globalization, Toyota worked on SMS reform since the late 1990s and completed the work in the early 2000s. Coupled with the increased speed of information and communication systems, Toyota's globalization obstacles were removed, and Toyota began globalization rather rapidly (see Wada 2015).

References

Cho, F. (1974). Toyota no seisan hōshiki [The production system of Toyota]. In *Gijutsu no Tomo* [Friends of Technology], Vol. 25, No. 3 Toyota: Toyota Jidōsha Kogyō Kabushiki Kaisha (Toyota Motor Co. Ltd).

Ohno, T. (1988). *Toyota production system: Beyond large-scale production*. Portland, Oregon: Productivity Press.

Sugimori, Y., Kusunoki, K., Cho, F., & Uchikawa, S. (1977). Toyota production system and Kanban system Materialization of just-in-time and respect-for-human system. *International Journal of Production Research, 15*(6). Oxford: Taylor & Francis.

Toyosaka, T., & Mano, M. (1978). Jūnen go no seisan ryō kanri to kōmu no yakuwari [The production management after 10 years and the role of the engineering department]. In *Toyota Manejiment (Toyota Mangement)*. Toyota: Toyota Motor Co. Ltd.

Toyota Jidōsha Kōgyō Kabushiki Kaisha (Toyota Motor Co., Ltd). (1978). *Toyota no ayumi: Toyota Jidōsha Kōgyō Kabushiki Kaisha sōritsu 40-shūnen kinen* [History of Toyota: 40th anniversary of Toyota Motor Co., Ltd]. Toyota: Toyota Jidōsha Kōgyō Kabushiki Kaisha.

Wada, Kazuo. (2015). Why did Toyota respond less quickly to globalization? *Enterprises et Histoire*, no. 80. Paris: ESKA.

Index

K. Wada, *The Evolution of the Toyota Production System*,
Studies in Economic History,
https://doi.org/10.1007/978-981-15-4928-1

The manufacturer's authorised representative in the EU is Springer Nature Customer Service Centre GmbH, Europaplatz 3, 69115 Heidelberg, Germany. If you have any concerns regarding our products, please contact ProductSafety@springernature.com

Printed and bound by CPI Group (UK) Ltd, Croydon, CR0 4YY
30/09/2026
02225472-0019